Resisting Violence

Morna Macleod • Natalia De Marinis
Editors

Resisting Violence

Emotional Communities in Latin America

Editors
Morna Macleod
Autonomous Morelos State University
Morelos, Mexico

Natalia De Marinis
Centre for Research and Postgraduate
Studies in Social Anthropology
Mexico

ISBN 978-3-319-88217-8   ISBN 978-3-319-66317-3 (eBook)
https://doi.org/10.1007/978-3-319-66317-3

© The Editor(s) (if applicable) and The Author(s) 2018
Softcover re-print of the Hardcover 1st edition 2018
This work is subject to copyright. All rights are solely and exclusively licensed by the Publisher, whether the whole or part of the material is concerned, specifically the rights of translation, reprinting, reuse of illustrations, recitation, broadcasting, reproduction on microfilms or in any other physical way, and transmission or information storage and retrieval, electronic adaptation, computer software, or by similar or dissimilar methodology now known or hereafter developed.
The use of general descriptive names, registered names, trademarks, service marks, etc. in this publication does not imply, even in the absence of a specific statement, that such names are exempt from the relevant protective laws and regulations and therefore free for general use.
The publisher, the authors and the editors are safe to assume that the advice and information in this book are believed to be true and accurate at the date of publication. Neither the publisher nor the authors or the editors give a warranty, express or implied, with respect to the material contained herein or for any errors or omissions that may have been made. The publisher remains neutral with regard to jurisdictional claims in published maps and institutional affiliations.

Cover Design Specs: Kaveh Kazemi/Contributor/gettyimages

Printed on acid-free paper

This Palgrave Macmillan imprint is published by Springer Nature
The registered company is Springer International Publishing AG
The registered company address is: Gewerbestrasse 11, 6330 Cham, Switzerland

To all the women and men who have created sparks of hope in the face of multifaceted and overwhelming violence.

Contents

1. Resisting Violence: Emotional Communities in Latin America — 1
   Natalia De Marinis and Morna Macleod

2. Violence, Emotional Communities, and Political Action in Colombia — 23
   Myriam Jimeno, Daniel Varela, and Angela Castillo

3. Testimony, Social Memory, and Strategic Emotional/Political Communities in Elena Poniatowska's *Crónicas* — 53
   Lynn Stephen

4. Emotional Histories: A Historiography of Resistances in Chalatenango, El Salvador — 77
   Jenny Pearce

5. Protesting Against Torture in Pinochet's Chile: Movimiento Contra la Tortura Sebastián Acevedo — 99
   Morna Macleod

6. Emotions, Experiences, and Communities: The Return of the Guatemalan Refugees — 123
   Angela Ixkic Bastian Duarte

7   Political-Affective Intersections: Testimonial Traces Among
    Forcibly Displaced Indigenous People of Oaxaca, Mexico   143
    Natalia De Marinis

8   Affective Contestations: Engaging Emotion Through
    the Sepur Zarco Trial   163
    Alison Crosby, M. Brinton Lykes, and Fabienne Doiron

9   Women Defending Women: Memories of Women Day
    Laborers and Emotional Communities   187
    Gisela Espinosa Damián

Index   211

Notes on Contributors

Angela Ixkic Bastian Duarte is a professor at the Autonomous Morelos State University, Mexico. She is an anthropologist who has done research on gender, ethnicity, and environmental topics. Her publications include, among others: "From the Margins of Latin American Feminism: Indigenous and Lesbian Feminisms", *Signs. The Journal of Women in Culture and Society*, vol. 38, num. 1: 153–178 (2012) and (co-authored with Lina Rosa Berrío Palomo, 2015) "Saberes en diálogos: mujeres indígenas y académicas en la construcción del conocimiento", 292–323, In Leyva et al., *Practicas Otras de Conocimiento(s)*. Mexico: IGWIA.

Angela Castillo graduated in Anthropology from the National University of Colombia, and holds a master's degree in Geography from University of Los Andes, Bogotá. Currently, she is a Ph.D. Anthropology student at the University of California, Berkeley. Her areas of interest include violence, state formation, land disputes, and socio-environmental conflicts. She is the co-author of the book *Después de la masacre: Emociones y política en el Cauca indio*.

Alison Crosby is an associate professor in the School of Gender, Sexuality and Women's Studies and Director of the Centre for Feminist Research at York University in Toronto, Canada. Her research and publications use an anti-racist, anti-colonial feminist lens to explore survivors' multifaceted struggles for agency and subjectivity in the aftermath of violence. She is currently completing a book manuscript with M. Brinton Lykes, *Mapping Mayan Women's Protagonism in Transitional Justice Processes in Postgenocide*

Guatemala. And with Malathi de Alwis, she is exploring memorialization as a site of contestation in Guatemala and Sri Lanka in the project "The Inhabitance of Loss: A Transnational Feminist Project on Memorialization."

Natalia De Marinis is Associate Professor of Social Anthropology at CIESAS (Center for Research and Postgraduate Studies in Social Anthropology) in Mexico. She has conducted extensive fieldwork in the indigenous Triqui region of Oaxaca and has written on indigenous collective rights, indigenous women, internal forced displacement, violence, (in)security, and the state. Her current research involves the access to justice and security of indigenous women in Veracruz, focusing on violence, state formation, and memories of organized indigenous women.

Fabienne Doiron is a PhD candidate in Gender, Feminist, and Women's Studies at York University in Toronto, Canada. Her MA and PhD research focus on gender issues in post-conflict Guatemala and have been informed by her solidarity and social justice work with the Maritimes-Guatemala Breaking the Silence Network. Her dissertation, focusing on femi(ni)cide and gendered and racialized violence in Guatemala, is grounded in intersectional feminist theory and informed by socio-legal studies, critical race theory, and anthropological work on the "violence of the everyday." She was a research assistant for Alison Crosby and M. Brinton Lykes' project on gender and reparations in post-genocidal Guatemala.

Gisela Espinosa Damián is a Mexican anthropologist and professor at the Metropolitan Autonomous University, Xochimilco Campus, and a member of the Mexican National System of Researchers. She specializes in participatory and collaborative research methodologies. Among her gender studies, she has analyzed Mexican feminisms, health, reproductive rights and maternal morbidity, violence, rural women and food supplies, migration and day laborer work. Her latest study, *Vivir para el surco. Trabajo y derechos en el Valle de San Quintín* (in process), was written in collaboration with Women in Defense of Women, an organization that promotes the labor rights in San Quintín Valley.

Myriam Jimeno is an anthropologist and National University of Colombia Professor (1974–2016). Her publications include *Crimen pasional. Contribución a una antropología de las emociones* (Bogotá: 2004) receiving merit award in Latin American Studies Association Ibero-American Book Prize, 2006; *Las sombras arbitrarias. Violencia y autoridad en Colombia* (Bogotá: 1996, co-authored), awarded the Ángel Escobar Foundation

Social Science and Humanities National Prize, 1995; *Juan Gregorio Palechor. The Story of my Life* (Duke University Press, 2014). *Después de la masacre: emociones y política en el Cauca indio*, co-authored (Bogotá: 2015). She was awarded research scholarship from John Simon Guggenheim Foundation 2010–2011, and professor emeritus Colciencias, 2016.

M. Brinton Lykes is Professor of Community-Cultural Psychology and Co-Director of the Center for Human Rights and International Justice at Boston College, USA. Her feminist participatory and action research collaborations include local cultural resources and the creative arts to analyze the causes and document the effects of gross violations of human rights. Her current work focuses on (1) racialized gender and sexual violence against Mayan women during armed conflict and their struggles for truth, justice, healing, and reparations; and (2) migration and post-deportation human rights violations and their effects for transnational families. She is co-founder and/or a board member of several local and international NGOs.

Morna Macleod is a professor in the Postgraduate Program in Social Science at the Autonomous Morelos State University, Mexico. She was a human rights activist after the Chilean military coup and during the armed conflict in Guatemala; she has also worked in aid agencies and as an independent consultant. Her research interests include rights and social justice; development; intersectional analysis; and in particular the Mayan movement, local power, and indigenous women in Guatemala. She is currently teaching and doing research on multiple violences in Mexico. Many of her publications are available on her website: http://mornamacleod.net/

Jenny Pearce is a research professor in the Latin America and Caribbean Centre at the London School of Economics. Previously she was Professor of Latin American Politics in the Department of Peace Studies, University of Bradford. She is a political scientist who works as an anthropologist and historian. Her research focuses on issues of violence, participation, and social change. She experiments with participatory methodologies working with communities experiencing multiple and chronic violences and is currently UK Principal Investigator on an ESRC/Conacyt project using such methodologies to build community security agendas in Mexico. She is also writing a book for Palgrave Macmillan on Politics and Violence.

Lynn Stephen is Distinguished Professor of Arts and Sciences and Professor of Anthropology at the University of Oregon where she founded the Center for Latino/a and Latin American Studies (CLLAS). From 2017 to 2019, she serves as president-elect and president of the Latin American Studies Association (LASA). Her scholarly work centers on the impact of globalization, migration, violence, nationalism and the politics of culture on indigenous communities in the Americas, with an emphasis on gender. She is currently researching indigenous women's access to justice in Guatemala, Mexico, and the USA and the impact of testimony on social movements and politics.

Daniel Varela is a researcher of the Colombian Institute of Anthropology and History (ICANH) and holds a master's degree in Anthropology from the National University of Colombia. He is a member of the research group: Social Conflict and Violence. His research interests include experiences of violence and the social and political recovery of the victims, social and political history of mining in an afro-descendant region, and the formation of agro industrial elites in Colombia. He is (co)author of *Después de la masacre: emociones y política en el Cauca indio* and *Las Compañías Chocó Pacífic y Tropical Oil a comienzos del siglo XX*.

List of Figures

Fig. 2.1 Massacre of Naya's victims at the 13th commemoration of the massacre holding the sign: "Life and Dignity of the People. No impunity, there is no forgiveness or forgetting, we want the culprits to be brought to justice." Photograph by Angela Castillo — 48

Fig. 2.2 Naya victims at the massacre's ninth commemoration holding the sign: "Nine years have passed since the massacre took place in the Naya River Valley." Photograph by Angela Castillo — 49

Fig. 3.1 Elena Poniatowska with Cuauhtémoc Abarca in the Museo de la Ciudad in July of 2015. Photograph by Lynn Stephen — 60

Fig. 4.1 Local Popular Power, Chaltenango 1984. Photograph by Mike Goldwater — 79

Fig. 5.1 The Sebastián Acevedo Movement Against torture. Photograph by Rosa Parissi — 107

Fig. 7.1 The wake for three murdered men at the Government Palace, Oaxaca city, August 2011. Photograph by Natalia De Marinis — 152

Fig. 8.1 Alliance to Break the Silence and Impunity banner: "Justice for sexual violence and sexual slavery." March commemorating the International Day for the Elimination of Violence against Women, Guatemala City, November 25, 2014. Photograph by Lisa Pauline Rankin — 174

Fig. 9.1 San Quintín Valley map by Mauricio Vázquez Techechil and Rigel Zaragoza Álvarez — 188

Fig. 9.2 Women Defending Women with the author. Photograph by Alfonso Zaragoza Álvarez — 194

Fig. 9.3 Woman day laborer. Photograph by Gisela Espinosa — 196

CHAPTER 1

Resisting Violence: Emotional Communities in Latin America

Natalia De Marinis and Morna Macleod

INTRODUCTION

This book maps different experiences in recent Latin American history of ordinary women and men's organized resistance to violence. Emotions in social movements have been the object of study in recent years (Jasper 2011), and growing attention has been paid to the role emotions play in social organizing, in the ways memories are evoked, testimony is given, and narratives of pain are transmitted (Das 1995; Taylor 2003; Jelin 2002). Our study takes us a step further. Developing the notion of "emotional communities," a term coined by Colombian anthropologist Myriam Jimeno, we explore the emotions and bonds established between victim-survivors, their political and emotional ties created with committed academics, social activists, and others, the ways in which emotions are embodied, enacted, and performed as a kind of cultural politics (Ahmed 2015) to reach a wider audience. The concept of "emotional communities" is our starting point to rethink experiences from new perspectives and becomes a hub where our concerns as researchers and activists intersect.

N. De Marinis (✉)
Center for Research and Postgraduate Studies
in Social Anthropology, Veracruz, Mexico

M. Macleod
Autonomous Morelos State University, Morelos, Mexico

© The Author(s) 2018
M. Macleod, N. De Marinis (eds.), *Resisting Violence*,
https://doi.org/10.1007/978-3-319-66317-3_1

Recent history, testimony, and memory work are the cornerstone of our study of emotions in contexts of resisting violence. We analyze various intentionally heterogeneous experiences and the political and affective bonds and alliances created between victim-survivors and ourselves as academics committed to social justice. Authors broaden the concept of emotional communities, adding new nuances, variations, and methodological approaches to think through the intersections between emotions and political action in diverse contexts of local collaborative research. Some experiences took place at the end of last century, but their testimonies have traveled through time acquiring new meanings in Latin America's current context of violence. Thus, examining, contributing, and adding to the notion of emotional communities is central to this book, in an exploration that takes the reader on a journey to different countries, experiences, periods of time, and forms of violence in Latin America.

Context

Over the past 40 years, Latin America has been wracked by different kinds of violence: military dictatorships, armed conflicts, and more recently, particularly in Mesoamerica, spiraling violence resulting from entrenched impunity and corruption, organized crime embedded in state institutions (Azaola 2012; Buscaglia 2014), and increasing inequality in wealth distribution (Reygadas 2008). During the Cold War, scholars and social actors tended to highlight political violence, isolating it from other forms of everyday violence, and thus not foreseeing the multiple forms of violence that would come into play after peace accords were signed and military regimes ceded power to civilian administrations (Scheper Hughes and Bourgois 2004).

This lack of breadth and foresight pushes us to assume a much broader concept, where political repression constantly interacts with other forms of everyday violence, including Galtung's trilogy of direct, structural, and cultural violence (2003), as well as Scheper Hughes and Bourgois' (2004) continuum of violence. A broader understanding of polyvalent violence allows us to understand the way intimate and domestic violence intertwines with public displays of brutality. It also highlights how traditional male socializing and gender roles illuminate the ways violence plays out, particularly among men (Pearce 2006).

The 1959 Cuban Revolution set an example that social change was possible, but political violence throughout the continent curtailed such expectations. Different strategies, including Chile's 1970 "peaceful road" to socialism and Nicaragua's armed struggle leading to revolutionary triumph in 1979, were fleeting experiences during which younger generations could yearn for brighter futures. Instead, military dictatorships, torture, imprisonment, forced disappearance, massacres, and scorched-earth national-security policies[1] squashed dreams of equality and social transformation in Latin America.

State violence, exemplified by Southern Cone military dictatorships in the 1970s and internal armed conflict in the 1980s in Central America, coincided with the critical juncture of crisis of the welfare state and the fight for socialism against new forms of increasingly entrenched neoliberal, free-market capitalism. The "drastic turn towards neoliberalism" affected "both practice and political-economic thought" (Harvey 2014, 19) through structural adjustment policies, privatization, and dismantling state social responsibility, while further exploiting and globalizing the workforce through free trade agreements, "treating workers and the environment as merchandise" (Harvey 2014, 89). Although Latin American neoliberalism was piloted in Pinochet's Chile with the "Chicago Boys" in the mid-1970s, it quickly spread into Central America following the peace accords signed there during the 1990s. Mexico's Zapatista uprising on precisely the day the North American Free Trade Agreement came into being bridges the old with the new, offering "other ways" of fighting neoliberalism, organizationally and discursively, while experimenting with innovative forms of resistance.

More recently, state violence is increasingly joined by other forms of public violence exercised by (il)legal and (il)licit corporate actors. Narcotics traffickers are closely allied with established private enterprise in money-laundering schemes that involve banks, transport firms, and construction companies, to name a few (Calveiro 2012). Traffickers also closely collude with government institutions, military and security forces, political parties, and leaders, particularly in Mexico and the "northern triangle" of Central America (El Salvador, Honduras, and Guatemala).

Against this bleak backdrop, the organizing of ordinary people, often led by women in local contexts of violence, and their daily struggles for social justice and human dignity provide glimmers of hope. This book looks at various experiences of organized ordinary people resisting violence and setting examples of hope. Despite dense and apparently impermeable contexts of extreme violence, human agency is possible and paves the road for further organization and human dignity. The volume also records the alliances formed between subject/victims and other actors, particularly committed scholars, and explores how these alliances form emotional communities, where emotions such as indignation, solidarity, empathy, and courage take central stage. These lived experiences of ordinary people provide "sparks of hope," recent accounts that need to be dug out and restored not only to history but as a groundwork for social justice in the future (Benjamin 2006; Pearce; and Macleod in this volume). Our focus will be on experiences of resistance to violence over the past 35 years that assume different expressions and contours in Mexico, Colombia, Guatemala, El Salvador, and Chile, in contexts of military dictatorship, armed conflicts, and their aftermath, structural and everyday violence, forced displacement, and organized crime. The authors' involvement in these experiences ranges from continual close accompaniment to less direct contact in a wider commitment to social justice.

Emotional Communities

The depth and breadth of Jimeno's notion of "emotional communities" are still in the making, nurtured by different lived experiences, theoretical debates, and reflections about the role of emotions in everyday life and social struggle. This collection of essays explores and enriches the concept by using this lens to reflect upon various experiences in Latin America over time. The notion of "emotional communities" coalesced in research carried out over several years by Jimeno and a team of students from the Center of Social Studies at the National University of Colombia with survivors of a massacre in southwest Colombia in 2001. The massacre forced the Nasa indigenous survivors to displace to lands allotted to them by the government in another part of the Cauca, where they rebuilt their lives and a new community, which they named Kitek Kiwe. Jimeno's team worked with the internally displaced survivors to reconstruct their memory both individually and collectively. The team realized the importance of the political and emotional dimensions of this work, which generated empathy among residents of the Kitek Kiwe community themselves, and between the community and the team of academics and students. The latter listened closely and annotated the displaced survivors' testimonies, becoming accomplices by strategizing how the community could denounce the massacre, tell their stories, and represent the massacre through annual public commemorations (also in this volume).

In this process of long-term accompaniment, Jimeno's research team wrote amply about the massacre, survival, reconstruction of people's lives, and reconfiguring of identities through Kitek Kiwe (Jimeno et al. 2011, 2015; Jimeno 2010, among others). The team also contributed to the commemorations and responded to Kitek Kiwe's requests, such as making a documentary video and documenting the recent history visually and through narratives.[2]

The notion of emotional communities offers a *bridge* between Jimeno's own genealogy of studying emotions and a conscious exploration of ethnography, collaborative research, and the connections between victims and academia. Because of diverse studies on violence since 1991, Jimeno concluded that there was a clear link between cognitive processes of reasoning, memories, assessments, and the role emotions play in experiences of violence (Jimeno 2004). By drawing on authors such as Reddy, Lila Abu-Lughod, and Catherine Lutz' cultural dimensions of emotions, Jimeno brings the marginal debate in the social sciences on emotions into the terrain of memory and collective action, after the in-depth and long-term collaboration with Kitek Kiwe.

Over the years, Myriam Jimeno's thinking on "emotional communities" greatly expanded. It currently brings together collective political, cultural, and emotional lived experience, the performative staging of traumatic events, and the relational nature of emotional communities, within Kitek Kiwe itself, its relations with close collaborators, such as Jimeno and her team, and with a wider audience during the annual commemorations. In the interview we carried out with Myriam Jimeno, she emphasizes the performative and cultural-political nature of emotional communities in contexts of violence, memory, and justice.

> [Emotional communities] are created through the process of narrating to another, testifying lived suffering through a story, a narrative, to someone else, and succeeding in the other identifying with their pain. Sometimes the narrative is performative, sometimes a ritual, in other cases it can be a political statement. I argue that this political narrative acquires great currency when it creates emotional community. That is, when the pain of the victim does not remain enclosed in the victim, but spreads to other audiences, who identify and are deeply moved by the narrative. This creates a political bond, not simply a compassionate moment. This *political* link contributes to enhance actions that seek justice, punish the guilty, set the record straight about what actually happened, and for victims to be holistically compensated. (Jimeno and Macleod, interview 2014)

Jimeno does not idealize communities, as she points out the risk of manipulation through certain kinds of charismatic leaders, the risk of trivializing pain and:

> exacerbating the dimension of suffering over and above restorative actions of the people themselves. It can become a pornography of violence, when horror fascinates the listener. This is a danger, because it locks people into their condition of victim, when what has been so important is the restructuring, converting victim into an active, not a passive category. (Jimeno and Macleod, interview 2014)

There are evident risks, including manipulation by charismatic leaders and official discourses, that appeal to emotions in order to appear close to victims in contexts of undeniable impunity. Emotional communities can be used for a variety of purposes and sometimes questionable ends. However, Jimeno's notion of emotional communities has multiple virtues, particularly in that it includes the emotions of victims-survivors in their struggles, and the emotions awakened among academics and wider audiences. The term also invokes the political-cultural nature of emotions. Pain expressed to others by a single subject is the point of departure of "emotional communities." The circularity of emotions in shared spaces and actions allows us to understand the pain, sadness, anger, and indignation pertaining not only to the victims; rather, these circulate through concrete political actions affecting "others" in their proximity. While incapable of feeling the experience of directly lived pain, we are permeated by it through the porous limits of our bodies, hearts, and minds.

Author and historian Barbara H. Rosenwein also coined the term "emotional communities" in a completely different context and discipline. Her book *Emotional Communities in the Early Middle Ages* (2006) and other writings have had a considerable impact on academic communities working on emotions. Rosenwein (2006, 2010) ingeniously fills a gap by recognizing not only the importance of emotions in the Middle Ages but also how groups are forged around values and shared sentiments:

> Emotional communities are largely the same as social communities – families, neighborhoods, syndicates, academic institutions, monasteries, factories, platoons, princely courts. But the researcher looking at them seeks above all to uncover systems of feeling, to establish what these communities (and the individuals within them) define and assess as valuable or harmful to them (for it is about such things that people express emotions); the emotions

that they value, devalue, or ignore; the nature of the affective bonds between people that they recognize; and the modes of emotional expression that they expect, encourage, tolerate, and deplore. (Rosenwein 2010, 11)

Rosenwein's concept of emotional communities varies substantially from Jimeno's, since the latter author's vision is more political and firmly grounded in violence, memory, and justice. However, Rosenwein and Jimeno's analyses share common aspects that distance them from academics in other disciplines: cognitive psychologists' concentration on individuals and biologists and geneticists' approaches to emotions that tend to freeze these in time. Jimeno and Rosenwein share a social constructionist approach to emotions—particularly apparent in the relationship established by Jimeno's anthropological team with the Nasa People. Rosenwein warns against universalistic approaches to emotions, clearly disagreeing with Nussbaum, who dislikes "the relativism that social constructionism implies" (Rosenwein 2006, 16). As a historian, Rosenwein is rightly wary of "presentism" (2010, 5), affirming that emotions can change over time: "how they are experienced, expressed, and interpreted—are shaped by the societies in which they are embedded" (ibid., 8–9). Jimeno and her team show that embedded societies can change suddenly, with the loss of place after a massacre, and the reconfiguration of identities as victim-survivors aim to rebuild their lives, with memory acting as a bridge between the "before" and "after" (Jimeno et al. 2011, 276). These are some of the reflections on emotions in the political that we will examine more deeply throughout this volume.

Thus, emotional communities constitute our point of departure to explore experiences of shared moments and places where memory acquires a sense of reparation imbued with the demand for justice, where the emotional and the political come together between victims and those in solidarity. There is a sense of joint belonging through emotional regimes (Rosenwein 2010; Cornejo 2016), as well as articulating this to processes of memory that transcend the group of victim-survivors themselves, to include the feelings of an audience, creating bonds of solidarity in political struggles for justice. Those called upon to become involved express solidarity in multiple ways: through documenting testimony, accompaniment, carrying out "expert witness" reports (putting one's social capital at the service of the aggrieved victims.) In these cases, emotions and the political coalesce and entwine through actions wich include justice, healing, and reparation. We highlight the salience of their materiality and the collective and intersubjective aspects of emotions and memory work with a view to justice.

Strategic emotional political communities emerged in this book as a new concept elaborating on Jimeno's notion of *emotional communities*. Lynn Stephen advances this term to think through the way Mexico City's 1985 earthquake victim testimonies traveled over time through Elena Poniatowska's *crónicas*. They also contribute to renewing traumatic memory in other political contexts. Stephen proposes in this volume that emotional communities result from the effect of traditional forms of protest and suggests placing them in a wider shared ethical context, bringing together past and present.

This opens up the possibility of authors engaging with events where they were not present: rather, past processes travel through time by way of testimonies. This broadening of the very notion of communities breaks time and space barriers: community is no longer perceived as closed and fixed, related simply to the present. Testimonies travel across time, and through different mechanisms that connect time and space. Morna Macleod makes another important contribution to this notion through the experience of the Movement Against Torture Sebastián Acevedo (MCTSA). The Movement mobilizes shared solidarities, emotions, and ethics across time. Macleod positions herself as a human rights activist against Chile's military dictatorship and recalls her closeness to some Movement members. However, she did not participate in any way in the Movement's activities. Her testimony gathering is recent, but she also retrieves the past testimonies through videos that circulate, capturing the power of the Movement's actions against torture, as well as their impact on others, and thus contributes to restoring to recent history this relatively unknown experience.

The analysis of audiences that accompany these memory processes provides another contribution to the book. Ixkic Bastian Duarte explores the experience of refugees in Mexico returning to Guatemala to resettle and create new communities before the signing of the 1996 peace accords. She achieves this through a novel form of analysis that brings together *acompañantes*, including herself: people that accompanied the return of refugees both practically and through committed solidarity.

There is great resonance among the chapters in terms of the intersection between political and emotional spheres. Gisela Espinosa describes her collaborative research work with women day laborers in San Quintín Valley, presenting a different kind of violence analyzed in other chapters. This chapter does not explore the violence of massacres, war, or forced displacement, but rather everyday violence and the violent trajectories of women day laborers. The 2015 insurrection of day laborers allows her to understand the emergence of traumatic memories and their impact charged with emotions, but also the political. It is from this intersection that the author positions her collaborative research with women day laborers.

While Myriam Jimeno and her team finally settle for the term *emotional communities*, in previous publications they put forward the notion of *political-affective communities*.[3] Fundamental differences do not exist between the two concepts; both form part of the same process of indignation and construction of knowledge. In some chapters in this volume, the term *political-affective communities* is used to highlight the intersection with the political. This is the case in Natalia De Marinis' chapter, as the author locates the importance of affects—as in affection—from a wider perspective than merely emotional dimensions, as we shall see later on. For the forcefully displaced Triqui women, the diverse emotions they express are also linked to affections produced by the *abject* environment/experience of displacement in which the displaced had to rebuild their lives and deal with unimagined political resistance. Jenny Pearce also takes up the notion of *political-affective communities* to analyze the nature of emotions as political consciousness, crucial to the process of turning memory into history for *campesinos* in postwar Chalatenango, El Salvador. The politicization of affects among *campesinos*, Pearce suggests, contributes to converting pain into acts of mutual support and cooperation in the reconstruction of memory and history.

The experiences of emotional communities in this volume portray a notion of community far from homogeneous and harmonious. As Crosby, Lykes, and Doiron point out, communities are permeated by racial, gender, class, and educational hierarchies, that is, power relations that also need to be unveiled in our own positioning as researchers. When we think about notions such as shared emotions, we are compelled to engage in an ethical reflection about the possibilities of empathy. By no means do we suggest that it is possible to feel the pain of others, nor that what we feel is commensurable to the pain of the victim-survivors we work with. Crosby, Lykes, and Doiron, and other authors in this volume emphasize these crossovers which nurture the ethical-political reflections in our approach to emotional communities.

Emotions, Performance, and Empathetic Engagement

Emotions as an analytical concept have received increasing interest in the social sciences since the 1970s. A major contribution consists of the study of emotions in human interaction and social movement collective action. This entails a critique of neurobiological and psychological perspectives, which relegate emotions to intimate, personal, and thus non-rational spheres. Dominant dichotomies between rational-emotional, public-private, mind-body have dismissed emotions from rational scientific thought and have linked them to the roots of gender differences, as characteristics associated with femininity and otherness. As Ahmed states, "The Darwinian model of emotions suggests that emotions are not only 'beneath' but also 'behind' the man/human, as a sign of an early and more primitive time" (Ahmed 2015, 3).

A hierarchy of emotions prevails, at once rational but also racial, where "being emotional" typifies some bodies but not others. Women, indigenous, Afro, and other subaltern bodies are considered "weaker," "primitive," and relegated to "otherness," "and are regarded as the strongholds of uncontrolled emotionality, unless mechanisms such as education can keep them in check" (Jimeno 2004, 28).[4] This naturalized western belief that links emotions to the irrational, as well as racializing and feminizing them, is precisely what has been brought into question in much research carried out in recent decades in different disciplinary fields.

In sociology, classical authors, such as Simmel, Weber, and Durkheim, have studied emotions, while Erving Goffman researched interactionism, followed by Randall Collins, Theodore Kemper, and others (see Sabido Ramos 2011; Ariza 2016). These studies have contributed to incorporating emotions into social action from a sociological and interactionist perspective, particularly in the study of social movements. Emotions are identified as a central part of knowledge and decision-making, on the par with rationality. Indeed, emotions drive social action (Jasper 2011).

Anthropological perspectives have also nurtured comprehension of cultural dimensions of emotions in different contexts. As Lutz (1986) affirms, when researchers seek their essence and focus narrowly on what comprises personhood, emotions are reduced to psychological dimensions, becoming "features of individuals rather than of situations, relationships, or moral positions. In other words, they are constructed as psychological, rather than social, phenomena" (Lutz 1986, 289). Le Breton (2013) suggests that emotions are not substances or fixed states; rather, they transform according to contexts, audiences, and personal analysis. Thus, in keeping with Lutz, cultural meanings assigned to emotions go unquestioned in Euro-American common sense passing itself off as universal. From this viewpoint, the essence of emotions can be identified, regarded as universal, and analyzed regardless of personal and social contexts (1986, 288). Renato Rosaldo's contribution illuminates these cultural differences. Initially understanding Ilongot head-hunting practices as an economic exchange, Rosaldo began to think otherwise following the death of his wife Michelle Zimbalist Rosaldo. Fourteen years after his work on the Ilongots, he realized that anger formed part of grief and recognized the place emotions merit in ethnographic study. Rosaldo calls this the *cultural force* of emotions that enhances the processing of grief (Rosaldo 1993). This led him to propose the notion of *positioned subject* recognizing the importance of situating one's own experience, critiquing pretensions of objectivity and universality.

Affectivity allows us to understand that the "inside" and the "outside" are interrelated rather than segregated entities. This understanding of emotions opens up the porous boundaries between body and space, and positions us as researchers in contexts of pain and cultural expressions of emotions. The so-called affective turn in social science (Clough and Halley 2007) raised the need to rethink the role of affection as affectation, the body's capacity to affect and be affected, to connect. This Spinozian perspective, adopted by Gilles Deleuze and Félix Guattari, is based on a critique of discursive construction and reason-based subjectivity, through incorporating bodies, matter, time, and environment; that is, subjectivity understood as a wider range of affectations (Clough and Halley 2007; Navaro-Yashin 2012).[5]

Anthropologist Naravo Yashin studied the way environmental affectations transmuted into emotional feelings among those displaced in Cyprus, analyzing the melancholy of the displaced as the effect/affectation of the milieu on their bodies. These alterations not only materialized in individual subjects but also permeated objects and the destroyed environment where the displaced were left to rebuild their lives (Navaro-Yashin 2012). For Sara Ahmed (2015), these new turns in the study of emotions transcend the advances made in psychology, and surpass sociological, individualizing, and biological arenas. Melancholy, pain, pleasure, anger, and joy cannot be understood as individual psychic states divorced from the circulation of energies and emotions that affect bodies. There are porous boundaries between "me" and the surface. Applying this specifically to narratives of pain, emotions circulate, project themselves, and affect us in multiple ways; thus, the idea of porosity of boundaries acquires greater acumen. Veena Das' analyses of pain include many of these arguments. Das claims that pain cannot be treated as something personal, as its expression is precisely an invitation to share. "It is this fact – that violence annihilates language, that terror cannot be brought into the realm of the utterable – which invites us to constitute the body as a mediating sign between the individual and society, and between the past and the present" (Das 1995, 184).

Sara Ahmed proposes that sentiments are crucial in forming surfaces and borders between one's own body and that external to it; she also argues that the emotions that create these frontiers also dissolve them, that is, "What separates us from others, also connects us to others. This paradox is clear if we think of the skin surface itself, as that which appears to contain us, but as where others impress upon us" (2015, 25). The circularity of emotions also emerges in post-structuralist feminist body and performance studies (Rosaldo and Lamphere 1974; Lutz and White 1986; Jaggar 1992; Butler 1990; Cornejo 2016; Taylor 2003). Since their debut in the 1970s, performance studies (Carlson 2004; Taylor 2003) emphasize emotions, attitudes, and events, dramatizing these for a wider public. Analyzed as embodied action (Taylor 2003; Butler 1990; Turner 1976), performance studies have been extensively nurtured by theatrics, ritual, and drama studies. For Butler (1990), performativity represents the embodiment of sexual normative and regulatory frames as part of the process of socialization.

In performance studies, there is a clear link between dramatizing (in this case) a grievance and its impact on the public. Diana Taylor (2003) has emphasized that, rather than focusing on what performance is, we should be asking what it enables and provokes. Taylor proposes a frame that situates performance as an act of transferring "knowledge" and critiques European logocentric knowledge that prioritized writing above embodied and expressive culture. Focusing on scenes that go beyond writing about the past invites a critical, situated methodology to emphasize our registers, interactions, and emotional engagement, no longer relegated to others, but rather including the implications that traumatic events have on all of us involved one way or another in these experiences.

In this volume, authors' standpoint and positionality as socially committed researchers is a cross-cutting theme throughout the book. This includes *situated knowledge* (De Marinis), *feminist participatory action research*

(Crosby, Lykes, and Doiron), *collaborative systematizing* (Espinosa), *collaborative research* (Jimeno, Varela, and Castillo), and Rappaport's (2008) metaphors of *inside/outside* (Macleod). Joanne Rappaport uses the metaphors "inside" and "outside" (Rappaport 2008) to name and understand the complexity of these different forms of positioning and collaboration between communities, and indigenous, national and foreign intellectuals. These metaphors, far from becoming fixed and essentialist locations, illuminate the diverse and ever-changing closeness and/or distance between different actors involved in collaborative strategies for academic, educational, and political processes. All authors reflect upon their diverse positionings and locations in relation to the subjects they work with, as well as the different possibilities and challenges facing the co-construction of knowledge with them.

The ways multiple hierarchies intersect relationships and interactions between researchers—volunteer *acompañantes* (Bastian), expert witnesses (Crosby, Lykes, and Doiron; and Stephen)—open up an ethical-political debate around the notion of community itself, and the reflection that more than harmony, conflictive heterogeneity gives rise to permanent, productive, and creative tensions. In Crosby, Lykes, and Doiron and Stephen's chapters, the notion of *nos-otras* (we-others) is explored to understand these tensions, and that naming them is the first step in decolonizing emotions, avoiding sensationalism and placing center stage the experience and authority of those who have directly suffered trauma.

History, Memory Testimonies, and Justice

Our book brings together experiences of extreme violence in recent history in Chile, Mexico, Colombia, El Salvador, and Guatemala. Rather than dwell on the copious documentation of atrocities committed during the 1970s dictatorships, Central American armed conflict in the 1980s, and increasing inequality and structural violence related to neoliberalism and state violence, we focus our lens on organized women and men's resistance to political repression, inequality, racism, sexism, and other forms of oppression. To do this we need to distinguish between memory and history, understanding the role of each. "Memory," Traverso (2016, 19–20) tells us, "is the sum of individual and collective memories; it is a present representation of the past created in the public sphere. History, in turn, is a critical discourse about the past. History is the work of reconstruction, contextualizing, interpreting the past through fabricating a story, a narrative, or various narratives about the past." The essays in this volume intertwine memory with recent history. And it is Walter Benjamin (2006, 392) who provides us with clues as to the importance of capturing "flashes" of history, to provide seeds of hope for the future: "Articulating the past historically does not mean recognizing it 'the way it really was.' It means appropriating a memory as it flashes up in a moment of danger." Our task as socially committed academics, is "to brush history against the grain" (ibid.), digging up flashes of history of organized everyday women and men, and their struggle for social justice in the context of extreme violence. By doing this, we overcome narratives of crushing violence that tend to minimize human agency and are able to establish "a conception of the present as now-time shot through with splinters of messianic time" (Benjamin 2006, 397).

This book offers different ways of understanding memory and the recent past, given authors' exploration of differing contexts and temporalities. Chapters that delve into experiences from the 1970s to 1980s include memory work, as in Pearce's involvement with the Museum of Historical Memory in postwar El Salvador and Bastian's experience of accompanying Guatemalan refugees in Mexico and their return to Guatemala. Macleod and Stephen also reconstruct processes in the 1980s; although the researchers did not participate directly in these particular cases, they were involved in related processes at the time; this then widens the very notion of involvement. In retrospect, they analyze the effects that testimonies have had over time. By gathering recent testimonies, they reconstruct recent history and make connections between memory and current contexts of violence.

The book does not focus on the much-studied literature of transitional justice, choosing testimony instead as a mechanism used both during and after periods of repression. Testimony has played a key role in Latin America during the five decades under review, forming part of a political-action repertoire particularly among the left and social movements. As Beverley (2008, 574) reminds us, "The word *testimonio* carries the connotation in Spanish of the act of testifying or bearing witness in a legal or religious sense," particularly among victim-survivors who do not have other channels to air their grievances. Testimonies in the context of violence and repression are key in "setting the record straight," providing voice and venue in public arenas to spokespersons who bear witness. "The question of *testimonio* – testimonial narrative – intertwines the 'desire for objectivity' and 'the desire for solidarity' in its very situation of production, circulation, and reception." (Beverley 2008, 571). Through testimony, the unsayable is uttered and solidarity is sought from those it addresses.

Testimony traverses time and becomes an effective form of denouncing situations of terror in the here and now. Thus, with indignation and bewilderment, Maya Achi' catechist Carmelita Santos, during the midst of the massacres in Guatemala, asks the federation of the relatives of the disappeared (FEDEFAM) at a 1983 meeting in Mexico City: "But why are they killing us like dogs?" She breaks the silence and highlights the cruelty and denial of human dignity perpetrated in indigenous communities, demanding action and solidarity. Elizabeth Lira, pioneer in therapeutic uses of testimony following the military coup d'état in Chile, worked with political prisoners and relatives of the disappeared, drawing the connections between personal pain and collective trauma, emotions, and events. This process enabled the most intimate impacts of torture and disappearance to be placed firmly in the context of military dictatorship, thus enabling victims to understand the political implications of methods used to destroy opponents: "Testimony as a therapeutic tool became a means to integrate aspects of traumatic experiences of political repression" (Lira 2007, 35).

All chapters discuss at length the role of testimony in visibilizing political struggle and resistance. Testimony contributes to memory work, to recuperating the collective and the personal, to highlighting voices and experience of violence that has been silenced, as in the case of indigenous peoples. We understand that testimony is both verbal and non-verbal, since there are other ways of testifying that are specific to indigenous peoples. In Jimeno, Varela and Castillo and De Marinis' chapters, both the displaced Nasa commemorations and the public acts of displaced Triquis broaden our notions of oral narrative to incorporate diverse cultural meanings of emotions and (in)justice and other forms of knowledge. These are brought into play through performative acts that include indigenous narratives and knowledges historically excluded from official spaces of justice, highlighting the continuity of injustice and their vindication as "millenary victims" (see Jimeno et al. this volume).

For their part, Lykes et al. and Espinosa analyze testimony orality in two dissimilar terrains involving indigenous women in Guatemala and Mexico, respectively. Espinosa's reflections derive from the act of testifying as part of a process of collaborative systematizing with indigenous day laborers. These testimonies are intersected by migratory and violent trajectories and continuums of violence in an agricultural laborer terrain. Crosby, Lykes, and Doiron scrutinize the roles of testimony of victims of sexual violence and of expert witnesses in an official court of justice in the Sepur Zarco trial, a public space fraught with gender, racial, and political hierarchies.

Testimonies are often not so immediate, but serve rather as a way to remember. Jelin (2002) suggests that the testimonial trace brings together both the experience of the survivor, narrating her/his experience, and the observer who literally bears witness to the referred to events. The relationship between telling and the responsibility of listening becomes a dialogically shared interaction. Lynn Stephen (2017) identifies different kinds of testimony, ranging from indigenous literacy, the voices of the subaltern, to "expert witness," that is, "professionals" who make use of their social capital and academic credibility to become translators defending those without a voice.

The sheer diversity of testimony constitutes its richness, captured in different experiences throughout this book. These dialogues also give us the opportunity to rethink testimony and memory, as narratives that allow certain kinds of denunciations, some curtailed and limited by frames imposed in different scenarios, particularly in contexts of transitional justice. It is therefore impossible to speak of memory, vision, and meaning in the singular, nor specify meanings in political and affective terms. Rather, we speak of memory and truth as a disputed terrain, with different narrative forms and political ends. Moreover, we speak especially of the present, as memory and the recent past take on meaning in the here and now, opening up the potential for future, creative transformation, the possibility of becoming. Thus, memory is not anchored in the past, or at least that is not its point of departure; rather it is the dangerous present that gives meaning to the past, where memory acts as a bridge that connects and articulates the unfolding of history (Calveiro 2006; Jelin 2002).

Memory is not antithetic to forgetting in various ways, including the political will to forget: Imposed erasure and absence of narrative frames can also impede the expression of memory. There is also "evasive forgetting" of those who prefer to forget to be able to live (Ricoeur 2004). The relationship between remembering and forgetting acquires great force in the face of current impunity; it colors the affectivity of memory. This affective burden takes its imprint from traumatic events; the unsayable becomes an inextricable nexus of memory, turning forgetting not into its opposite, but rather integrating it as one of its vital components.

Memory is necessarily related to emotions such as suffering, joy, sadness. It is also intimately linked to collectivity, as highlighted by memory theorists. Halbwachs' pioneer reflections on "social memory frameworks" point to the collective (2004), articulating and giving meaning to a shared past. Pollak (2006) speaks of events "lived indirectly," deeply appropriated by group members who may not have experienced them in person. This identification also occurs in reference to place, emblematic figures, and is transferred by legacy, where it is almost impossible, Pollak claims, to separate the limits between individual and collective memory.

In our experiences, testimony becomes a possibility to narrate, wherein affections circulate between body limits and what is possible to say or to name. Our contact with victims implies an ongoing reflection about the ethics of listening and empathy. Sadness arising from body ailments, fear, or terror annuls the possibility of naming. This contributes to impunity curtailing the capacity to denounce, as does the lack of protection mechanisms for those who testify in different arenas. The inability to denounce and be understood is further complicated by culturally diverse contexts where emotions are expressed, become embodied, are circulated and impact on others. In several chapters, emphasis is given to listening, as well as to audience members where testimonies are transmitted. The concept of *empathetic listener* synthesizes these interactions in order to rethink the notion of *testimonial trace*, and suggests that testimony necessarily involves others, an audience that bears witness.

We adhere to critiquing the emerging testimony and trauma industry: a procession of "trauma experts" in the words of Castillejo Cuellar (2009; also see Fassin 2009). Much of this critical analysis concerns the silence of victims, the political use of testimonies and power, gender, and racialized relations in contexts that involve indigenous and/or Afro peoples. These power relations are created between those obliged to give testimony and those who are located in the moral space of listening (Crosby and Lykes 2011; Theidon 2009).

Some authors suggest that the core problem resides in a notion of victim enclosed in specific normative and enunciatory frames that define who is a victim and who is not: the conditions that allow one to situate oneself as a victim; the ways victims are expected to act, what victims can say, and what they cannot say and must remain hidden. These limitations stem from unequal relations with the state, whereby victims have to position themselves within institutional limits. The only way to question power is curtailed by the very logics of power. Truth commissions and compensatory policies can also have unexpected outcomes: Many reports are simply archived and their recommendations ignored; reparation measures may become bureaucratized, inaccessible, and even morally offensive. Jimeno, Varela and Castillo, and Pearce discuss social actors' reluctance to position themselves as victims as this contributes to dispossession and a loss of agency: "Are we victims or survivors?" ask the *campesinos* of Chalatenango, El Salvador.

As Alison Crosby and Brinton Lykes (2011; and Crosby, Lykes, and Doiron in this volume) propose, "truth-telling" and reconstructing the past are not neutral acts; on the contrary, they necessarily involve gender, political, and cultural constructions. Supposed gender-neutrality constitutes a central critique of truth commissions. The invisibilizing of women's grievances derives from two sources: the universalizing nature of human rights that suppresses differences through the principle of equality and generalized undervaluing of violence against women in times of war, explained in part by invisibilizing violence against women in times of peace. Crosby and Lykes (2011), Ross (2010), and Theidon (2006) in Guatemala, South Africa, and Peru, respectively, refer to silence as a form of survival when women are faced with impunity, sexism, and a lack of justice. The perpetrators are usually still "out there" in most cases, and this creates greater defenselessness among the women.

Our experiences are not only based on these critiques but are also rooted in the commitment to revert deplorable situations that abound in diverse forms of political violence in Latin America. Here the feminist notion of *situated knowledge* (Haraway 1988), shared by certain currents of collaborative and activist research (Speed 2008; Hernández Castillo 2016; Sieder 2017), allows us to analyze our experiences as a way of generating various collaborative processes between researchers and victims. These perspectives are rooted in the context of decades of popular education (Freire 1969), participatory research (Fals Borda 1987), activist anthropology, and feminist research in Latin America. We intend to go a bit further as we make explicit how relationships between victim-survivors and researchers are woven together through political bonds, but also emotional and affective commitments in the resistance to violence in Latin America.

Notes

1. Much has been written on the marked differences and certain similarities between political repression in South and Central America; our intention here is to emphasize that social transformation was not tolerable for local elites and the US government.
2. "Kitek Kiwe, nuestra memoria," is a documentary directed by Pedro Tattay Bolaños. See https://www.youtube.com/watch?v=hfcdfBdsvEk
3. This concept was proposed in Jimeno (2007).
4. All translations from Spanish are ours, save documents translated and published in English.
5. The influential assumption of an inner being conceptualized as a separate entity excluded the possibility of this circular approach to emotions, where inside and outside are more porous, and where materiality affects subjectivity. Foucault privileges this "outside" through his critique of philosophy of the subject. He states that subjectivity cannot be understood outside specific regimes of truth and governmentality that affect bodies and subjectivity (Foucault 1997).

References

Ahmed, Sara. 2015 [2004]. *The Cultural Politics of Emotions*. New York/London: Routledge.

Ariza, Marina, ed. 2016. *Emociones, Afectos y Sociología: Diálogos desde la investigación social y la interdisciplina*. Mexico: Instituto de Investigaciones Sociales, Universidad Nacional Autónoma de México.

Azaola, Elena. 2012. La violencia hoy, las violencias de siempre. *Desacatos* 40, September–December, pp. 13–32.

Benjamin, Walter. 2006 [1940]. On the Concept of History. In *Walter Benjamin, Selected Writings, Volume 4, 1938–1949*, ed. Howard Eiland and Michael W. Jennings, 389–400. Cambridge, MA/London: Harvard University Press.

Beverley, John. 2008. Testimonio, Subalternity, and Narrative Authority. In *A Companion to Latin American Literature and Culture*, ed. Sara Castro-Klaren, 571–583. Oxford/Maden: Blackwell Publishing.

Buscaglia, Edgardo. 2014 [2013]. Vacíos de poder en México. *Debate*, pp. 11–38.

Butler, Judith. 1990. *Gender Trouble: Feminism and the Subversion of Identity*. London/New York: Routledge.

Calveiro, Pilar. 2006. Los usos políticos de la memoria. In *Sujetos sociales y nuevas formas de protesta en la historia reciente de América Latina*, ed. Gerardo Caetano, 359–382. Buenos Aires: CLACSO.

———. 2012. *Violencias de Estado, la guerra antiterrorista y la guerra contra el crimen como medios de control global*. México: Siglo XXI.

Carlson, Marvin. 2004. *Performance: A Critical Introduction*. Nueva York: Routledge.
Castillejo Cuellar, Alejandro. 2009. *Archivos del dolor: ensayos sobre la violencia y el recuerdo en la Sudáfrica contemporánea*. Bogotá: Universidad de los Andes.
Clough, Patricia, and Jean Halley, eds. 2007. *The Affective Turn: Theorizing the Social*. Durham/London: Duke University Press.
Cornejo, Amaranta. 2016. Una relectura feminista de algunas propuestas teóricas del estudio social de las emociones. *Revista Interdisciplina* 4 (8): 89–104.
Crosby, Alison, and Brinton Lykes. 2011. Mayan Women Survivors Speak: The Gendered Relations of Truth Telling in Postwar Guatemala. *The International Journal of Transitional Justice* 5 (3): 456–476.
Das, Veena. 1995. *Critical Events: An anthropological Perspective on Contemporary Indian*. Oxford: Oxford University Press.
Fals Borda, Orlando. 1987. The Application of Participatory Action-Research in Latin America. *International Sociology* 2 (4): 329–347.
Fassin, Didier. 2009. *The Empire of Trauma: An Inquiry of the Condition of Victimhood*. Princeton/Oxford: Princeton University Press.
Foucault, Michel. 1997. *Society Must Be Defended*. New York: Picador.
Freire, Paulo. 1969. *Pedagogía del oprimido*. México: Siglo XXI.
Galtung, Johan. 2003 [1989]. *Violencia Cultural*, Documento. Vol. 14, 1–36. GuerniKa-Lumo: Gernika Gogoratuz.
Halbwachs, Maurice. 2004 [1968]. *La memoria colectiva*. Zaragoza: Prensas Universitarias de Zaragoza.
Haraway, Donna. 1988. Situated Knowledges: The Science Question in Feminism and the Privilege of Partial Perspective. *Feminist Studies* 14 (3): 575–599.
Harvey, David. 2014. *Breve historia del neoliberalismo*. Bolivia: Vicepresidencia del Estado.
Hernández Castillo, R. Aída. 2016. *Multiple InJustices: Indigenous Women, Law and Political Struggle in Latin America*. Arizona: The Arizona of University Press.
Jaggar, Alison. 1992. *Gender/Body/Knowledge: Feminist Reconstruction of Being and Knowing*. New Brunswick: Rutgers University Press.
Jasper, James. 2011. Emotions and Social Movements: Twenty Years of Theory and Research. *Annual Review of Sociology* 37 (14): 14.1–14.9.
Jelin, Elizabeth. 2002. *Los trabajos de la memoria*. Buenos Aires: Siglo XXI.
Jimeno, Myriam. 2004. *Crimen pasional: contribución a una antropología de las emociones*. Bogotá: Universidad Nacional de Colombia.
———. 2007. Cuerpo personal y cuerpo politico: violencia, cultura y ciudadanía neoliberal. *Universitas Humanísticas* 63 (January–June): 15–34.
———. 2010. Emocoes e política: A vitima e a construcao de comunidades emocionais. *Revista Mana* 16 (1): 99–121.
Jimeno, Myriam, and Morna Macleod. 2014. Interview with Myriam Jimeno. November 2014. Available at http://mornamacleod.net/?p=767

Jimeno, Myriam, Daniel Varela, and Ángela Castillo. 2011. Experiencias de violencia: etnografía y recomposición social en Colombia. *Sociedade e Cultura* 14 (2): 275–285.
Jimeno, Myriam, Daniel Varela, and Angeles Castillo. 2015. *Después de la masacre, emociones y política en el Cauca Indio*. Bogotá: ICANH y CES: Universidad Nacional de Colombia.
Le Breton, David. 2013. Por una antropología de las emociones. *Revista Latinoamericana sobre Cuerpo, Emociones y Sociedad* 4 (10): 69–79.
Lira, Elizabeth. 2007. El testimonio de experiencias políticas traumáticas: terapia y denuncia en Chile (1973–1985). In *Historizar el pasado, serie digital*, dir. Anne Pérotin-Dumon, 1–40. Available at www.historizarelpasadovivo.cl/es_contenido.php
Lutz, Catherine. 1986. Emotion, Thought and Estrangement: Emotion as a Cultural Category. *Cultural Anthropology* 1 (3): 287–309.
Lutz, Catherine, and Geoffrey White. 1986. The Anthropology of Emotions. *Annual Review of Anthropology* 15: 405–436.
Navaro-Yashin, Yael. 2012. *The Make Believe Space: Affective Geography in a Postwar Polity*. Durham/Londres: Duke University Press.
Pearce, Jenny. 2006. Bringing Violence 'Back Home': Gender Socialisation and the Transmission of Violence Through Time and Space. In *Global Civil Society 2006/7*, ed. Marlies Glasius, Mary Kaldor, and Helmut Anheier, 42–60. London: Sage Knowledge.
Pollak, Michael. 2006. *Memoria, Olvido y Silencio: La producción de identidades frente a situaciones límite*. Trans. Christian Gebauer, Renata Oliveira Rufino and Mariana Tello. La Plata: Al margen.
Ramos, Sabido. 2011. El cuerpo y la afectividad como objetos de estudio en América Latina: Intereses temáticos y procesos de institucionalización reciente. *Revista Sociológica* 26 (74): 33–78.
Rappaport, Joanne. 2008. *Utopías interculturales. Intelectuales públicos, experimentos con la cultura y pluralismo étnico en Colombia*. Bogotá: Escuela de Ciencias Humanas, Editorial Universidad del Rosario.
Reygadas, Luis. 2008. *La apropiación: Destejiendo las redes de la desigualdad*. Barcelona: Anthropos Editorial; México: Universidad Autónoma Metropolitana, Iztapalapa.
Ricoeur, Paul. 2004. *Memory, History, Forgetting*. Chicago/London: Chicago University Press.
Rosaldo, Renato. 1993. *Culture and Truth: The Remarking of Social Analysis*. Boston: Beacon Press.
Rosaldo, Michelle Zimbalist, and Louise Lamphere, eds. 1974. *Women, Culture and Society*. Stanford: Stanford University Press.
Rosenwein, Barbara H. 2006. *Emotional Communities in the Early Middle Ages*. Ithaca/London: Cornell University Press.

———. 2010. Problems and Methods in the History of Emotions. *Passions in Context: Journal of the History and Philosophy of Emotions* 1 (1). Available at http://www.passionsincontext.de/index.php/?id=557

Ross, Fiona. 2010. An Acknowledged Failure: Women, Voice, Violence and the South African Truth and Reconciliation Commission. In *Localizing Transitional Justice*, ed. Rosalind Shaw and Lars Waldorf, 69–91. Stanford: Stanford University Press.

Scheper-Hughes, Nancy, and Philippe Bourgois, eds. 2004. *Violence in War and Peace: An Anthology*. Oxford: Blackwell Publishing.

Sieder, Rachel, ed. 2017. *Demanding Justice and Security: Indigenous Women and Legal Pluralism in Latin America*. New Brunswick: Rutgers University Press.

Speed, Shannon. 2008. *Rights in Rebellion: Indigenous Struggle and Human Rights in Chiapas*. Stanford: Stanford University Press.

Stephen, Lynn. 2017. Bearing Witness: Testimony in Latin American Anthropology and Related Fields. *The Journal of Latin American and Caribbean Anthropology* 22 (1): 85–109.

Taylor, Diana. 2003. *The Archive and the Repertoire: Performing Cultural Memories in the Americas*. Durham: Duke University Press.

Theidon, Kimberly. 2006. Género en transición: Sentido común, mujeres y guerra. *Cuadernos de Antropología Social* 24: 69–92.

———. 2009. La teta asustada: Una teoría sobre la violencia de la memoria. *Ideele Revista del Instituto de defensa legal* 191: 56–63.

Traverso, Enzo. 2016. Memoria y Historia del Siglo XXI. In *Archivos y Memoria de la Represión en América Latina (1973–1990)*, ed. María Graciela Acuna et al., 17–29. Santiago de Chile: LOM ediciones/FASIC.

Turner, Victor. 1976. *The Ritual Process: Structure and Anti-structure*. Chicago: Aldine Publishing Company.

CHAPTER 2

Violence, Emotional Communities, and Political Action in Colombia

Myriam Jimeno, Daniel Varela, and Angela Castillo

SETTING THE STAGE

During Holy Week of 2001, the armed group *Autodefensas Unidas de Colombia*, AUC,[1] entered the Naya, a remote region in southwest Colombia, traversed by a river of the same name. During this incursion they murdered more than 40 persons (including Nasa indigenous people, Afro-Colombians, peasants, and traders) and forced thousands more to flee and take refuge in shelters in nearby municipalities. Shortly after the massacre, most of the families that fled from the Naya returned due to overcrowding at the shelters. However, 56 families from various ethnic backgrounds, but mainly indigenous Nasa, decided not to return because they feared renewed violent assaults. They began a fight to redress their violated rights, which guided their process of personal reconstruction and gave life to a new social

---

M. Jimeno (✉)
National University of Colombia, Bogotá, Colombia

D. Varela
Colombian Institute of Anthropology and History,
National University of Colombia, Bogotá, Colombia

A. Castillo
University of California, Berkeley, CA, USA

group, a new community far from their region of origin, with elements of new identity and self-identification. Due to legal proceedings, in 2004 the Colombian state allocated another piece of land to this group near Popayán, capital of the Cauca Province. Here they founded the *Kitek Kiwe* ("blooming land" in Nasa language) Indigenous Council.[2]

Between 2008 and 2014, we focused on understanding the complex context in which the new life and the social re-composition of this group developed following the violent event. Group reconstruction involved small and continuous actions aimed at economic recovery; activation of kinship relationships, political alliances and new leaderships; new liaisons with governmental and non-governmental institutions; and adoption of new ways of dialoguing with the larger Colombian society. We found that the common thread of these actions was the construction of a narrative about the traumatic events that focused on a particular category: *victim* with violated rights. It was evident, both in the public scenarios where this narrative was disseminated and in our ethnographic experience and intimate coexistence with members of this group, that they imbued the victim category with an emotional and affective content that allowed it to transcend beyond a simple and imposed bureaucratic category. We came to understand that the social re-composition and political action of these actors required rebuilding their emotional bond with society through the creation of *emotional communities*. These communities of meaning allow a link to be established between grief as subjective emotion and grief as a publicly shared political feeling.

In this chapter, we examine three commemorations of the massacre. The purpose of these events is not limited to remembering the dead; they also endeavor to encourage processes of social transformation. Our ethnographic approach to Kitek Kiwe's commemorations enables us to study their effect on the restoration of this group's agency as citizens. It is also an approach for exploring the political and restorative potential of these events and the processes of memory building in general. Hannah Arendt suggests that narration opens the possibility of reflecting on horror, the *shoah*[3] specifically, because through narration the story becomes visible for the individuals participating in a political action (Arendt 1993, 203–204). Giving public testimony of injury removes the violent event from a personal perspective (or that of a closed community) and places it on a scenario of memory building and citizen action, within the perspective of a wider community that can acknowledge its moral outrage and sympathize with the victim. The Kitek Kiwe commemorations presented testimony through a shared narrative construction that situates the event and identifies it as injury to a wider social body through the bond of emotional identification.

We are aware that one of the effects of violence on people is their feeling of mistrust toward the social environment, which leads to the isolation of the victims and their confinement around their conflicting emotions. This has an impact on society's public sphere because confinement hinders both individual and community capacity for citizen action (Jimeno et al. 1996; Jimeno 2008).

In contrast to the isolation brought on by violent acts, people and social groups may choose to visibilize traumatic events. Actions that focus on memory building and testimony, besides their links to a search for justice, become deeply affective moral judgments. During recent decades, Colombia has seen its citizens affected by violence mobilize politically. Mobilization symbolically centers on the victim as a category that connects personal and subjective domains with the public sphere. It turns personal grief into a matter of social justice: That is what we, from an analytical vantage point, call emotional communities, communities of meaning and affection, linking persons, and even far removed social actors; here grief transcends indignation and encourages organization and mobilization. The symbolic power of the victim to convene and strengthen political action is grounded principally in bonds of an emotional nature.

Thus, it is important to understand emotions as relational acts, interwoven in a sociocultural structure, and not purely as personal emotions. It is precisely the emotional nature of the victim category that enables grief to be communicated as social criticism and to become a political tool to strengthen weak institutions. The assertion and power of the victim are part of a progressive social process in which civil society is strengthened in spite of the impact of two decades of violence. The victim-focused mobilization allows victims who have experienced violence to articulate those violent acts from their perspective, in a way that is unprecedented in Colombia. It also enables a narrative expressing feelings of grief, anger, and compassion to become political action.

Memory, Narrative, and Emotional Communities in Commemoration Ceremonies of the Massacre

In this section, we examine three events undertaken in April 2008, 2009, and 2013 by the Kitek Kiwe community in commemoration of the Naya massacre. We approach them as central events of production and transmission of *memory* as proposed by Connerton (1989): special methods that enable a common remembrance. We also view these commemorations as ritual or performative events (Alexander 2006) that depict a unified *narrative* of the trauma in the form of public testimonies and express the community's political search for redress. However, we mainly focus on the potential of these events to connect the event's spectators and performers through emotional bonds, creating what we call emotional communities.

The term *commemoration* relates to the memory of an incident or a person through a collective ceremony. Recently in Colombia, groups of victims of the armed conflict have begun using this concept to refer to the events by which they remember violent acts such as murders, forced displacements, and massacres carried out by paramilitaries, guerrilla groups, and state agents. Thus, events similar to Kitek Kiwe's are hardly unique. Rather, they constitute collective expressions of armed conflict in Colombia from victims' viewpoint. The commemoration as a ritual or performative action makes it an ideal space to depict a collective and agreed performance about the facts and meanings of the massacre.

The role of the *victim* as a witness narrating the facts and building memory can be seen as a hinge that allows passage from an individual and particular domain to the field of shared action and wider audiences. According to Hannah Arendt (1993), the ability to act in the world and create stories that are able to become history is the source of the political nature of the *human condition*. Human beings "actively reveal their unique and personal identity" through narrated action and story, which is an action itself.

The affective bonds arising from the narrative in these commemorative events have a special centrality. We consider emotions to be the language by which facts are expressed and not as universal categories or instinctive answers (Le Breton 1999). As with any other language, emotions are cultural and historical, and as such, they only exist in social and inter-subjective terrains. We thus conceive of the concept of emotional communities as the social and semantic space where narration and action are possible and make sense. Accordingly, the narration links certain persons, victims of a particular violent event, with a wider audience. The bonds between the community that experienced the violence and the spectators of the commemoration coalesce in the construction of common feelings of moral indignation. Shared indignation strengthens the public political exercise of people who have been harmed because it grants legitimacy and transformative capacity to their social critiques and their demands for justice and truth. Emotional communities encourage spectators who are part of the government to take concrete steps within their institutions; they also inspire audiences removed from the events that transpired to undertake similar acts. In the particular case of the Kitek Kiwe community, this meant highlighting the responsibility that paramilitary groups had in carrying out acts of violence, in collusion with the police, state agents, and other regional social sectors.

In the process of understanding emotional communities as the semantic field where action occurs, it was necessary—and inevitable—for us to be affectively touched in order to understand the meaning of the commemorations. As researchers, we were immersed in the process of staging, sometimes as participants and other times as mere spectators, but always as persons who were emotionally touched, due to the empathy we felt with the community's demands for truth and justice. Emotional involvement is not only part of the relationships that we as ethnographers establish in our fieldwork; it is also an important asset as an approach to knowledge when it is the key to participating in the universes of meaning that emerge in these research contexts. The emotional commitment with this community forced us at certain moments to put aside our simple objective of analyzing the political meaning of the memories about the massacre and get directly involved in the construction and dissemination of those recollections. As a result, we produced, along with this community, a text and a documentary video of their remembrances called *Kitek Kiwe: nuestra memoria* (Jimeno et al. 2011).

As with any social action, commemorations also have external and internal restrictions. The former have to do with the power structures that block demands for justice and social change; the latter refer to political disputes inside the group. In this chapter, we will approach different actions of memory, symbolic and cultural conciliation, and affective mediation that transformed these ritual acts into events at which the victims could recover socially and strengthen their civic agency.

The analysis of the seventh commemoration (2008) describes how a unified narrative is created and staged through various symbolic mechanisms. The story of the eighth commemoration (2009) shows how this narrative is mediated by cultural and emotional devices that transform it into an extension of an identity of indignation caused by the massacre. Regarding the thirteenth commemoration (2013), we highlight how the narrative staged therein revealed the internal tensions surrounding the group's political leadership and the dispute about different forms of solidarity. The disputes that surfaced regarding who articulates the narrative and who uses it in spaces of political advocacy ended up restricting the impact of the commemoration as a citizen action. In the context of this event, the staging of the narrative turned out to be more important for strengthening internal leaderships, at the expense of its potential for external symbolic dissemination.

2008. The Staging of a Unified Narrative

In 2008, we visited the Kitek Kiwe Council's territory for the first time. Our visit took place in April because we wanted to attend the seventh commemoration of the massacre, an event organized by community members. We designed a set of methodological strategies to approach people through both individual interviews and a collective reflection based on a sociodrama related to the massacre and subsequent events. We saw that the Elías Trochez Educational Center[4] was one of the most accessible places, due to its location and educational activities.

The Elías Trochez School is a vibrant space for this new community, located right in the center, over a high terrace, also shared by the Council's office. In one of the first assemblies we attended, we discussed how a sociodrama could tell the story of the violent event. We suggested that they represent actions, thoughts, and feelings, personified initially by three groups within the community: women, children, and adult men. In the end, the community agreed to let the children take the stage under the direction of one of the teachers. In the following week, we went to the Educational Center during school hours to help develop the sociodrama.

Gerson Acosta, then a teacher, agreed to divide the presentation in three acts. He started by asking the children (around 20 were selected) to convey what they knew and to share their most important memories. Some of them did not remember the events or did not experience them, but were well acquainted with the massacre due to the stories they heard from parents and others. Based on these remembrances they developed the story and defined characters and scenes. The cast included three families: The first including a father, mother, and children; the second had a grandmother and a granddaughter; and the last one was a couple. They also incorporated a messenger, a trader, a *raspachín* (young person who collects coca leaves), a *the'wala* (Nasa doctor-spiritual/religiuos leader), an Afro-Colombian, a group of workers, and the paramilitaries (*paracos*). However, during the rehearsals they decided to replace the paramilitaries with a character called "death" because for them it was better to represent violence instead of personalizing it; in addition, "the main characters should be the victims instead of the armed groups." A heated debate arose over whether to include the *raspachín* character or not. The group rehearsed for three days stopping only for short breaks, as onlookers voiced approval or displeasure.

The first act was divided into three scenes: the life in the Naya region and the news of the attack, the flight, and arrival at the refugee camps.

The first scene depicted everyday life in the Naya region: farmers, a trader, a mule driver, an indigenous person chewing coca, a black miner, and a coca *raspachín*, all of them focused on their own tasks in the rural setting. Suddenly, a character dressed in black (death) arrives and kills them instantly with her scythe. Only one person, the messenger, is able to escape. The families are sleeping until wakened by his shouts, "The paramilitaries are coming, the paramilitaries are coming, you must leave immediately!" Each family reacts differently: One family rushes and runs away with just the clothes they are wearing; another is reluctant to believe the messenger and stays put; the third family focuses on what to take with them (the granddaughter argues with her grandmother because she does not want to leave her doll). The *the'wala*, an older man, tells the families who refuse to leave that it is better to flee because those people "do not have the best intentions." The next scene shows the characters hurrying along a country path, afraid, some stumble and others fall. During their flight, they see dead people and the adults cover the children's eyes; some of them are barefoot and decide to take the shoes off the dead bodies to escape more quickly. It is dark and late at night; people hurry to escape, showing fear, exhaustion, and anxiety.

Camera operators and television reporters arrive at the death scene. Gerson asked these actors to act in a jovial and carefree manner. He also asked Daniel (coauthor of this chapter) to create and rehearse a script with the television reporter in which he forces people who are crying over their dead relatives to grant interviews, while the children (representing the families of the dead) ignore him. Gerson suggested that a boy shout out to the television crew "pair of vultures!" Other children role-played public workers performing "external examinations on the dead," while a girl spontaneously corrected them, "They are not dead people, they are victims!" The children personified women crying and shouting "my husband!", "my father!", "my brother!", "my uncle!" as well as a woman who could not find her relatives. Gerson taught the children how to scream and cry, and at one point, he asked them not to laugh because "we are communicating a part of our history." The first act ends when the refugees reach a village called Timba.

At that point, Leandro, then director of the Educational Center and a leader of the Kitek Kiwe Council, made a suggestion for the sociodrama. While the children rehearsed, he wrote on the blackboard: (1) Displacement, (2) Shelter 1, (3) Shelter 2, and (4) Process of self-education. Those were the steps according to Leandro that needed to be represented onstage, particularly the last one. He was opposed to the onstage presence of the *raspachín* character, associated with illicit coca crops in Naya life. He also thought that the flight scene should include more Afro-Colombians and that a reference should be included to remind spectators that in Timba "we also received threats from the paramilitaries."

The second act narrated their initial experience in Timba: distress, anxiety, and the improvised construction of shacks. Threats began reaching the shelter and a large group of people decided to seek safety by moving to another municipality, Santander de Quilichao. Gerson employed the same strategy he used in the first act.[5] He said, "Children, recall our situation in the bull ring and in Tóez. Who wants to share some words about that? We cannot forget those moments!" A boy said, "People were living in shacks and tents." "They called us *indios*,"[6] added Gerson, "there were two fights: one with the outer world, the inhabitants of Santander de Quilichao and Tóez who saw us as invaders and discriminated against us. The other fight occurred within our group, because we were struggling with the consequences of displacement, like losing our relatives, lands, houses, and then conflicts arose among ourselves." A girl said, "In Tóez at first they lent us houses and gave us food, but then they stopped helping, they discriminated against us, and called us 'displaced people'."

The rehearsal continued with the third and last act regarding regrouping and relocation at *La Laguna* estate, near Popayán, nowadays renamed as Kitek Kiwe community's collective territory. The children brought different clothes and chose the music for each scene. The act began with the chaos of life at the shelters and people discussing a proposal to "organize ourselves." The children remembered that they heard words such as committee, association, group, organization; and the final decision to create a "displaced people's association."[7]

The children proposed that a *the'wala* talk about the need to ask the Association of Indigenous Councils of Northern Cauca (*Asociación de Cabildos Indígenas del Norte del Cauca*—ACIN) for support. This idea led to the creation of the Association of Displaced Peasants and Indigenous People of the Naya region (*Asociación de Campesinos e Indígenas Desplazados del Naya*—Asocaidena). The children took on the roles of leaders filing a writ of protection of fundamental rights and people signing several documents, hoping to receive a new piece of land. Suddenly, the messenger comes with great news: The writ was issued in their favor and a plot of land in the municipality of Timbío was now theirs. The act ends as families arrive at *La Laguna* and begin adapting land, houses, and the school. The rehearsal concluded with a collective shout: "You can see it, you can feel it, the Naya is present!"

That night, the Kitek Kiwe Council convened a meeting attended by many men and women and by Asocaidena's governing board. They decided that the sociodrama prepared by the schoolchildren would be the massacre commemoration's central highlight. They then discussed in detail the declaration to be presented at the event and decided on speakers: Lisinia Collazos (representing the Naya widows), the Council's governor, and the president of Asocaidena.[8]

The morning of the commemoration, we took a bus to the village of Timba and entered the main square amid the noise of bus horns and children shouting the news of our arrival. Timba is a settlement near Santander de Quilichao (the second largest municipality in the Cauca Province) and the gateway to the Naya region. That year the families of victims, survivors, and the displaced gathered in the marketplace, together with peasants, indigenous peoples, and Afro-Colombians of the Naya region. Allied communities were also present, including members of indigenous and communitarian councils of neighboring municipalities. This commemoration was particularly important because different kinds of victims participated. It was an inclusive ritual act because, previously, victims had carried out commemorations alone, due to the significant distance that separates the Naya river's high and the low basins. The constitution of the Kitek Kiwe Council strengthened the resolve of the people who decided against returning to the region after the massacre, so they also attended the commemoration as a united community.

This new social cohesion surfaced as the sociodrama coalesced. Although Gerson, the teacher, staged the play, it was the students and members of the Council who gathered all the elements to construct the narrative. The fact that the children who created the dramatization were forced to experience the violence and displacement at such a young age indicates that community's bonds are largely structured around common memories of the massacre.

We noticed when we arrived that the event was more massive than we expected and calculated nearly 800 participants. The children quickly occupied the dais and took their place onstage. The mayor of Buenos Aires, the largest municipality where Timba is located, opened the event and asked for a round of applause for the children, who wove their batons, a symbol of indigenous authority, and shouted, "You can live it, you can feel it, the Naya are present." Everybody clapped. The mayor spoke emphatically about an agreement reached with the National Commission of Reparation and Reconciliation (*Comisión Nacional de Reparación y Reconciliación*—CNRR) to develop a pilot project to reconstruct Buenos Aires. CNRR representatives had a place at the event's main table. Then there was an "ecumenical act" involving greetings by representatives of several faiths: the Catholic Church, the Christian Congregation of the New Universal Pact, and the Bethesda Christian church, represented by Lisinia Collazos, clothed in a red dress. She raised her voice to say, "We, as victims, believe in what we have created. We need justice!" She read a brief verse from the Bible. She was followed by representatives of community organizations, most of them Afro-Colombian. Then, Enrique, governor of the Kitek Kiwe Council said, "We are talking as victims and also as indigenous people. We are interested in remaining in the Naya because this land belongs to us in our own right; we have been living there for eighty years and the navels of our children are buried there." Statements followed by representatives of the Naya community organizations, a leading member of Cauca's Regional Indigenous Council (*Consejo Regional Indígena del Cauca*— CRIC)[9] gave a long, thoughtful, and well-structured speech prefaced by words in the Nasa language. He said, "This is an event for the victims. It is not a space to legitimize unilateral government decisions. It is the victims who have struggled so that the truth is not blurred; progress must be made in bringing the murderers to justice, every one of them."

Subsequently, Jorge, a member of Kitek Kiwe, spoke on behalf of Asocaidena. He spoke at length about the Association's lawsuit against the government seeking collective compensation for the victims. He also mentioned the flaws in the Law of Justice and Peace,[10] particularly in terms of Decree 1290 of 2008 (which focuses on individual reparation by means of administrative procedures) and the lack of guarantees for the non-repetition of violent acts. Other interventions followed, such as the reading of a carefully worded text by an Afro-Colombian teacher regarding the victims' cultural diversity. Several hours went by and, with the heat, people got distracted and on edge. Although the children were restless, they remained onstage. At that point, we wondered if perhaps there would be changes to the program because there were other speeches pending, including one by the CNRR representative. Suddenly and unpredictably, Lisinia raised her high-pitched voice and said, "Where are the victims? Are they asleep?" Everybody woke up; this small woman helped the audience recover its focus. She wanted to make her voice heard, denounce the authorities as accomplices of the massacre, and insist that the government had to compensate the victims.

She concluded by saying, "We want to blossom again and we want to do it together, as a community."

After Lisinia's intervention, Leandro joined the children onstage and read "Our life project in the high basin of the Naya river in Cauca, Colombia, South America," a narration similar to the children's dramatization. We confirmed that the narrative structure had been useful in interpreting the violent event. It comprised several phases: life in the Naya region, violence and displacement, life in the shelters, and the organizational process. When Leandro finished reading, Gerson took the stage and the sociodrama started. It was around two o'clock in the afternoon, but still the audience was moved and interested in seeing the children in action. Gerson, with an announcer's intonation, acted as narrator. The last scene of the sociodrama had greater impact than in previous rehearsals, driving home a message that the solution would come through organization, as manifested by examples such as Asocaidena, the Kitek Kiwe Council, and the writ that allowed them to receive *La Laguna* territory. "With *mingas*,[11] with community work, and with assemblies, we are fighting for life," Gerson shouted, adding, "We share a final message with you: We demand truth, justice, reparation, and the right of non-repetition."

This exercise in community memory highlighted individual testimonies of victims who were to become leaders, such as Lisinia, Jorge, Enrique, and Leandro. They emphasized public dialogue and reaffirmed their rights as citizens. The commemoration also allowed the emergence of new leadership that encouraged participation of other community members (the children) and greater use of stage narrative, in contrast to political rhetoric. The young teacher Gerson Acosta was one of the new leaders.

The activity created a unified narration about the massacre shared by a very diverse group of people and institutional representatives. They seemed moved. As Alexander (2006) states, trauma and its narration are remembered and re-created from the group's cultural perspectives, from its historical models, and from new categories constructed in the face of new challenges. That is what the community did in the commemoration: There is an overlap of traditional and new elements from varied sources, such as the framework of International Humanitarian Law and the sociodrama's staging elements. Different styles of narration and leadership also emerged. Rhetorical construction and its symbolic and affective impact results from individuals and groups' active work that led to wide emotional identification and political impact, as we describe below.

2009. A Staging for Social Transformation

The following year we came back for another commemoration. Unlike 2008 when we encouraged staging the sociodrama, in 2009 the people of Kitek Kiwe organized their own memorial. They decided to present it on their own Kitek Kiwe territorial land, *La Laguna*. The ceremony took place in the main room of the Educational Center Elías Trochez. Although fewer people participated than the previous year, there were peasant families from neighboring rural areas, employees from Timbío's municipal administration, representatives of the Department of Protection of Citizens' Rights and the National Public Prosecutor's Office, students from Cauca University, members of the CNRR, and people from several non-governmental organizations supporting this community.

Aída Quilcué, the Chairwoman of the CRIC, was a special guest at the event. In 2008, she led an enormous indigenous demonstration in the cities of Popayán, Cali, and Bogota.

Minga was the name given to this mass protest of thousands of indigenous people. Unfortunately, it ended in personal tragedy for Aída: One month after the demonstration, a group from the Colombian National Army murdered her husband under circumstances that remain unclear. For the community leaders, the presence of representatives of the Human Rights Unit and the National Prosecutor's Office for Human Right Violations was very important. They came from the capital Bogotá exclusively for this event. One of them was the prosecutor in charge of investigating this case. We were unaware that the commemoration had been carefully planned as a way to demand justice and pressure the government institution to punish those responsible for the massacre.

We arrived in the morning in Kitek Kiwe territory. As a sign of mourning, the entrance was decorated with an arch of white and purple balloons. The indigenous guard, an institution created by the CRIC in an act of civil resistance to confront armed groups, protected the entrance. We were asked to register a few meters away, where four girls were using an improvised wooden table to take participants' data on lists drawn up by the Kitek Kiwe Council. We walked into the school's main hall. The act was presided over by Chairwoman Aída Quilcué. The National Public Prosecutor's Office representatives, the Cauca Province Ombudsman, and public workers from the Solicitor General's Office sat to the sides of the room right under big banners emblazoned with the words, "For the defense of people's life and dignity," "No impunity, there is no forgiveness or forgetting, we want the culprits to be brought to justice."

One Kitek Kiwe leader said, "What we demand as victims is to know what the Public Prosecutor's Office has done for our case." A peasant who returned to the Naya region added, "I had to witness how they threw the bodies into the rivers. If only La Balsa River could talk...so many things that it could say! [...] I do not understand why today, when the victims demand their rights in national and international arenas, the government only complains and says that we are overreacting! [...] I want to deeply criticize the measures to guarantee victims' rights in public hearings [against the paramilitary leaders]. Someone has to guarantee our protection as victims." Several members of victims associations also intervened and the final event dramatized the "rights of the victims," prepared by a group from the Kitek Kiwe Council. The characters were Mrs. Justice, Mrs. Reparation, Mrs. Guarantee of Non-Repetition, and Mr. Victim, embodied by three women and Gerson, the teacher who had become governor of the Kitek Kiwe Council. The four of them were talking to each other and seemed concerned and eager to discover the truth about the massacre.

Mr. Victim (played by Gerson), with his back toward the audience and facing the women said, "Mrs. Justice, I am a victim, how can I get redress? Mrs. Reparation, how can I get the truth? Mrs. Guarantee, what can I do to prevent the repetition of violent events?" The three embodied rights answered that they doubted that Álvaro Uribe's[12] government was going to guarantee their existence. "So nothing can be done? Is there anything I can do? Please, help me!" demanded Mr. Victim. The embodied rights added, "Perhaps if there was somebody in the government who was really committed, the situation might improve." Gerson said, "Who can we turn to? Is the Public Prosecutor's Office present here?" "Yes!" answered the audience. Mr. Victim carried on, "What do you say, should we ask this office to sign the document?" "Yes!" was the overwhelming answer. "Is the Ombudsman here?" "Yes!" The mentioned civil servants stood up in silence. Mr. Victim carried on, "Is there anybody here from the Solicitor General's Office?" "Yes!" shouted the audience. "Let's do a *minga* to clear up the facts. Who wants to join me? Mr. Ombudsman, Mr. Representative of the Public Prosecutor's Office, do you agree to help us discover the truth about the Naya massacre and guarantee the rights of the victims?" The audience shouted, "They have to agree!" "Will you sign this agreement and give your word to the victims, the children, and the widows?" "They must sign, they must sign!" echoed the participants. The Cauca Province Ombudsman raised his right hand and said falteringly, "I swear." One by one, the other civil servants repeated his words, swore, and signed the "agreement" (as it is called by Kitek Kiwe), followed by loud applause. Many participants gathered around the civil servants, taking photographs and videos. It was the climax of the event. Subsequently, the Council's governor said, "I am going to pay a simple tribute to a woman role model of resistance and struggle, who embodies the words 'it is possible'. This is a very humble homage, so that you continue being the voice of this process, because the victims need voices like yours. Please join me, dear friend, Aída Quilqué." The honored chairwoman of the CRIC received presents from the women of the Council: a hat with the national colors, a bracelet to keep her force intact, and a necklace symbolizing the Naya region victims. She answered in Nasa language and in Spanish:

> I want to start by remembering Cacica Gaitana and her fight along with five thousand Nasas who died in Tierradentro [the fight against the Spanish conquest in the seventeenth century]. After that first massacre, other similar events have been taking place. That is why today we 'walk the talk' together in a *minga*, to demand respect. We started the *minga* [last year] after many murders in Northern Cauca. Then they attacked my husband. They could not deny the attack [...] they tried to pass it off, but it was just another case of false positives.[13] Investigation is not enough; we want these murders in our community to stop! What can we do to keep them from killing us? [...] I would like to invite the Afro-Colombian communities to keep on working together and demand respect for our people's dignity. We have to join our experiences and become a *minga*, so that we can shout louder demanding respect for the dignity of our people.

Aída concluded by explaining the steps needed to appeal to the International Criminal Court and denounce state-sponsored crimes.

This commemoration demonstrated the emotional richness of testimonies and their staging have concrete effects on listeners. In this case (as in many others in Colombia), shared indignation was disseminated by the victims themselves. As mentioned earlier, for at least a decade several groups of survivors and displaced people have promoted scenarios where testimonies of grief cease being a private story and create opportunities for new communities to gather and express their moral indignation. The narrative of the trauma staged at the commemoration eight years after the massacre established affective bonds between the community of victims and the spectators of the performative act. These new bonds contributed to the foundation of an emotional community with the spectators, grounded in a shared version of the violent event but mostly based on an emotional and psychological identification with victims' pain.

The audience participated through its applause and cheers in an event that demanded justice in the presence of the representative of the Public Prosecutor's Office. The event illustrates how staged commemorations and memories create bonds of empathy. After the commemoration, one of the public prosecutors who signed the agreement did indeed set in motion concrete actions regarding the case. In August 2009, five months after the commemoration, a public prosecutor of the Unit of Justice and Peace ordered the arrest of René Pedraza, Brigadier General of the National Army. This high-level official commanded the National Army's Third Division had jurisdiction over the Naya region. Comments by members of the Calima Block of the AUC paramilitary group revealed that men from the Pichincha battalion (which belonged to the Third Division) helped the massacre to happen as they provided transportation and war material to the paramilitaries. However, the following month the public prosecutor was removed from the case and the arrest warrant was revoked. The public prosecutor was forced to flee the country given his participation in the case.

The transformative nature of the commemoration is evident: this symbolic performance constitutes civic action given the impact it had on institutional procedures. In this case, a demand for justice led to criminal procedures against those responsible, even though more powerful higher government echelons reverted the public prosecutor's legal actions.

2013. A Commemoration "for Ourselves"

In 2010 and 2011, we participated in two massive commemorations of the massacre, while accompanying the Kitek Kiwe community.[14] After finishing our fieldwork in April 2013, we thought that it was the right time to go back. Lisinia told us that they were expecting institutional support for a ceremony in the city of Popayán. As the day of the commemoration drew near, we called her again. She told us that the event had been canceled because they did not get support and there were "other kinds of problems." We hesitated about returning to Kitek Kiwe. We thought that the commemoration had been canceled because the date of the event almost coincided with another significant date: the first National Victims' Day, April 9th, as decreed by 2011 Law 1448. The attention of the country, and the media was focused on that day, so the event organized by Kitek Kiwe would not capture the public's eye in that context. Yet before April 11, Lisinia told us, "We will organize a small, internal event, it will be just us. We just decided, so please join us." We arrived the night before the commemoration.

The morning of the event, on the high terrace of *La Laguna* estate (where the school is located), the children were sitting in a circle on plastic chairs, waiting under the sun. Half an hour later they were impatient and started to move about, to stand up and talk to each other, some of them asked us to take photos of them and wanted to check the camera. The energetic voice of Gerson, former teacher and governor, warned, "Be patient, children!" and Edwin, a young man and then governor, said, "We are going to start the event. We ask the coordinator of each station to be ready. Children, we are about to begin this meaningful memory ritual."

Big loudspeakers played songs by Joaquín Sabina and slowly people began to fall into a long row, similar to Catholic processions or troupes in carnival parades. Gerson was the main organizer of the event, so he knew the script by heart. He was giving orders, encouraging and thanking people for participating. After being governor of the Council for three consecutive periods, he was now the director of Asocaidena. He was no longer the thin and youthful schoolteacher we had met the first time; he had gained weight and now exercised authority on behalf of his community. All the members of the Indigenous Council and the community in general attended the event, some 170 persons, according to a careful registry made by Leonilde Mestizo. Participants were mainly children from the Elías Trochez School, parents, and teachers; we were the only outsiders.

We missed the presence of Naya representatives, civil servants, journalists, neighbors, NGOs, representatives of the ACIN and the CRIC, and mostly, some longtime Kitek Kiwe leaders such as Leandro and both Enriques. Their absence signaled tension among political community leaders that threatened to weaken the process. The community fabric was fraught with tensions stemming from decision-making, particularly between the Council and Asocaidena. The tensions had to do with intergenerational disputes and community leaders' diverse family, religious, and regional alliances.

The commemoration began with the national, indigenous-guard and CRIC anthems. Gerson explained how the ritual would proceed and highlighted the spiritual rewards awaiting participants; he asked everyone to exhibit their "injuries" and said that they were "millenary." Another teacher displayed a list she called the "victimizing quilt: torture, kidnap, homicide, disappearance." Lisinia, Leonilde, and Rubiela, the widows, asked in unison, "What do the victims want? Justice, truth, reparation, guarantees for non-repetition."

After a brief evocation of "the blow they gave us twelve years ago," the children performed a dance dressed in coarse sack fabrics to the sound of southern Andean music. Edwin explained that the first station referred to the time of the Spanish invasion:

> Christopher Columbus was a sailor who wanted to navigate the ocean. He asked for ships but he also needed a crew. Since the army didn't have enough men, the solution was to release people from jails, on the orders of the Spanish Crown. The indigenous civilization enjoyed good health in this paradise, but those outsiders violated our trust, and we were victims of that army. The massacre of the Naya was a repetition of that first mass murder [...] however, since then, we've learned from Cacica Gaitana how to resist.

After mentioning the struggle of other caciques during the Spanish conquest, Edwin emphasized the continuity of injustice and their vindication as "millenary victims." At that point, we recalled the narrative strategy used by the Cauca indigenous movement: record violent acts on a wide time line going back to the conquest (Espinosa 2007). We continued in a row toward the second station, led by a two-meter baton ornamented with the characteristic Nasa multicolor tassels and held by the *the'wala* José Dolores Guasaquillo. That baton represented the Council's authority and several elderly males carried it during the procession. One banner read "We walk in remembrance of the victims murdered in the armed conflict," and another full-color banner said "The Naya massacre. A present-day memory and a resilient people." At the back of the parade, two children held a placard that read "Memory ritual. Strengthening the autonomy, identity, customs, and traditions now and always. Nasa community Kitek Kiwe." While we walked, an elderly man, Eugenio, sprinkled water with a bouquet of herbs in a purifying ritual. Meanwhile, Gerson continued giving instructions, going back and forth, asking people to clear the path or keep their voices down. It was now clear that Gerson had monopolized the organization of the event. What might this mean for building inclusive emotional communities and their ability to be politically influential?

Following the banners, two youngsters walked as pageboys, dressed up in CRIC scarves and flags. Another four boys marched as if they were at the Holy Week processions in Popayán carrying a box on their shoulders, "the memory chest," where they put away the words written on papers at every station. Apparently, that memory chest also recalled the Jewish people's exodus in the Holy Ark, a reference that was coherent with Gerson's affiliation and that of the wider community to ecumenical Christian churches in Timbío.

The schoolteachers also participated in the march and some members of the community held placards and banners on which they referenced rights that had been violated and demands on the government. A big banner said, "No impunity, there is no forgiveness or forgetting, we want culprits brought to justice." Two young people held white poster boards with the words "Victims of forced disappearance" and a list of 20 names. Yet another poster board listed the names of 30 "victims of homicide." Bayardo, a young man from the Council, recorded every detail with a camcorder.

The procession carried on from station to station, following a provisional rope on which were tied papers referring to events about the history of the community's victimization. The preparation of the venue, the banners, the children's dress, the music, and the objects spoke to the time and attention that families had invested in planning the event. Previously, all tasks had been distributed among families and now they had the opportunity to explain the meaning of every detail to participants. The event plainly had significance for the community as it strongly vindicated their violated rights. Even though the event was supposed to be "internal," it was also a dialogue with disgruntled or dissident members, as well as a demand made to the external world.

The second station was located inside a small kiosk on the path. A sign announced "Years 1940–1960, death of Jorge Eliécer Gaitán and founders of the Naya". Blanca Ulchur read a short text: "We remember Jorge Eliécer Gaitán, who fought for his people [...] when he was assassinated by the two political parties, our elders began to be murdered as well, which is why they migrated to the Naya region." She then read the names of the founders one by one while the participants answered in unison "may they live forever!" Blanca also recalled that many peasants were then fleeing in many regions of Colombia, just as they had.

We walked to the third station called "1970–1980, we follow the footprints of our elders," in charge of "major" Eugenio Garcés. He stopped under an arch decorated with small flags and colored balloons and told participants that during those years a group of indigenous people decided to found an organization to address several forms of oppression. It worked at first as an agrarian union and then, in 1971, it became the CRIC, a platform from which to fight on behalf of indigenous peoples.

The fourth station covered the period 1990–1999. A white sunshade rested on the path, decorated with colored ribbons. The person in charge was one of the Ulchur sisters (Gerson's sister-in-law), who stressed the fact that by the end of the nineties the *Autodefensas Unidas de Colombia* AUC were very strong in Valle and Cauca Provinces and received the support of landowners and regional authorities because they were supposedly fighting the guerrillas. She mentioned some of the AUC majors and the eight or more massacres they committed. "The Cauca River is a clandestine cemetery," she said.

The procession continued to another arch embellished with flowers, where one of the first leaders, Jorge, together with Mariela and Ana Delia, held a piece of poster board that said: "Welcome to the year 2000, entrance to the 21st century, the Third Millennium." Most of the participants sat on the side of the path. Jorge narrated an event, a kidnapping undertaken by the ELN (National Liberation Army) on the road connecting Cali and Buenaventura in 2000. He said that in the ensuing years their community received threats from the paramilitaries who five years later carried out the massacre. Mariela Cruz added:

> In 2000, we endured threats and targeted murders. The AUC settled in Timba and chose this settlement as their base, restricting the entrance of food and making accusations against the people. When they thought that somebody was a collaborator [of the guerrilla], they took them to a small room and tied them up. This happened to one of my cousins who was only twelve years old. We women plucked up courage and decided not to let the child alone and the people of the ACIN supported us. The AUC threatened us with their guns but we were spiritually strong and the child was one of our sons. We went to talk with two men named Arturo and Bocanegra [AUC officers in Timba]. They asked us to turn over the boy's father. At 5 pm the father came down from the Naya. They were very vulgar and told him that his son was an accomplice [of the guerrilla]. Then they killed the boy's father, Marcos Peña.

Mariela continued narrating the murder of Pedro Campo and Luis Eduardo Yule in 2000 by the AUC, and the assassination of Elías Trochez by the ELN. "They thought that we were collaborating with [state] institutions to rid ourselves of armed groups. All of the armed groups, even by the Army, accused us because people kidnapped by the ELN along the Cali-Buenaventura road dumped them at our schools." She concluded, "Now we demand justice, truth, and non-repetition. We must not allow the victims to be forgotten." They then dedicated a song ("*Un beso y una flor*" by Nino Bravo) to the victims of those years.

Lisinia and her family were in charge of the sixth station. There was a table covered by a white tablecloth and placards decorated with palms and *platanillo* flowers from her farm. The biggest placard said, "We Naya victims reject every form of violence." Under the table, there were eight photos of persons killed in the massacre, including Lisinia's husband Audilio Rivera, informally known as William or Willy. On display were pages with tables full of statistics about the country's displaced population; the data confirmed that the highest number of displaced people in Colombia occurred between 2000 and 2003. The organizers also exhibited photos with slogans chanted by activists at several national victims' movement events: "We want truth, but the real truth," "We want to live with dignity." The station made clear that the Kitek Kiwe group felt it belonged to the national victims' movement.[15]

Lisinia turned to the people and said, "We still have so much to learn from this memory. Jorge Eliécer Gaitán said he was going to fight for the people but we are not there yet." She then explained every placard and thanked the families for contributing to the station's display. Gerson read a list of 24 victims of the massacre. A song by Nino Bravo wafted from the loudspeakers: "*Más allá del mar habrá un lugar*...[beyond the sea there will be a place...]." Most of the participants were crying when we continued the procession. At the seventh station a teacher and José Roosevelt, one of the young men who held positions in the Council, recalled several massacres in Cauca Province, with a list of missing persons.

We walked toward the last station, located on a hilltop. Several years ago, this place was named "Memory Park." We were accompanied by the music of Grupo Niche, "*A lo lejos se ve mi pueblo natal, no veo la santa hora de estar allá* [in the distance you can see my home town, I cannot wait for the sacred moment of my arrival]". At the top of the hill, Gerson thanked those who "believed" and opened the space for people's participation. Rubiela said, "We must stop fighting with each other and keep on being brothers and sisters," and Leonilde, with a similar message, remembered all the names of the absent leaders and their importance to the movement. Slowly, the procession scattered and the participants headed to Lisinia's house for a community lunch, at about three in the afternoon.

The tour of the stations at this twelfth commemoration helped reaffirm the Naya people's possession of its territory. It resembled the tours made at certain times of the year in the indigenous reserves of Tierradentro (Rappaport 2005). The stations recalled moments or milestones selected out of the Naya people's history, and brought together a varied spectrum of external events, bound by two central ideas: the need to build memory and to face continuing injustices with resistance, whose origin is clear, that is, the conquest of America beginning in the fifteenth century. The narration of abuses throughout the centuries paused to clearly identify the victims, as well as the courageous persons who faced atrocities with acts of integrity and resistance. The theatrical narration tied current suffering to previous experiences that occurred in repetitive cycles, clearly connecting facts that initially seem discontinuous and unrelated. The dominant references to injustice, suffering, dispossession, and violence as a continuously lived experience is a common element in contemporary, public indigenous discourse and in the ideas of earlier indigenous intellectuals, such as Quintín Lame.

Commemorations, such as ritual acts and staging, successfully narrate events as a lived trauma, producing symbolic extension and emotional identification. The narrative constructions that in 2008 and 2009 were dramatized in public endeavored to influence the conflicts of everyday life, particularly since they attempt to connect what is untied, or address underlying tension and disagreements within the community, in this case different ways of exercising leadership. For this reason, organizers insisted on having entire families involved in staging the event and, compared to previous commemorations, were less interested in having outsiders participate.

The narrative of unity that we observed in the previous commemorations persisted in 2013. However, this time the ceremony focused internally on Kitek Kiwe and thus the performative act was restricted in terms of building emotional communities. This strategy sought to strengthen political supremacy of one sector of the community. The absence of historical leaders, whose political strategy emphasized dialogue with other sectors of national society, reduced this commemoration's public impact.

The staging of the narrative helped strengthen certain internal leaderships, at the expense of its potential for external symbolic outreach. Kitek Kiwe has experienced structural tension since its origin. It surfaced at the commemoration due to two current perspectives: on the one hand groups of relatives and [religious] believers and, on the other, historical leaders who favor institutional action. The commemoration revealed internal divisions, even though the narration was still constructed around a utopia of a cohesive community. Thus, the event, as a space to restore victims' civil and public action, turned into a tool for empowering some members at the expense of the rest of the community.

Beyond the external struggles and demands, the commemoration highlighted the internal conflicts and the fact that construction of emotional communities is also a micro-political field in which personal leaderships and some sectors of the community are empowered over others: Social differences and internal splits depend on who capitalizes the influence and mobilizes the bonds of affective identity.

The temporality of emotional communities depends on the specific scope of the actions undertaken by social agents and on changes in the sociopolitical context. Thus, since the displacement in 2001, Kitek Kiwe witnessed the appearance of solidarity bonds, joint action, and affection among people who were distant and unknown to each other in the Naya. Those relationships go beyond the boundaries of this community: Their foundation involved jointly demanding justice, obtaining the support of institutions, civil and social organizations, and undertaking symbolic construction work in which the commemorations became a tool that acted as a sounding board. This common purpose, however, did not prevent the appearance of conflicts between the existing organizations (the Indigenous Council and Asocaidena) involving control, alternating leadership, managing economic resources, and disputes over the unevenness of external aid. Other issues persisted, such as the role of young people versus the elders, women versus men, Christians versus other faiths, or the strength of kinship relationships versus adherence to ethnic policy. In this context, does the emotional community lose strength and validity? Is its moral and political strength weakened? It is too early to venture answers. On April 19, 2017, a terrible incident occurred: Gerson, who had become the new governor of the Council, was murdered by a young man from his community. The underlying motives of the murder have yet to be disclosed and it is uncertain how this tragedy will affect the future of the group. We only know that in spite of the mistrust and the fears, the internal mobilization to mourn Gerson's death was well organized and powerful.

Conclusions

Despite the internal divisions, Kitek Kiwe has continued to work together over two decades, through shared experience and autonomous life plans (as they call them). Community members have benefited from measures that have brought reparation and justice, both individually and as a group.[16] Most importantly, they created a narrative about events and culprits that comply with a general frame of reference; this has had an impact on the justice system and has produced some relative though solid outcomes. Their narrative has spread to national hearings and other victims' rights movements; it found allies and support in the indigenous movement and secured a process of personal recovery and re-configuration.

Morna Macleod suggests in her chapter in this book that the concept of emotional communities does not refer to a homogenous, defined, and stable group, but to bonds constructed under certain circumstances, of variable durability, and with diverse and fluctuating space-time spans. The *Movimiento Contra la Tortura Sebastián Acevedo* (Sebastián Acevedo Movement Against Torture) forged in Chile after the 1973 coup d'état united a group of people who became bold activists supported by pedestrian onlookers, and this bond was forged across distant spaces and time. Activists would begin their activities by chanting slogans, "A man is being tortured here," and "I name you Freedom" One of the participants recently remembered, "It was powerful, forceful, full of unity and tremendous energy." This kind of action was necessary to challenge the silence surrounding the topic of torture (see the chapter "Protesting Against Torture in Pinochet's Chile: Movimiento contra la tortura Sebastián Acevedo" this volume). Thus, Macleod suggests that the concept of emotional communities may be ephemeral and limited, but it may contribute to the creation of strong bonds that have a lasting impact on memory.

Lynn Stephen (see Chapter "Testimony, Social Memory, and Strategic Emotional/Political Communities in Elena Poniatowska's *Crónicas*" this volume) adds an important element by pointing out that oral testimony forges bonds that persist over time and connects people who live in distant contexts. This testimony is not about structural social identities, but rather establishing emotional links. As we have seen in the case of Kitek Kiwe, ethical and political bonds are a source of civil action. Stephen argues that Elena Poniatowska ties together three events in the same political-sentimental structure: the 1968 massacre at Tlatelolco Square in Mexico City, the earthquake in the Mexican capital in 1985, and the disappearance of 43 student teachers of Ayotzinapa in 2014. She relates these events through her chronicles about people's suffering and social struggles in light of these historical events in Mexico. The chronicles and their active dissemination created a new identity and an affective community, which implied a discursive work, the construction of shared symbols, and the production of common elements in spite of differences. Stephen proposes the concept of *strategic emotional political communities* to highlight their varied character and potential to encourage mobilization and public action. The emotional communities that are shaped in this way "include empathetic listeners who have not suffered but who are willing to act and take risks to bring tragic and horrific events to light and work to prevent their recurrence" (Stephen this volume).

People's social bonds are shaken when forced to experience violence and as a result they doubt and mistrust the social environment; this in turn influences their resolve for citizen action. Authorities and their guarantees to provide security to individuals are deemed unreliable. The experience of violence damages self-appraisal skills and psycho-emotional mechanisms to face life. The challenge, then, is to overcome these losses as an individual and as a member of a social group (Jimeno et al. 1996; Jimeno 2007). One way to do this is by narrating, telling the facts, sharing the lived experiences with others, as a form of private therapy or as social narration (Jimeno 2008). The people of Kitek Kiwe did not cling to trauma, nor insist on their grief, they did not lock themselves into a narrative that was incomprehensible outside the group. The narration of the traumatic event and its theatrical testimony has been, in its periodic repetitions, at the service of psychological reparation and new public action, as described above. Here, narration is a form of political action, as Hannah Arendt (1993) puts it, and not a compulsive series of repetitions that hinder overcoming trauma. The act of narrating in public aims to connect a particular event with a wider explanation that identifies the perpetrators in a long chain of events seen as a historical process that can be reversed through denunciating and by refusing to forget. Viewed this way, violence is defeated by remembering.

The Naya massacre commemorations held by the Kitek Kiwe community emerge in the current context of Colombia and the world in which victims are singularly present in the figure of the witness and through the power of testimonial memory (Hartog 2012; Reyes Mate 2008; Fassin and Rechtman 2009; Mesnard 2011; Agamben 2002). *El tiempo de las víctimas* [the time of the victims] is the title of an article by Francois Hartog, who reviews the history of this subject up until its current configuration in modern consciousness. From another perspective, Alfonso Reyes Mate (2008) and Didier Fassin (2009) discuss the dawn of a new era in terms of the meaning of victims. Victims have been invisible throughout history and their only public moment is their burial ceremony, according to Reyes Mate. The conviction that progress produces victims, so to progress we must forget the past is an idea strongly associated with modernity and modern notions of the autonomous subject, that is, a figure who does not depend on traditions or old bonds. The novelty, says Reyes Mate, is that those ideas are no longer valid and the suffering of the victims has ceased to be insignificant because their condition represents injustice. This sign of our times manifests in several ways, including renewed conditions of slavery and colonialism; this has tangible effects within new conceptions of justice and restorative ethics.

The coming of a new era, to use such an expression, involves changes in the law that benefit victims, so a link is forged between justice and reparation for victims, and the notion of punishment is re-established. Clear examples are the actions carried out by the public prosecutor in charge of bringing those responsible for the Naya massacre to justice. He focused on the case after experiencing the powerful feelings that surrounded the eighth commemoration and perceiving people's general feeling of moral indignation. Only after those memories had been revitalized could a new era begin.

We know that the victim complains, suffers, and may be trapped and isolated in the grief he or she experiences. The victim may remain silent and become engrossed in suffering. In this case, we say that the person causes pity. However, the victims we know in Kitek Kiwe called for solidarity and successfully united a fragmented civil society through the commemorations, at least temporarily. The power of the narrative embodied in the figure of the victim as witness is paradoxically its main weakness, when it becomes the object of dispute between micro-powers that hope to dominate the narrative voice. As we saw in the 2013 commemoration, the leadership dispute within Kitek Kiwe led testimonials to be limited to the community, thus losing their symbolic outreach to wider audiences and, thus, hindering their role as a means to reactivate public action. But these are just episodes in a chain of deliberate actions that expand their linkages in order to go beyond and confirm what Natalia De Marinis and Morna Macleod underscore in this book's introduction: how memory, denunciation, and emotions are related in the narration of grief and how created emotional communities are key elements in the joint search for justice.

Beyond their relationship with justice, memory and bearing witness become moral judgments with deep affective burdens. The political mobilization of the victims in Colombia is an act of affirming citizenship that involves their emotional renovation, intercultural dialogue, and transforming emotional bonds of empathy and identification through political action. The category of victim establishes a link between what is merely subjective and personal and the public sphere, and turns personal grief into a matter of political justice. This is the creation of emotional communities, in which shared grief transcends indignation and encourages organization and mobilization. The symbolic power of the victim to convene and strengthen political action lies primarily in bonds of an emotional nature.

For this reason, it is important to understand emotions as relational acts, interwoven in the sociocultural structure, and not only as personal emotions. It is precisely the emotional nature of the victim category that enables pain to be communicated as social criticism and become a political tool to strengthen weak institutions. The affirmation and power of the victim are part of an ongoing social process of reasserting civil society, after having suffered the impact of violence during the past two decades. This category allows victims to express, in an unprecedented way in Colombia, violent events from their perspective and for a narrative to be constructed in which feelings of grief, anger, and compassion can be expressed and political action can be encouraged.

The commemorations reviewed herein frame the emotional richness of testimonies through dramatization and the staging produces concrete effects on a listening audience. In this case (as in many others in Colombia), shared indignation was promoted by the victims themselves. As we mentioned at the beginning of this chapter, for at least a decade several groups of survivors and displaced people have promoted venues, at which

Fig. 2.1 Massacre of Naya's victims at the 13th commemoration of the massacre holding the sign: "Life and Dignity of the People. No impunity, there is no forgiveness or forgetting, we want the culprits to be brought to justice." Photograph by Angela Castillo

the testimony of grief ceases to be a private story and becomes the element that unites communities around feelings of moral indignation. The commemorations we reviewed herein narrated the trauma through performative events that created a shared version of a violent incident, but more importantly encouraged emotional and psychological identification around grief and the need for justice.

To summarize, we have suggested that emotions are a political language and not just an intimate feeling. That language, when it is public and shared, allows moral communities to emerge, grounded in the ethics of recognizing that creating emotional communities encourages political action. The notion of victim endeavors to condense the magnitude of events and become a cultural symbol of thousands of Colombians' feelings of grief and anger. If this symbol is mainstreamed and achieves the sympathy of wider sectors of the country, then we will have found a way of sharing and acting as a society within the bounds of civility (Figs. 2.1 and 2.2).

Fig. 2.2 Naya victims at the massacre's ninth commemoration holding the sign: "Nine years have passed since the massacre took place in the Naya River Valley." Photograph by Angela Castillo

Notes

1. In 1995, along the northern border between Colombia and Panama, the majors of nine illegal, paramilitary organizations met to establish "an anti-subversive military-political movement," known subsequently as *Autodefensas Unidas de Colombia*—AUC. In 1999, they formed the Calima Block that operated in Colombia's southwestern region and in 2001 perpetrated the Naya massacre (CNMH 2013, 160).
2. The indigenous council is one of the forms of organization and political representation of the indigenous communities. Although this concept comes from Hispanic colonial regulations, the organization was reconfigured as a political tool of the contemporary indigenous movement in the Cauca region.
3. Hannah Arendt rejected the term "holocaust" due to its religious connotations.
4. This Educational Center was founded by the community in 2004 and was named after an indigenous Nasa governor who was murdered by the National Liberation Army—ELN guerrilla, days before the paramilitary massacre.
5. Tóez is one of the three municipalities located in Cauca, Colombia, along with Santander de Quilichao and Timba, where the people of the Naya region settled down after running away from the massacre.
6. This word refers to indigenous people but here it is pejorative.
7. Displaced people is a Colombian category to refer to victims of the armed conflict who lost relatives and land. This term can be equated, though is not completely similar to the international category of internal refugee.
8. Asocaidena was one of the initial organizations created by Naya's displaced people. It brought together indigenous Nasa and non-indigenous campesino families. It coexists with the Kitek Kiwe Council.
9. The CRIC was created in 1971 by several indigenous communities of Cauca Province. Its main and historical objective has been to protect and expand indigenous territories, strengthen their political representation, and defend their culture in the face of government policies that would blur indigenous identity.
10. Law of the Justice and Peace, enacted in 2005, regulates both paramilitary group's demobilization and victims of paramilitaries' compensation.
11. A *minga* in the Andes is a group of people from a community who gather to help one of its individuals or families (e.g., building a house or harvesting) or to pursue a common initiative. The indigenous movement in Cauca has extended its meaning to collective political actions, marches, and public demonstrations, among other activities.
12. President of Colombia between 2002 and 2010.

13. The "false positives" are civilians who were murdered by the National Army as supposed guerrillas in order to inflate military progress reports of fights against armed groups.
14. For other aspects of our fieldwork, see Jimeno et al. (2015).
15. For further information about the value of testimony and the Colombian victims' movement, see *El testimonio. Aportes a la construcción de la memoria histórica* (Roldán 2013).
16. Several families received economic compensation through the administrative reparation program and some official institutions have supported economic programs for agricultural crops (coffee, plantain, cassava), cattle breeding, housing, electricity and other services. A special court of the Peace and Justice jurisdiction decreed protection measures to support the community in security matters and issued a guarantee over the land they are currently occupying. The National Lands Agency allocated the community an additional piece of land that members hope to expand in the future.

References

Agamben, Giorgio. 2002. On Security and Terror. *Theory & Event* 5 (4): 1–6.
Alexander, Jeffrey. 2006. Cultural Pragmatics: Social Performance Between Ritual and Strategy. In *Social Performance Symbolic Action, Cultural Pragmatics, and Ritual*, ed. Jeffrey Alexander, Bernhard Giesen, and Jason L. Mast, 29–90. New York: Cambridge University Press.
Arendt, Hannah. [1958] 1993. *La condición humana*. Barcelona: Paidós.
Centro Nacional de Memoria Histórica (CNMH). 2013. *Basta Ya. Colombia: memorias de guerra y dignidad*. Bogotá: Centro Nacional de Memoria Histórica and Departamento para la Prosperidad Social (DPS).
Connerton, Paul. 1989. *How Societies Remember*. Cambridge: Cambridge University Press.
Espinosa, Mónica. 2007. Memoria cultural y el continuo del genocidio: lo indígena en Colombia. *Antípoda: Revista de Antropología y Arqueología* 5: 51–62.
Fassin, Didier, and Richard Rechtman. 2009. *The Empire of Trauma: An Inquiry into the Condition of Victimhood*. Princeton: Princeton University Press.
Hartog, Francois. 2012. El tiempo de las víctimas. *Revista de Estudios Sociales* 44: 12–19.
Jimeno, Myriam. 2007. Cuerpo personal y cuerpo político. Violencia, cultura y ciudadanía neoliberal. In *Cultura y neoliberalismo*, ed. Alejandro Grimson, 195–211. Buenos Aires: Consejo Latinoamericano de Ciencias Sociales.
———. 2008. Lenguaje, subjetividad y experiencias de violencia. In *Veena Das: Sujetos del dolor, agentes de dignidad*, ed. Francisco Ortega, 261–291. Bogotá:

Universidad Nacional de Colombia, Facultad de Ciencias Humanas, Centro de Estudios Sociales (CES), and Instituto Pensar, Pontificia Universidad Javeriana.

Jimeno, Myriam, Ismael Roldán, David Ospina, Luis Jaramillo, José Maria Calvo, and Sonia Chaparro. 1996. *Las sombras arbitrarias. Violencia y autoridad en Colombia*. Bogotá: Universidad Nacional de Colombia.

Jimeno, Myriam, Leandro Güetio, Ángela Castillo, and Daniel Varela. 2011. *Kitek Kiwe: reasentamiento del Naya. Nuestra memoria*. Bogotá: Centro de Estudios Sociales (CES), Universidad Nacional de Colombia, Cabildo Indígena Nasa Kitek Kiwe y U.S. Agency for International Development (USAID).

Jimeno, Myriam, Daniel Varela, and Ángela Castillo. 2015. *Después de la masacre. Emociones y política en el Cauca indio*. Bogotá: Universidad Nacional de Colombia, Instituto Colombiano de Antropología.

Le Breton, David. 1999. *Las pasiones ordinarias: antropología de las emociones*. Buenos Aires: Nueva Visión Argentina.

Mesnard, Philippe. 2011. *Testimonio en resistencia*. Buenos Aires: Editorial Waldhuter.

Rappaport, Joanne. 2005. *Retornando la mirada: una investigación colaborativa interétnica sobre el Cauca a la entrada del milenio*. Bogotá: Editorial Universidad del Cauca.

Reyes Mate, Manuel. 2008. *Justicia de las víctimas. Terrorismo, memoria, reconciliación*. Barcelona: Anthropos Editorial.

Roldán, Ismael. 2013. El testimonio. Aportes a la construcción de la memoria histórica. *Revista Colombiana de Psiquiatría* 42 (2): 68-72.

CHAPTER 3

Testimony, Social Memory, and Strategic Emotional/Political Communities in Elena Poniatowska's *Crónicas*

Lynn Stephen

INTRODUCTION

The *crónica* is a major genre in Mexican letters that is elastic in nature and can be tied to earlier narrative forms such as the Durán Codex or "The History of the Indies of New Spain" by Diego Durán, published around 1581. In Mexico the *crónica* is the literary genre that serves as the major bridge between politics and culture.[1] Elena Poniatowska has excelled in both short and long forms of *crónicas*; analysts of her early career (as a journalist who specialized in interviews) even credit her with inventing a particular Mexican *crónica* style and a unique style of fiction built on real life characters and situations. Her longer *crónicas* are known for their gripping narratives. Oral testimonies are key ingredients in her longer *crónicas*.

The practice of oral testimony has been broadly defined as a form of retrospective public witnessing of shattering events of a history that is "essentially not over" and is "in some sense brought into being by the (itself interminable) process of testimonial witnessing."[2] Oral testimony thus becomes a vehicle for broadening historical truth through opening up who legitimately speaks and is heard in a given society. While there is an emerging literature on the ways in which people giving public

L. Stephen (✉)
Department of Athropology, University of Oregon, Eugene, OR, USA

testimony on repression and trauma and those listening to it become emotionally connected (from differential standpoints) and can act together to denounce, document, and create political impact through narrative as emotional communities (Jimeno et al. 2015; Stephen 2013; Bhaskar and Walker 2010), these processes have not been explored in textualized testimonies through time.

My standpoint in this discussion is unusual in this collection. I am not a collaborator in a direct process of creating a current strategic emotional community. Rather, I am a chronicler of *crónicas* and of their influence in Mexico, most recently in relation to the 30th anniversary of the tragic 1985 Mexico City earthquake. I was living in Mexico at the time of the earthquake and was in Mexico City for the second day of quakes and the aftermath of this tragic event. I thus shared in the experience of the event and in the amazing emergence of civil society organizing and had a small role in providing assistance. Because of the emotional impact of that shared experience, I feel a part of what I argue is the strategic emotional/political network or community that developed out of that event and continued through its ongoing documentation in the *crónicas* of Elena Poniatowska, among others.

Crónica and Emotional Communities

Here I argue that Poniatowska's use of oral testimony in her *crónicas*—often containing descriptions of intense suffering, trauma, and resilience—results in the construction of what Colombian anthropologist Myriam Jimeno has called "emotional community." I build on Jimeno's concept to explore how textualized oral narrative/testimony becomes a container for the conjoining of emotional and political connections, often across economic and social difference. This is not to deny the often-entrenched racial, ethnic, socio-economic, and gender hierarchies that permeate the network of people who provide and listen to testimony around a traumatic event. Rather, it is to suggest the ways in which emotion can serve as a strategic link across difference in the forging of strategic emotional/political communities that can have an impact on the ways that tragic events are remembered and through historical memory may suggest paths for current political action. In most cases this network of testifiers and readers through time, what I here call a strategic emotional/political community, are brought together in a shared political ethic that may not result in traditional protest actions as measured by bodies in the street. At key political moments, however, such strategic emotional/political communities may be mobilized.

Jimeno suggests that people who have lived through and commemorate horrible events such as the massacre of Naya carried out in Timba, Cauca, in 2001 create an emotional identity (Jimeno 2010; Jimeno and Macleod 2014). Jimeno has zeroed in on the process of identification, which Stuart Hall proposes as an ongoing construction, a process never completed. Identification, Hall writes, "is conditional, lodged in contingency. Once secured, it does not obliterate difference….Identification is, then, a process of articulation, a suturing, an over-determination not a subsumption….and since as a process it operates across difference, it entails discursive work, the binding and making of symbolic boundaries, the production of 'frontier-effects'" (Hall 1996, 2–3).

Jimeno labels the process of identification that trauma survivors engage in through public narration of their experience of tragedy as "emotional community." Following the characteristics of identification proposed by Stuart Hall, we can see that the identification process involved in creating emotional community does not center on concepts of identity such as ethnicity, class, race, or gender, but rather on creating networks of connection through shared emotion. Such connections may eventually articulate into political action and in that context result in shared identities, but the processes of identification involved in creating emotional community work somewhat differently than those linked to structural identity categories of difference. The concept of emotional community requires important discursive work, the creation of shared symbols, and the production of connection across difference—processes which work against compartmentalization and tensions emanating from the production of conflict-based identity categories in opposition.

The process of creating emotional community is centered in the act of one person narrating their experience of suffering to another so that it is not identified only with the victim "but is extended to other audiences who can identify with the experience and be moved by it" (Jimeno and Macleod 2014, 2). It produces not just a moment of compassion, but also a connection, sometimes political, that that can be translated into concrete actions. Jimeno's insight works well together with what I have written about the role of testimony in the building of social movements. In my analysis of the 2006 social movement of Oaxaca, I suggested the crucial role of public testimony and its reproduction in textual, audio, and visual forms in creating widespread emotional connections and moving people to act. "Testimony has the ability to reactivate not only past events but the emotions linked to them; in this way, testimony attaches those past emotions of the tellers to the present emotions of the listeners. In social movements, this can be a particularly powerful dimension of testimonies, as they reconnect listeners, readers, and observers to events that have already happened but that, through testimony, become alive again and motivate some to want to act" (Stephen 2013, 112).

We may want to ask the question of whether we can separate emotional and political communities. My prior research on social movements would suggest that we can find the answer to this question in the very ways that people talk about and narrate their own experiences of repression, resilience, and action. In human experience and narration there is not a neat analytical hiving off of emotions as experienced in the body (rapid heartbeat, tightening of the neck, tensing of the muscles, perhaps a rise in body temperature in the case of anger and fear), the description of events, and then how an individual felt. The emotional experience is hardwired into narration, into the experience of listening—and while not as intense in visual, audio, or textual documentation of testimony—it is also present. Humans have used oral narrative for a very long time as mode of knowledge transmission. If we want to truly understand the ways that emotions work in narrative, the creation of memory, and in ethical-political viewpoints and in strategic actions, it does not make sense to conceptualize them as separate.

The experiences of testifying, of listening, of reading the testimonies of others are key to how political perspectives develop not only in individuals, but also in how these individuals connect with others to analyze the world from a partially shared optic (often cognizant of difference at the same time), and how groups of people can participate in shifting public political discourses and perceptions. An analysis of this process entails scaling down to document the pivotal, emotive experiences of individuals, scaling across to see how actors who experience a shared trauma connect with one another, scaling out to see the networks constructed through testifying, listening, and reading, and scaling up to see how this strategic network or emotional/political community can take on a larger ideological life in relation to other public discourses and ideologies.

In the case of social movements, the motivation to act may be aimed at fellow citizens who identify with wrongs committed against a large group of people. In other cases, such as that of a Tribunal of Conscience for Women survivors of Sexual Violence during the Armed Conflict in

Guatemala held in 2010 by several Guatemalan civil society organizations, eight Mayan and *Ladina* women testified for a large audience of about 800 people. The audience included "women survivors, members of Guatemalan civil society, state officials, and a cross-section of the international community" (Crosby and Lykes 2011, 457). Crosby and Lykes interrogate what they call "the pain of others" in relation to the listeners of the tribunal, some of whom seemed to question the genuineness of the narratives that were shared. They considered whether the tribunal permitted national and international elites to "steal the pain of others," in the words of Sharene Razack, who suggests that the unreflexive consumption of other's pain is "the antithesis of genuine outrage" (Razack 2007). Crosby and Lykes consideration of Razack's concept is an important check on the concept of emotional communities, which cut across difference and unite people from different subject positions. If emotional communities do involve creating emotional connections between sufferers and non-sufferers, how do we honor the subjectivity, agency, and complex reality of the survivor? (Crosby and Lykes 2011, 475).

In this volume, they suggest recognizing their very different position in relation to the courageous indigenous women who testified in the trail of military officers who subjected them to years of sexual and domestic slavery as "Nos-otras," or "we-others."

This clever double meaning that emerges through acknowledging a shared "We" but also a separation of "we-others: in relation to the Spanish "*Nosotras*" suggests a strategy for engaged listening, alliance and solidarity rooted in and acknowledging difference. They suggest that such positioning is a way to decolonize emotions, avoid sensationalizing and dignify the pain of others, and center the experience and authority of the Mayan women who were the centerpiece of the Sepur Zarco trial.

In a larger sense, we might think of different levels and kinds of participation in emotional communities. There are the emotional communities formed by those who share an immediate experience of suffering from the same event and those who share a similar experience in a different context. Emotional communities can also include those who are empathetic listeners who are non-sufferers, but who are willing to act and take risks to bring tragic and horrific events to light and work to prevent their recurrence. Such listeners might be considered as part of a strategic emotional community.

Here I want to focus down on the role of testimonial narratives in creating strategic emotional/political communities. The textualization, digitization, and dissemination of testimonial narratives can play an important role in whose voices are heard, and by whom and in the construction of strategic emotional communities. Testimonial narratives widely disseminated through *crónicas* and in other forms can influence social memory, cultural politics, and the way that historical events are remembered, canonized, and even shape the kind of future that can be imagined.[3] As anthropologist Rosalind Shaw writes, "memories shape the capacity to produce the future (e.g. Werbner 1998), and are themselves shaped by the kind of future we think we're heading for (e.g., West 2000)" (2013). The work of collecting testimonials used in *crónicas* that influence individual and national memory belongs to the future as well as the past and in its practice offers "new techniques for a politics of future making" (see Shaw 2013).

In what follows, I explore how *crónica* writing, which relies heavily on testimonial narratives, participates in the construction of strategic emotional/political communities in Mexico that influence social memory and new political futures. My case study will focus on Elena Poniatowska's *crónica Nada, Nadie* (about the 1985 earthquake) and the ways that the work first as *crónica* articles for *La Jornada*, later as a book, and then as a part of a museum exhibit and gathering celebrating 30 years since the earthquake connected the trauma of the earthquake to the trauma of the disappearance of 43 student teachers from Ayotzinapa in 2014. Through an analysis first of her writing about the earthquake and then the ways that her writing traveled and was remembered three decades later on the 30th anniversary of the earthquake in 2015, I seek to demonstrate how the recording of testimony, its textualization, and dissemination link together a wide range of victims and survivors of the 1985 earthquake to non-sufferers and empathetic listeners some 30 years later in an emotional community through time.

Chronicling the 1985 Mexico City Earthquake

Elena Poniatowska first collected narratives with a tape recorder on a daily basis right after the 1985 Mexico City earthquake, wrote them up, and published them in *La Jornada*. Later in 1988 they were published as a book titled *Nada, nadie: Las voces del temblor* (Poniatowska 1988). The book was published in English in 1995 as *Nothing, Nobody: The Voices of the Mexico City Earthquake* (Poniatowska 1995). In 2015 she participated in a series of activities that commemorated the 30th anniversary of the earthquake.

July 28, 2015. I am sitting in the back seat of a car with Elena Poniatowska, two of her friends and a representative of the *Comité 19 de Septiembre de 1985*—a community organization formed to commemorate the Mexico City earthquake of 1985. We are on our way to a public discussion held by several organizations that were constituted during the earthquake. Some of them have remained active and others have been reactivated. Elena has been invited to share some thoughts about the upcoming 30th anniversary of the powerful earthquakes that shook Mexico City on the 19th and 20th September in 1985. We are on our way to a discussion in the *Museo de la Ciudad*, housed in the former palace of Count of Santiago de Calimaya, in the center of Mexico City.

We park the car across from the museum and cross Pino Suárez Street. The seventeenth-century *palacio* glows a bright orange in the later afternoon sunlight. As we approach the building, a crowd converges on Elena. Selfie sticks come out and she begins to pose for pictures with a succession of young women who come up to her. She keeps walking as one of the hosts tries to keep her moving forward into the central courtyard on the first floor where the event is to take place. An old friend of Elena's, Cuauhtémoc Abarca, founder and representative of the *Coordinadora de Residentes de Tlatelolco* (Coordinator of the Residents of Tlatelolco, an organization of residents suffering damages, trauma, and loss of relatives' lives), approaches.

Elena gives him a big hug and walks into the courtyard. She sits down next to him. On the other side sits a woman from the *Comité 19 de Septiembre 1985* (19th September Committee, an organization of earthquake survivors) and next to her, Super Barrio—a kind of super hero who represents the Assembly of Neighborhoods, formed two years after the earthquake in 1987.

The event begins. The event moderator states:

> We are going to get started. I would like to welcome Elena Poniatowska and the 19th of September committee in commemoration of the 30th anniversary of the Earthquake. This is a history we cannot forget. It is a history that is present every day. Because of this, we are profoundly grateful for the presence today of Elena Poniatowska who is here to talk with us today.

Applause sounds (Fig. 3.1)

Fig. 3.1 Elena Poniatowska with Cuauhtémoc Abarca in the Museo de la Ciudad in July of 2015. Photograph by Lynn Stephen

This Is a History We Cannot Forget

This is a history we cannot forget. On September 29 and 20, 1985, two powerful earthquakes measuring up to magnitude 8.1 shook Mexico City. Between 10,000 and 40,000 people were killed. Thousands of buildings collapsed. More than 4000 people were rescued alive up to ten days after quake. Mexico's President, Miguel de la Madrid, waited for more than three days to respond to the crises. After his first survey of the damage he stated, "We are prepared to respond to this situation, and we do not need to request foreign assistance. Mexico has enough resources and together people and government will overcome. We are grateful for the good will extended to us, but we are self-sufficient" (Poniatowska 1995, 15).

In the absence of any kind of government response, the people of Mexico began the rescue effort. Local Boy Scout troops were some of the first to respond and many others followed in their wake. Neighbors, students, people young and old stopped their lives to dig for survivors, loan their cars for transport, and deliver medicine. Brigades were formed of students, volunteers of all kinds joined in. Among some indigenous peoples, the explanation was that the gods had been angered and sat up, causing the ground to buckle. In the midst of this widespread tragedy, not only the gods sat up, but also people in Mexico City population stood should to shoulder to aid in the recovery. Discovering what was possible through the autonomous organizing of civil society on top of the ruins created a sense of hope and the possibility for change that morphed into a major political upheaval—eventually resulting in the creation of a new political party, the National Democratic Front with Cuauhtémoc Cárdenas as its presidential candidate that challenged the Institutional Revolutionary Party (PRI) in 1988 federal elections.

In September 1985 Elena Poniatowska immediately began to record testimonies of earthquake survivors and joined the efforts to support the survivors, particularly the group of seamstresses known as *El Sindicato de Costureras "19 de Septiembre"* in San Antonio Abad. She developed a close friendship with union leader Evangelina Corona that continues to this day and served as treasurer of a group that acted in solidarity with the *Sindicato de Costureras*. Poniatowska wrote not only about the plight of the seamstresses and many others whose lives were turned upside down by the earthquake, but also about government ineptness and corruption at a time when the incompetency of the PRI government was at a high point. Some of the most striking testimonials she collected pins the blame for the massive death toll on the government, not on the temblor. Judith García states:

> I want to state that the people who died didn't die because of the earthquake. This is a lie. People died because of poor construction, because of fraud, because of the criminal incapacity and the inefficiency of a corrupt government that doesn't give a damn about people living and working in buildings that can collapse.
> ... this was not a seismic problem but a problem of having assassins in power who couldn't care less about the life of children, the life of what could have been a future for this country. Thousands of dead cannot be erased overnight. (Poniatowska 1995, 83–84)

Elena's *cronica* not only documented and analyzed the earthquake and its aftermath, but the voices she highlighted became a part of civil society (see Monsiváis 2005) and contributed to the political democratization of Mexico in future decades. The voice of Judith García symbolizes the discontent and beliefs of many Mexicans who survived the earthquake, witnessed the lack of government accountability, and believed that a better political future lay ahead. Through the testimony of Judith García, other earthquake survivors and those who did not suffer but were outraged made an emotional connection. The conversion of emotional community to political community happened quickly in the aftermath of the 1985 earthquake, particularly in the face of an initially pathetic state response.

Poniatowska's newspaper articles and chronicle *Nothing, Nobody* also documents the organization of Mexican civil society and how groups such as the 19th of September Garment Workers' Union, the Coordinator of the Residents of Tlatelolco, the Unique Coordinator of Earthquake Victims (*Coordinadora Unica de los Damnificados*), and Wake up the Neighborhood (*Amanecer el Barrio*) emerged in 1985 to form the pillars of civil society. Reflecting the voices of some of the poorest Mexicans, "*los damnificados de siempre*" ("those who are always the victims") (Poniatowska 2015, 16), Poniatowska's writing and its duplication, reproduction, endless citations and references, travels, and 20th and 30th earthquake anniversary rememberings document how Mexicans governed themselves from an ethic of mutual solidarity which shook the political pillars of the country. Hundreds of thousands of people organized themselves to rescue survivors, helped one another survive, and then created permanent organizations to hold the government responsible for what happened. The emotional connections created through widespread processes of documentation and the rituals of remembering such as the 30th anniversary activities suggest the power of strategic emotional/political communities through time as well as their ability to incorporate additional narratives that resonate with the original ones shared.

In a 2015, 30th anniversary special edition of the magazine *Proceso* commemorating the earthquake and all it represents Elena wrote of 1985:

> A revolution could break out around each fallen building. It has been years since Mexicans have mobilized in this way, it's a new phenomenon. They discover that instead of the government it is they who are saving themselves and everyone else.... The fear and the pain make each person think that it could have been they who were left with nothing. Out of the ruins, another city emerges.
>
> Carlos Monsiváis considers the city's transformation. In 1985 the term "civil society" acquired an unexpected credibility and it is the poorest Mexicans who organized themselves and Mexico. (Poniatowska 2015, 9)

In a conversation we had in October 2015, Elena recalled the intelligence and insight Monsiváis had into the transformation that occurred in the city. "He had a phrase that I always repeat because it moves me so much." He said:

> On the 19th of September, and in response to the victims, Mexico City saw one of the most noble take-overs of power in its history, one that transcended the limits of mere solidarity. It was the conversion of a people into a government and of official disorder into civil order. "Democracy can be, also, the sudden importance of each person." (Interview with Elena Poniatowska, October 12, 2015, Mexico City)

Linking Strategic Emotional/Political Communities Through Time

Through their emotional content, testimonials open and close space and time. They can travel from the past to the present and into the future. They can connect the old with the young, can distill intense moments of history, and project those moments into a new time and space, allowing new interpretations and imagination to take place. They can connect the past with a future that is yet to happen. Testimonials can rewrite history one experience at a time by highlighting invisible inequalities in moments of crises. But much of their endurance can be found in the creation of strategic emotional communities that consist of connected testifiers and listeners whose mutual empathies can be politically mobilized in critical historical junctures.

Elena Poniatowska's documentation and interpretation of the 1985 earthquake through testimonies created a permanent fissure in the imaginary world of politics as understood by Mexico's political elites at the time. An important source of the force of this rupture can be found in the conjoining of emotional and political experiences and their dissemination and connection to a wide network of readers. Consider the words of Juana de la Rosa Osorno shortly after the earthquake as she stares into the textile sweatshop building where many of her co-workers died buried alive and where she labored for years.

> Seated on the sidewalk of Lorenzo Boturini Street is Juana de la Rosa Osorno, 55 who works for Dimension Weld employed by Elías Serur: Now with this disaster, she says, putting her hands under her green and checkered apron, we are here in the street waiting for people's charity to be able to eat.

The boss is not a bad person; he is just fickle. He offers one thing then, then another; he changes his mind; we can never come to an agreement. He first yelled at us, "The machinery is yours with my compliments. I've lost it all, my life is buried here."

His life is not buried there; if any lives are buried, it's those of the *compañeras*. The boss came running when he heard that the building had fallen. And the dead were here, bleeding among concrete and steel mesh. Elías did not suffer a scratch. So why would he say that his life had been buried here? (October 3, *La Jornada*; Poniatowska 1988, 145; Poniatowska 1995, 143)

Words uttered into a tape recorder in October 1985 in the Mexico City neighborhood of San Antonio Abad appear in print in *La Jornada* newspaper a week or two later. The paper is Xeroxed in multiple copies and transported to Monterrey, Guadalajara, and other cities by activists who worked with the Victims Coordinating Council (CUD). People in these cities read the words aloud to their families and make more copies. In 1988, the words appear as part of the book *Nada, Nadie* on pages 145–146. In 1995, they are translated into English and published as part of *Nothing, Nobody* on page 143. In September 2015, words from the same testimony are placed on the wall of the *Museo de la Ciudad* as part of an exhibit titled "*19/09/1985 7:19 A 30 años del sismo.*" (September 19, 1985, 7:19,[4] 30 years after the earthquake) curated by Sergio Raúl Arroyo (Colorado Nates 2015). On October 11, 2015, I walk through the exhibit and listen to a 15-year-old girl marvel to her mother, "How could they leave so many people buried in those buildings? Could this happen now?," while standing in front of Juana de la Rosa Osorno's words and a series of pictures showing the utter destruction of the sweatshops where thousands of garment workers labored and hundreds died. "How could we stop this from happening again?" she wonders.

The testimony of suffering and surviving of Juana de la Rosa Osorno in a public forum published in 1985 has connected her 30 years later to a young girl touring a museum exhibit documenting the earthquake in graphic detail. As an empathetic listener and observer this young woman has become connected to the strategic emotional/political community created by earthquake survivors and many who worked with them, including Poniatowska. While we do not know how this young woman will act in the future, her question about whether what happened in 1985 could happen "now" suggests that she is reading the experiences of earthquake survivors in the present and even projecting that into the future. She is, at the very least, sharing in an ethical/political standpoint that links her to a wide network of people. The narrative of de la Rosa Osorno is having a "real effect" through its continual construction of strategic emotional/political community on the wall of the museum exhibit (Jimeno and Macleod 2014, 2).

On Not Forgetting

Thirty years after the earthquake, Evangelina Corona (General Secretary of the Garment workers Union "19th of September") and Cuauhtémoc Abarca (Leader of the Front of the Residents of Tlatelolco and the Coordinator of the Residents of Tlatelolco) and also of the CUD (Single Coordinator of Earthquake Victims) were still in the public eye and were important figures in the social memory production to mark the 30th anniversary of the earthquake in 2015. Evangelina Corona went on to be elected to the Mexican legislature as a representative of the Democratic Revolutionary Party (PRD) and served as Secretary of the Environment of Mexico City (Meneses Arias 2015). In 2007, she published her own testimony titled "*Contar las cosas como fueron*" (Corona Cadena 2007). Elena Poniatowska wrote of Evangelina's book that it:

> results in a freshness, a moving frankness, because Doña Eva (as she is called by her *compañeras*) reveals her intimate self without hiding anything, and she hands us everything so that we can drink it like a glass of pure water… She doesn't paint herself as a victim or a martyr, she tells of her life experiences and the changes in her life naturally. (Poniatowska 2008)

Here, testimonies begat other testimonies and the strategic emotional/political community emanating from Evangelina's original testimonies in *La Jornada* and *Nada, Nadie* created a public for her own book. Textualizing allows testimonies to travel, be reshaped, and re-appear in new forms. They can be art on the wall, read into movies, or repeated into a microphone 20 or 30 years after their original recording. Here are two other examples.

We are sitting in a large circle at the *Museo de la Ciudad*. The event featuring Elena Poniatowska's conversation with the public on July 28, 2015, is well underway. Elena begins her remarks and then reads two testimonies from her 1988 book. She begins with a comment that acknowledges her place as a non-sufferer and person of privilege in the emotional community connected to the 1985 earthquake:

> It gives me a great deal of pleasure to see Cuauhtémoc Abarca who I knew when he didn't have gray hair and was thin. He also knew me without gray hair and when I was skinny. We were talking together in that time (of 1985). But he knows much more about it than me because I didn't live in Tlatelolco. I didn't live in the Nuevo León. On the contrary, I was one of the privileged ones. One part of the people in the city—the people from Las Lomas, the people from the south, of the city, I live near the University City—we didn't even know what had happened because we lost electricity. We only had the radios in the cars and the only person who began to talk about what was going on was Zabludowsky (long-time TV anchor for state-run Televisa), because I think he had a special radio, a luxury radio in his car. So half of us didn't know and we are always the privileged people who nothing happens too.
>
> Things always happen to the same people…Great misfortunes always befall the same people, the same Mexicans.
>
> Rather than talk to you about the earthquake, because there are many more people here much better prepared to talk about this than me, those who lived it in flesh and blood….I only arrived the day after the earthquake to record the testimonials of the people. To go to the funerals. To go to the buildings that had fallen. After a while, I arrived where Cuauhtémoc was working and I spoke with him. We were in the streets, some of us, for three months. Three months after that fatal date. I prefer, if you all will agree, to read you a testimony.

After clarifying her role as a witness and empathetic listener in the strategic emotional/political community of the earthquake whose participation emanates from an elite class and social position very different from most of the victims and survivors of the earthquake, Elena proceeded to read the testimony of Alonso Mixteco who came to work in Mexico City from Guerrero. In the process she also made a critical connection, linking the strategic emotional/political community of the earthquake with the emerging emotional/political community of the families and supporters of the 43 student teachers who attended normal school in Ayotzinapa who were disappeared in September 2014 while commandeering buses for an event to memorialize the killing of hundreds of students in the plaza de Tlatelolco in 1968. Poniatowska made this link verbally stating, "We all are wearing Guerrero like a brand that has been burned onto us with a hot iron." ("*Guerrero, lo tenemos todo con una marca de fuego aquí en la frente*"). (Interview with Elena Poniatowska, July 28, 2015, Mexico City).

She then proceeded to read from the *testimonio* of Alonso Mixteco, partially excerpted below.

I am Mixtec on my father's side, that's why I write my name as Alonso Mixteco; I am Nahuatl on my mother's side. I come from two indigenous cultures. I came to work all the way from Guerrero. I came with some affection for the capital city, but now I am sad to relate all that has happened here. On September 19, at seven in the morning, I left the place where I live and ten minutes after seven I arrived at the building that housed the National Commission on Seniority at Manuel Doblado 39. ...
...the building roared, falling into pieces. Suddenly the wall the *compañera* (Virginia) was standing by fell on her, and still another wall tumbled on top. I then covered my head with my briefcase. Something fell on my head and I fell in a sitting position. ....When the building crumpled, just imagine that someone pushed it toward the north. If you pay attention, you'll see that all of the buildings fell towards the north except for a few that fell on this side. Then I managed to say only, "My children, goodbye to my children, I'll never see them again".
Everything turned dark and I was wholly covered, wholly buried on the floor where I remained seated, well, not completely seated, almost in a standing position, I had no space to move, but I found a little can and I began to hit the floor with it, over and over again, Because I could move my arm, and I shouted for more than fifteen minutes, "Help, come and get me out of here, please. Help.".......
...a ray of sun came in, but at a distance of a hundred feet. I said to myself, "Here's my salvation."
Crawling, holding my head like this, with all the strength of my whole body I went [to] that opening. ....My head is good and hard, my bones are as iron, and even if I went bald, I was going to open that hole, and I opened it so much that I was able to pull the rest of my body, and with my body I excavated about a hundred feet of tunnel by creeping, holding my head like this until I arrived at the place where there was light. I didn't even have a scratch on my noggin...I saw my eight-story building compressed into one. I ran shouting "Virginia, Virginia," I shouted "Virginia" a lot, but Virginia never answered.
"She's dead."
Then I ran in a different direction...
...What I wanted was a volunteer *compañero* who could help me get Garnica out, along with the other *compañero* and *compañera* Virginia....
"Hey, you, stop it," the others shouted contemptuously. "Stop it, you, you are not from the rescue brigades....I insisted and I would point to them, the place where the *compañero* Javier and the *compañera* Virginia were buried.

"Get out, you; we are the ones who know how; you don't know how, you can't do this."

How couldn't I do it when I was the only one who knew where they were. But in their eyes I couldn't get my hands in because I was not from Rescue. They were the sole authorities. This why I, as an Indian, do not like those rescue people because they don't do things as they should. All they want is to be heroes. …had they ever been under the wreckage, or could they share my despair. (Poniatowska 1995, 27–30)

The words of Alonso, struggling to move and finally extracting himself by tunneling forward with his head 100 feet through the eight-story building collapsed into one, are a gripping narrative of determination and survival. Unable to find his friend and officemate Virginia, he insists on looking himself in the wreckage for her only to be told by the official rescuers that he should stay away, since he does not know how to work in the collapsed building. He identifies himself as an Indian to distinguish himself from the all-knowing urban rescuers. "Could they share my despair?" he asks. By articulating his physical and emotional pain in the narrative through rejection and the loss of Virginia, Alonso provides emotional tendrils for readers to grab on to.

The monumental sense of struggle and emergence into the light is also a powerful metaphor. Through invoking Alonso's words from 1985 and connecting them to the tragedy of the disappeared students of 2014, who in turn were seeking to memorialize hundreds of students massacred in the *Plaza of Tlatelolco* in 1968, Poniatowska built another layer of memory and emotional connection among the 150 people gathered at the museum listening to her.

To further solidify that connection and link the disappearance of students in 2014 with the earthquake, the second testimony she read was of Antonio Lazcano Araujo. He specialized in evolutionary biology and was teaching at the National Autonomous University of Mexico (UNAM) before he worked as a volunteer identifying bodies and trying to return them to grieving family members. Before beginning to read his testimony at the earthquake memorial event in 2015, Elena stated, "Now Parque Delta is a giant store, like Liverpool or Palacio de Hierro…He tells about how he went to that park to fumigate bodies and ….it was a stadium where all the seats were empty and the actors in the center of the arena were dead."

In 1985, Mexico City's Social Security Baseball Park was converted into a giant morgue shortly after the earthquake. Unclaimed bodies and remains were stored there. Often relatives who survived the earthquake and had searched in the rubble, in hospitals, and elsewhere would go there to try and find their loved ones. Hundreds of bodies in mounds were covered with limestone and ice and covered with plastic. Rows and rows of coffins and the smell of decomposing bodies confronted all who entered. Some came as volunteers to help with identification and burial. Others came hoping to identify a missing relative. From all walks of life, volunteers, public servants, and survivors met one another. In the space of this national morgue, humanity was stripped down to its essentials. It is here where Professor Antonio Lazcano Araujo helped people to find their unidentified relatives. He spoke with the dead and with the living, such as the thin man he describes helping to locate his sister and two nieces and get coffins for them. The living and the dead were all connected. Here is a partial excerpt from Antonio's testimony about this scene, in Poniatowska's 1988 *Nada, Nadie*. The version here is from the 1995 translation to English.

> What's the Deal on the Coffins—in the voice of Professor Antonio Lazcano Araujo:
> When I turned my head to the left I saw a little girl with eyes wide open and the grimace of an interrupted smile, an eight-year-old: "Little girl, why on earth didn't you run? Why did the beam fall on you?" I insistently spoke to the cadavers to the point of rage, wrath, and hatred: "This isn't fair." "It's not fair that in this country hospitals, schools, government buildings, and public buildings should collapse just like that"....
> ....A small, skinny, brown guy appeared, the typical Mexican who has had to work very hard from birth, someone who probably lived in some lost tenement in some lost slum, with a sweater that was all too thin, Jesus! Really! Why are our people so unprotected? What helplessness. God! Really! It makes you mad to see people like that, with nothing. "And the coffins?" he asked, "What's the deal on the coffins?" He needed three of them. Three coffins. He wanted to know how much they were. And how would he have paid for them, the poor bastard?
> "Have you identified your family?"
> "Yes, they are there. But tell me how much do those caskets run?"
> "No, the coffins are free; we'll give them to you right away. Are you here by yourself?"
> He was there to claim his sister and two nieces, one fourteen, the other nine years old....Then I asked the skinny man, "Listen, can we sprinkle limestone on your relatives?"
> "Yes."
> The fourteen-year old had to be transferred to an adult casket because she was too big for the other one. As I sprinkled her, I thought of Hamlet, when Ophelia, after losing her mind drowns. ....I had exactly the same sensation:

"Girl, I am sprinkling limestone on you, so you'll go all whitened up, you who have not lived at all, fourteen-year-old girl." .....I could only sprinkle limestone on her. Not a single flower, just a lot of white dust. (Poniatowska 1995, 89–90)

Juxtaposing the narrative of the heroic escape of Alonso with Antonio's tragic encounter with three young women and the man who came to claim their bodies brings multiple public voices and experiences from the earthquake to light. The question about whether lime can be sprinkled on the body of the 14-year-old girl echoes the tragic loss of the disappeared students who the Mexican government falsely claimed had been burned with no trace of their remains to be found. The man who came to claim his sister and two nieces stands in as an echo of the parents of the Ayotzinapa students searching for their remains or evidence of what happened to them.

After reading the second testimony, Elena concluded, "I hope that by reading these to all of you that it gives to all of us an understanding of the dimensions of the terrible pain of the earthquake in all of those who died." She is very deliberately bringing to the public these two testimonies that can connect to the present and bring her audience back to 1985. This is a self-conscious effort on the part of Poniatowska to build out the strategic emotional/political community of 1985 earthquake survivors and their supporters and connect them to the 2015 emotional/political community of the parents of the disappeared students and the international network of those who support them.

One Man's Testimony Through Time

About 40 minutes into the event to commemorate the 30th anniversary of the 1985 earthquake at *El Museo de la Ciudad*, a man in his fifties with a shaved head, fashionable dark-framed glasses, and a suit and tie raised his hand. He was clutching a yellowed copy of *La Jornada* newspaper. His exchange with Elena consolidated 30 years of the recording, publishing, dissemination, and then transformation of one testimonial about the 1985 earthquake. I was watching, I thought at the moment, the undulating motion of a wave of social memory and emotional community that could be thought of like a cyclical tide. Lapping at the shores of the center of Mexico City where the earthquake wrought its greatest destruction, the testimonies Elena recorded in 1985 spun out in many lives, continued to appear in new forms, and remained strong emotional connectors for a wide range of people through time.

The man in the suit rose to his feet, took the microphone and addressed the crowd:

> My name is Andrés. ...I have been fascinated to read the testimonies written by Elena Poniatowska. On the 19th of September, 1985 I had a very difficult experience. On this day my brother died in the collapse of a building that was in Colonia Roma in Chihuahua number 156. But thanks to God, I didn't feel as bad as I could have. I wanted to share my testimony by telephone. I contacted Señora Elena and she gave me an appointment to come to her house. It was thirty years ago and I still had hair. I went to her house there in Chimalistac and I was very accelerated, and very nervous. I was feeling really bad, really bad because I had lost my younger brother who was like a son to me. He was 26 years old and I was 33.
>
> Elena interviewed me and to my surprise, two months after the earthquake happened, on November 28th, La Señora Elena Poniatowska published my testimony.

Andrés stopped there, held up a copy of the *La Jornada* newspaper from November 28, 1985, and the crowd broke out in wild applause. He continued:

> This testimony impacted me in a big way. It motivated me to carry out further investigation, to study, and to take on another life. In 1989, I went to visit Señora Elena with my wife, on January 6, 1989, and she gave us a copy of her book Las *Voces del Temblor,* which included my testimony on pages 246, 247 and 248.
>
> After this I was motivated to do much more. I started attending workshops, working on my writing. All of this permitted me, although I am not a writer, to produce a book. ....I know that you (facing Elena) are a great writer, but thanks to God here is my book. I am going to write about this in an open letter to *La Jornada* this Sunday, I have the printed version for you here on a USB.
>
> And I tell you. I am an architect, not a writer, but I am an apprentice. The fact that you took my testimony and published it had a very big impact on me. On the basis of that testimony which you published, I have written my own book which is called *"Thirty Years After the Earthquake: The Jornada del Lobo: A spiritual awakening."* Thank you.

Andres' original testimony published in *La Jornada* and in *Nada Nadie* was titled "El Lobo Who Would Never Get Mad: Those who want to cooperate, please plant a flower." Andrés brother, Alejandro Escoto, died in a poorly built school in Colonia Roma, the University of Chapultepec, "which buried him with other students, who like him, studied tourism." Andrés stated in his 1985 testimony, "I'm not going to place a tombstone or a memorial there. I am going to have a little garden, and whoever wants to cooperate can plant a flower....I don't know where Alejandro is, but I feel that I may be a little better as a person because I reflect something of my brother" (Poniatowska 1995, 249).

As Andrés spoke in the *Museo de la Ciudad* in front of some of the primary political actors of the 1985 earthquake, the press took his picture and some (including me) recorded his words. His image is on Facebook along with other pictures from that day. Although his original testimony was 30 years old, he remained connected to it, and was able to launch his own writing from that experience. His book is another link in the strategic emotional/political community created through Poniatowska's newspaper chronicles and book *Nada, Nadie* about the earthquake.

Testimony, Strategic Emotional Communities, and Alternative Political Futures

Did the *crónicas* and book of Elena Poniatowska change the way Mexico remembers the earthquake? Did the publication of the experiences and words of everyday people and those outside the political elite change the outcome? Did those words and the strategic emotional/political communities they are connected to help to build a political opening in Mexico? Many would say yes. Others would say perhaps.

The earthquake did spawn a wave of urban social activism that ultimately had an impact on the transformation on the governance of the city itself. It changed the governance of Mexico City from the mid-1990s to the present, consolidating a leftist city government. The occasion of the 30th anniversary of the earthquake and the recirculation of *Nada Nadie*, public forums at which many of its protagonists appeared, museum exhibits and films, created a wider public space for testimonies of the 1985 quake connected to other social and political traumas. Through this process, testimonies from the past and present circulated, crossed paths, and connected disparate historical events, disrupting a linear sense of history in Mexico and telescoping the events of Ayotzinapa, the massacre of Tlaltelolco, and the *terremoto* into a shared space.

Common-sense understandings of western history tell us that events happen in a linear fashion with one experience following another. Studies in the humanities of how social memory is constructed, however, emphasize that memory of the past is always influenced by the context of the present (see Fentress and Wickham 1992; Samuel 1994). In fact, the act of "remembering" joins the past with the present. To remember can mean "to have or keep an image or idea in your mind of (something or someone from the past): to think of (something or someone from the past) again; to cause (something) to come back into your mind; to keep (information) in your mind: to not forget (something)" (Merriam-Webster 2015). To remember connects a person to the linguistic skills linked to oral testimony and to participation in a speech community. Oral testimony refers to a person's account of an event or experience as delivered from the lips of a person through a speech act. It is an oral telling of a person's perception of a past event through seeing, hearing, smelling, and other sensory information. It signifies witnessing and is often performative and public (see Stephen 2013, 109–110). The act of remembering a specific event through testimony thus acquires its meaning only in the context of the specific interpretive practices and framework of a community of speakers (Backhurst 1990, 220). Writing about memory, Backhurst states that for Soviet linguist Voloshinov, "memory can never be understood as an intermediate relation between the thinking subject and some private mental image of the past. The image, he argues, becomes a phenomenon of consciousness only when clothed with words, and these owe their meaning to social practices of communication" (Backhurst 1990, 220).

Linking memory to the social practices of communication is crucial to understanding how social memory is crafted in different contextual moments and changes through time, depending on the specific social and political conditions in which it is deployed. And we cannot divorce memory from the emotions linked to specific instances of trauma or painful events, as evidenced in the testimonies of the earthquake discussed above. Documentation of testimonies at a particular point in time—as Poniatowska does in her *crónicas*—does not freeze the meaning or significance of those testimonies. Each time they are recited, read, and remembered, they acquire new meaning in a new context. And it is the emotion embedded in such public testimonies that allows them to transcend specific historical contexts. In this way, social memory can be thought of as having ever-changing and distinct relationships with time. Rather than trying to equate social memory and testimonies with specific events at an actual point in linear time, it makes more sense to think of social memories as flexible containers that can operate in circular, layered, or even spiraled fields of time.

The models of time that many Native peoples work with can provide us with important insights here. Rather than assume that time is linear and that we as humans exist on one plane marked by a distinct past, present, and future, the knowledge systems of Native peoples such as the Nahua (Maffie 2014), Maya (León Portillo 1990), Nasa (Rappaport 1998, 2005), Mixtec (Terraciano 2002), and Kahnawake Mohawks (Simpson 2014) can link the past, present, and future together through one event, one feature of the landscape that marks a significant occurrence, a ritual, a song, a prayer, or a map. Here I argue that these varied models of time and how time links to specific material (landmarks, ritual objects, art), speech (testimonies of events, genealogies, prayers, songs), and objects provide important models for how the *crónicas* about specific historical events and processes in Mexico are remembered, canonized, challenged, shape and reshape the kind of future that can be imagined and move people to political action. If we think of a public testimonial as a symbolic object like a ritual object, a prayer or genealogy that has emotional force through its telling and reproduction, then we can see it as a continual generator of emotional communities and memories. Memories shape the capacity to produce the future, and are themselves shaped by the kind of future we think we are heading for. Through their participation in the ways that national events are remembered and strategic emotional/political communities are created and sustained through time, the *crónicas* of Elena Poniatowska and the testimonies they contain are doing important work in shaping future political imaginaries in Mexico.

Notes

1. The genre known in the United States as slave narratives was an important part of the abolition movement in the United States.
2. Shoshona Felman and Dori Laub, 1992, Testimony: *Crises in Witnessing in Literature, Psychoanalysis, and History.* New York: Routledge, xv–xvii; Bhaskar Sarkar, and Janet Walker, 2010, *Documentary Testimonies: Global Archives of Suffering.* New York: Routledge, 7.
3. For example, the genre known as slave narratives which recounted the experiences of those who escaped slavery were an important part of the abolition movement in the United States (see Smith Foster 1994).
4. 7:19 AM was the exact time of the earthquake.

References

Backhurst, David. 1990. Social Memory in Soviet Thought. In *Collective Remembering*, ed. David Middleton and Derek Edwards, 203–226. London: Sage.

Bhaskar, Sarkar, and Janet Walker, eds. 2010. *Documentary Testimonies. Global Archives of Suffering*. New York: Routledge.

Colorado Nates, Oscar. 2015. A 31 años del terremoto del 19 de septiembre de 1985 en la Cd. de México: Una memoria gráfica. Oscarenfotos.com. https://oscarenfotos.com/2015/09/19/30-aniversario-terremoto-cd-de-mexico/. Accessed 29 Mar 2017.

Corona Cadena, Evangelina. 2007. *Contar las cosas Como fueron*. México: DEMAC.

Crosby, Alison, and M. Brinton Lykes. 2011. Mayan Women Survivors Speak: The Gendered Relations of Truth Telling in Postwar Guatemala. *The International Journal of Transitional Justice* 5: 456–576. https://doi.org/10.1093/ojtj/tjr017.

Fentress, James, and Chris Wickham. 1992. *Social Memory*. Oxford: Blackwell.

Hall, Stuart. 1996. Introduction: Who Need "Identity"? In *Questions of Cultural Identity*, ed. Stuart Hall and Paul du Gay, 1–17. London: Sage.

Jimeno, Myriam. 2010. Emoções e Política: A *Vítima* e a Construção de Comunidades Emocionais. *Mana: Estudos de Antropologia Social* 16 (1): 99–121.

Jimeno, Myriam, and Morna Macleod. 2014. *Interview with Myriam Jimeno*, November 2014. http://mornamacleod.net/?p=767

Jimeno, Myriam, Daniel Varela, and Ángeles Castillo. 2015. *Después de la masacre: emociones y política en el Cauca Indio*. Bogotá: ICANH-CES-Universidad Nacional de Colombia.

León Portillo, Miguel. 1990. *Time and Reality in the Thought of the Maya*. Norman: University of Oklahoma Press.

Maffie, James. 2014. *Aztec Philosophy: Understanding a World in Motion*. Denver: University Press of Colorado.

Meneses Arias, Natyelly. 2015. Costureras de 85: la lucha sindical que surgió de la tragedia. *Milenio*, September 18, 2015. http://www.milenio.com/df/Terremoto_85-costureras_San_Antonio_Abad_sismo_85-terremoto_85_costureras_0_593940695.html

Merriam-Webster. 2015. Dictionary. To Remember. http://www.merriam-webster.com/dictionary/remember

Monsiváis, Carlos. 2005. *"No sin Nosotros": Los días del terremoto 1985–2005*. Santiago de Chile/México D.F: Ediciones Era, México/LOM Ediciones.

Poniatowska, Elena. 1988. *Nada, nadie: Las voces del temblor*. Mexico City: Ediciones Era.

———. 1995. *Nothing, Nobody: The Voices of the Mexico City Earthquake*. Philadelphia: Temple University Press. Translated, with a Foreword by Aurora Camacho de Schmidt and Arthur Schmidt.
———. 2008. Las memorias de una costurera: Evangelina Corona. Opinión. *La Jornada*, May 11, 2008. http://www.jornada.unam.mx/2008/05/11/index.php?section=cultura&article=a06a1cul
———. 2015. Nuestro Peor Enemigo es el Olvido. *Proceso Special Edition* 51: 8–19.
Rappaport, Joanne. 1998. *The Politics of Memory: Native Historical Interpretation in the Colombian Andes*. Durham: Duke University Press.
———. 2005. *Intercultural Utopias: Public Intellectuals, Cultural Experimentation, and Ethnic Pluralism in Colombia*. Durham: Duke University Press.
Razack, Sharene. 2007. Stealing the Pain of Others: Reflections on Canadian Humanitarian Responses. *Review of Education, Pedagogy, and Cultural Studies* 29 (4): 375–395.
Samuel, Raphael. 1994. *Theatres of Memory, Vol. 1. Past and Present in Contemporary Culture*. London: Verso.
Shaw, Rosalind. 2013. Provocation: Futurizing Memory. Field notes: The Politics of Memory. *Cultural Anthropology*, September 5, 2013. http://www.culanth.org/fieldsights/376-provocation-futurizing-memory
Simpson, Audra. 2014. *Mohawk Interruptus: Political Life across the Borders of Settler States*. Durham: Duke University Press.
Smith Foster, Frances. 1994. *Witnessing Slavery: The Development of Ante-bellum Slave Narratives*. 2nd ed. Madison: University of Wisconsin Press.
Stephen, Lynn. 2013. *We Are the Face of Oaxaca: Testimony and Social Movements*. Durham/London: Duke University Press.
Terraciano, Kevin. 2002. *The Mixtecs of Colonial Oaxaca*. Palo Alto: Stanford University Press.
Werbner, Richard, ed. 1998. *Memory and the Postcolony*. London: Zed Books.
West, Harry. 2000. Girls with Guns: Narrating the Experience of War of FRELIMO's "Female Detachment". *Anthropological Quarterly* 73: 180–194.

CHAPTER 4

Emotional Histories: A Historiography of Resistances in Chalatenango, El Salvador

Jenny Pearce

INTRODUCTION

Language has unmistakably made plain that memory is not an instrument for exploring the past, but rather a medium. It is the medium of that which is experienced, just as the earth is the medium in which ancient cities lie buried. He who seeks to approach his own buried past must conduct himself like a man digging. Above all, he must not be afraid to return again and again to the same matter; to scatter it as one scatters earth, to turn it over as one turns over soil. For the *matter itself* is no more than the strata which yield their long-sought secrets only to the most meticulous investigation. That is to say, they yield those images that, severed from all earlier associations, reside as treasures in the sober rooms of our later insights—like torsos in a collector's gallery.... In this sense, for authentic memories, it is far less important that the investigator report on them than

---

A longer version of this chapter was published: Pearce J. (2016) The Past Is Not History: Co-constructing an Historiography of Resistances in El Salvador. Conflicto armado, justicia y memoria. Tomo I: Teoría política y experiencias de memoria. Editorial: Universidad Pontificia Bolivariana. Medellín: Grupo de Investigación sobre Estudios Críticos, pp. 125–156.

J. Pearce (✉)
Latin America and Caribbean Centre, London School of Economics, London, UK

that he mark, quite precisely, the site where he gained possession of them. Epic and rhapsodic in the strictest sense, genuine memory must therefore yield an image of the person who remembers, in the same way a good archaeological report not only informs us about the strata from which its findings originate but also gives an account of the strata which first had to be broken through (Benjamin 1932, 576).

This chapter explores the idea of a "historiography of resistances" based on Walter Benjamin's *Concept of History*. The aim is to find ways to excavate uncounted and discounted memories in Latin America as sources of contingent agency for political and social change. It connects to the themes of this volume because such a historiography is imbued with emotion within and between all those involved in its construction. Narratives of resistance in Latin America involve experiences of violence, suffering and solidarity. The historiographer has to embrace these emotional histories in order to grasp the full character of the past. Recognizing the emotionality of history and historization is an important advance in human sensibilities. The "memory boom" is widely credited with putting the mind and emotions of the historical actor *and the* historian center stage (Tumblety 2013, 3). Enzo Traverso (2016) links his reflections on memory and history in the twentieth century to the emergence of a figure of fundamental importance: the victim: "Previously very discrete and marginal from the point of view of its public dimension, the victim now is projected to the center of the scene, where he/she occupies the entire scene. The victim appears today as the true hero of the twentieth century and generates very strong attention, sometimes obsessional" (Traverso 2016, 24).

Interestingly, the resistant "emotional community" of Chalatenango, El Salvador, which is the subject of this chapter, was insistent that they did not want to be considered "victims", and their Committee which came together to build their museum of "historical memory" was consciously named: the *Comité de Memoria Sobreviviente* (Committee of Surviving Memory). Natalia De Marinis' nomenclature of the "political affective" community (De Marinis this volume) captures well the interface between the emotional processes among people who have been through unspeakable trauma and the political processes they can engender through the analytical consciousness they gain in turning their memories into history. This politicization of affect is a bridge between *emotion* and *resistance*. The idea of *resistance* requires acknowledgement of forms of agency that a given epoch might not recognize as such. These forms are, as Benjamin argues, often mere traces or just an image that "flashes up at the moment of its recognizability, and is never seen again" (Benjamin 1940, Thesis V. 390). They are lost to history when the present does not recognize itself in the image, unless, that is, the historian acts. This chapter suggests one way of acting for the historian, or of enacting Benjamin.[1] It involves a process of excavating "reserves of memory" *with* resistant makers of history in the Salvadoran civil war/revolution, in order to restore to them their "historical capital" (Nora 1989, 7). These are (mostly) illiterate peasants of the remote north east of Chalatenango on the Honduran border, who organized a peasant union in the early 1970s, only to face savage repression. When the peasants began to organize, "they made war on us" (*Nos hicieron la guerra*), the peasants say (interviews, September 2014). This led to a growth of active support for the nascent guerrilla movement in the region (the Popular Forces of Liberation, FPL), and which joined with other groups in 1980, to form the Farabundo Marti Liberation Movement (FMLN). However, this was no ideological or manipulated mobilization. It produced real conflicts within peasant communities who shared a profound spirituality and rejection of violence. Support for the armed struggle began with the need for defense, a "negative" resistance which gradually became a "positive" resistance, and I argue, took a revolutionary turn, when the peasants began to build what was called Local Popular Power (PPL, *Poder Popular Local*), as a form of civil defense and self-government in their zone of guerilla control in Chalatenango (Fig. 4.1).

Fig. 4.1 Local Popular Power, Chaltenango 1984. Photograph by Mike Goldwater

I shared a brief few months with these peasants in 1984, writing an oral history of the peasant movement and the construction of PPL, when the war had been taken—under US advice—into the air, resulting in almost daily bombardment. I returned three decades later to work with the Museum of Historical Memory, Arcatao, Chalatenango, set up by the peasants in 2010, on their memories of resistance, repression and revolution and to explore with them what kind of history emerged from their memories. Such a process of digging around in the "strata of memory" with the subjects of memory exemplifies the spirit of Benjamin's argument for an historiography which offers "sparks of hope"[2] in the past rather than predicting revolutionary agency for the future. Benjamin's focus on the "radical fragments of history" (Benjamin 1940, Thesis V 424) rather than its rational unfolding toward the revolutionary project accords with the way many resistances never gain a place in the history books, precisely because they "fail" to bring about a revolutionary change. Yet these fragments themselves tell an important story, one of which is the core of this article. At the same time, the historian who uses memory is confronted by many challenges around the kind of history that he or she is writing and how to validate this source of knowledge and address its incompletenesses. If the aim is to restore "historical capital" to peasants, there are many additional challenges in terms of scholarship, ownership and voice. These cannot be ignored when building emotional histories.

This chapter will first of all briefly summarize how Benjamin encourages us to think about history and resistance. Second, it will offer some background context to the Memory and History *Conversatorios* (Conversations) organized with the Museum of Historical Memory of Arcatao in 2014, and the difficulty the peasants' faced in translating memories into a historical narrative which could influence the politics of the present in El Salvador. Third, it will briefly discuss the themes of agency amidst violence, articulated by the peasants as they began to turn their past into history. Finally, it will reflect on the challenges of building history from memory with peasants who remain mostly unable to read or *write* their own history.

Benjamin and the "Radical Fragments" of History

Benjamin in the quote at the beginning of this chapter reminds of us of two things. The first is that the past leaves us "treasures in the sober rooms of our later insights". However, these treasures are just torsos in a gallery; they are not full-bodied parts of our present. They are uprooted from their past and the contextual strata which gave them form. We have to break through layers and layers of earth to uncover these treasures in their full meaning and import. Under the strata are *buried* the sources of our later insights. If we do not dig and dig, we have only a faint trace rather than the rich seam of learning from memory.

Second, Benjamin highlights the importance of the remembering person, how they are today as well as how they remember their lives in the past. In my interpretation, the remembering person is a subject in all his or her embodied complexity. The subject is always potentially capable of agency in the world, of acting on the world rather than the passive bearer of the structural constraints they are born into or of the dominating, coercive or consent forming action of others. The remembering subject is also connected emotionally to others, and the construction of a politically affective community is contingently related to the relationships of which he or she is part and the experiences they share.

Read alongside his *Concept of History*, Benjamin's "Excavation and Memory", points us toward a historiography for those who seek the buried treasures of emancipatory struggles and to understand the agents who have taken them forward. Benjamin challenges the "historicist", epitomized by influential nineteenth-century historians, such as Leopold von Ranke (1795–1886) who saw history as eternal time, which the historian excavates for the facts that remain waiting his (or her) attention. It assumes a universal history and is content to establish a causal nexus between moments of history that once constructed, demonstrate an inevitable progress of human perfectibility.[3] There is no room in such a view of history for those possibilities which were never actualized. Werner Hamacher in his essay on "'Now': Walter Benjamin on Historical Time", clarifies the importance of Benjamin's dispute with the historicist, when he discusses the role of possibility and contingency in Benjamin's essay, as the essence of what makes history history: "Historical is that which only can be recognized as historical from its contingent possibility to yet have been different and to yet become different, and thus from its after-history" (Hamacher 2005, 65). Thus, the fleeting possibilities and "flashes" of history, the resistances which are the subject of this chapter, are historical by virtue of the possibility that they might not be realized and are exposed to the danger of being missed:

> Because there is no reservoir fixed for all time, in which the treasures of possibility for ever accumulate, but only a reservoir whose stock dissolves with every missed chance, history is no progression where given possibilities, one by one, one out of the other, are actualized, so that in the end all possibilities

will have been exhausted and all possible actualities established. Where there is history, there is no continuum between the possible and the actual. (Hamacher 2005, 67)

Benjamin points us toward a historiography that uses memory to dig for resistances and ruptures, for possibilities and contingencies. Resistance is a complex word, which Howard Caygill (2013, 223) argues remains intangible, "a peculiar condition of possibility of both power and defiance: without it there is no power". This captures the idea that resistance at its minimum involves a "stand"[4] against more powerful forces, and that in turn generates power to act. I use resistance in this chapter to convey the efforts by peasants first to make such a stand, initially through their peasant union and against rising repression. Gradually this turned into resistance as action to change the course of "history" in their favor. In the course of this "stand" and the violence unleashed against them, the peasants grasped a sense that they could build on values of mutual support and cooperation to build a vision for their future as well as a rejection of their past. Many recount how this process enabled members of their communities to overcome alcoholism and interpersonal violence, traditional responses of, in particular, the downtrodden male.

Howard Caygill shows how resistance has also been linked to consciousness and subjectivity, with attitudes to violence a major dividing line among those who make use of this concept. Resistance was incorporated into Marxist theory and attached to national and class consciousness, with some seeing resistance as a first step toward a revolutionary class war and a classless society. This, as Caygill points out, was the position of Che Guevara, who influenced some of the revolutionary movements in El Salvador. However, in Chalatenango, the guerrilla leadership took the North Vietnamese military position of General Giap, and the founder and leader of the FPL, Salvador Cayetano Carpio (known as Marcial), famously responded to Che Guevara when he dismissed the possibility of a revolution in El Salvador due to the lack of appropriate terrain for a guerrilla rearguard, that "in El Salvador, the people are our mountains" (Pearce 1985, 127). The emphasis on popular organizing and consciousness by the guerrilla theorists gave space to peasants to reach an acceptance through experience rather than ideology, of armed struggle as their only option, but on terms which recognized their own political agency. In conversations, they still talk of the original theory of political organization promulgated by Carpio and the FPL, that the voices of the base of the movement should be heard by the leadership and returned downward in strategies which reflect those voices and opinions. They were also very aware of how this was abandoned as the armed struggle intensified and after the suicide of Marcial in 1983. The theology of liberation brought to the region by radical, if not yet revolutionary, priests in the late 1960s and 1970s, had also literally liberated mindsets, supplemented by simple Marxist messages.[5] Experiences of marches in the capital city with workers and students are etched on memories as moments of great risk—their buses to the city were frequently stopped and people arrested—but of gaining a sense of belonging to a wider resistance. The Sunday sermons of Archbishop Romero, urging the government to halt its violence toward the peasants, gave validation and moral support to their struggles.

These experiences strengthened the "resistant subjectivity", Caygill also associates with the concept of resistance. Such resistant subjectivity is often mobilized, he argues, around virtues of justice, courage/fortitude and prudence. Such virtues and others emerged strongly in the peasant resistance, but not as discursive or rhetorical memes. They were practical tools which peasants used to withstand the enormous hardships of life in the guerrilla controlled zone. They are also deeply emotional in the way they draw on feelings of fear and solidarity. The skills the peasants learnt and their organizational creativity enabled them eventually to negotiate their return to their homes in the late 1980s, after a brutal army invasion which forced most of them to refugee camps in Honduras in 1985.

Why then, is this peasant resistance a "fleeting" moment of history that has to be excavated with those who created it because it is in "danger" of being lost? Why, does it require the insight of Walter Benjamin's essay to explain its full import? The answers lie in the way, gradually, the logic of resistance and revolution ceded space to the logic of war in El Salvador. The emancipatory dimensions of the resistance were lost as the military dimensions overcame them, and the Peace Accord of 1992 was based on what came to be accepted as a military stalemate and was agreed between military commanders. The uncounted and discounted memories of resistance in El Salvador are still apparent in how the peasants continue to conduct their lives. However, Salvadoran society does not recognize itself in these memories. This is why this chapter discusses a methodology for restoring the "historical capital" within the memories, working with the peasants to re-discover their significance for them and ultimately for Salvadoran society. Above all it taps into the long-term emotional affects and effects of savage violence, in which the politicization of affects enabled the peasants to turn their pain into cooperation with each other. As the historian, reluctantly (due to my training) I acknowledge my emotional as well as intellectual participation in this history. Returning to Chalatenango 30 years after my time with the peasants, was because the intensive months we shared, shaped my own life and understanding of the role of the intellectual.

THE PAST IS NOT HISTORY IN EL SALVADOR

Salvadorans have taken some time to address the history of the Salvadoran civil war. There are still many histories and, as Jorge Juárez, Director of the Center of the History of the Salvadoran Civil War, expressed it in an interview, many memories:

> How do you build a narrative from so many memories? How do you build a narrative that enables us to live together? There is still a lot of pain within people – too much pain still. Perhaps, history constructed "from below" could be a more real history, but it is complex to do it because there are varied problematic psychological factors. For example, as a form of protection, people close down their memories…people self-repress, there is much constraint. However, in the long term, it is important to construct this history. Places of memory are also important and controversial. In this moment there is a big show in the country – it is a struggle to make and name streets, places, monuments, etc. The Armed Forces also build memory. This construction of spaces of memory is conflictive- for example, where to put D'Aubuisson and the extreme right in this exercise? (Interview with Jorge Juárez, August 2014)

The FMLN, the guerrilla organization which fought the war, came to power through elections in 2009 and again in 2014.Although some of its commanders have written their versions of history, El Salvador certainly has no "official" history and no history *desde abajo* ("from below"), over 20 years after the war formally ended. This is also despite a considerable literature written by international academics on the civil war and its aftermath. Thus, El Salvador is not an example of a victor's history as such, but of contested memories, perhaps reflecting the stalemate that brought the civil war to a close. The past is not history in El Salvador. And the conditions for violence remain. El Salvador is among the most violent countries in the world today, despite the end of the war (Insight Crime 2015).

The stalemate of the 1992 peace agreement disguised the victory of the modernizing elites of the country, well prepared before the final peace process through the neoliberal think tank, the Salvadoran Foundation for

Economic and Social Development (FUSADES), funded by United States Agency for International Development (USAID), to integrate El Salvador firmly within the post-Cold War economic paradigm of neoliberal globalization. The issues for which the peasants, workers, students and radical intellectuals had fought, such as agrarian reform and a model of state led inclusive development, were not on the agenda at the peace talks nor in their wake. The FMLN won the right to participate politically, but regions such as Chalatenango, remained as marginal to the development of the country as before the war, even though they received considerable international aid in the war's immediate aftermath, mostly due to the grass roots organizing which international NGOs and other bodies had come to respect. The story of the reconstruction process after the war in Chalatenango has been told in Salazar and Carmen Cruz (2012), Van Der Borgh (2003), Silber (2004, 2011) and Todd (2010). The history of self-organizing continued to play a role as the communities' negotiated solutions to their problems, with the support of national NGOs close to the communities. Yet Silber (2011) records through her fieldwork in the region a "palpable disillusionment" among the population of the area. She suggests that post-war Chalatenango "is a story of a resocialization of survivors of the civil war into contentious citizens who engage in a politics of resistance to continued processes of exclusion" (2011, 8). Todd (2010, 222) captures the significance of peasant organizing and collective action even in the post-war period, but argues that "governments, observers, and analysts have displaced *campesinos* from Salvadoran national history".

The legacy of the history of self-organizing during the war remains palpable. The peasants have constructed small museums of historical memory, such as in Las Flores, Las Vueltas as well as the one to be discussed in this chapter in Arcatao. Many from the region have also played a significant role in movements, such as *ProBúsqueda* which had been set up in Guarjila with *Padre* Jon de Cortina, to search for the children of victims of the war who had been disappeared or handed out for adoption. Chalatenango was one of the worst affected by such practices. There is evidence that by maintaining the social cohesion that had served the communities so well during the war, these communities have also resisted the efforts by gangs from the cities to build a base in this important borderland and drug trafficking route. Las Flores, for example, was reported in 2015 to have had not a single homicide in a decade (El Faro 2015). Some of the infrastructure projects the state had brought to the region have also been deeply contested, such as the Transversal del Norte, a road linking Chalatenango to

Honduras, and which many felt would facilitate the drugs rather than other trades. And a mining project in 2013 has generated organized opposition in the municipality of Las Flores, under a Mayor who had played an active role in the peasant movement and the Local Popular Power of Chalatenango during the war. In 2014, following a popular consultation the town declared itself "free of mining" and in 2017, El Salvador became the first country in the world to ban metal mining.

This capacity for self-organizing could have been harnessed for post-war development and given state support and resources. Without the latter and with dwindling international aid and cooperation, their actions enabled them to preserve community but not offer opportunities to new generations or influence national policy on agriculture and food security, for instance. Lack of recognition of the extraordinary savagery these peasants endured in their struggle for a dignified life and of the creative way they responded to the collapse of the state in their region leaves them with memories but no history which could be capitalized into their inclusion into the political debates of the country. Poverty and associated social problems persist and there is little to keep young people in the region. For many, *el norte* or migration to the USA remains the dream of the future.

I became aware in my return visits that armed actors on both sides of the civil war were unwilling to recognize the ongoing value of the peasants' contribution to the development of the country. As entry to political competition beckoned in 1992, so guerrilla commanders paid less and less attention to this peripheral region (Sprenkels 2014) and focused on the struggle for political power in the center. Narratives about the civil war rarely referred to the political role of the peasants. They were at most "base" to the wider struggle waged by the guerrilla army. Many have found it difficult to accept that there was some role for the peasants that was not reducible to the logic of armed struggle, or that they offer a wisdom of ongoing value to the society as a whole.

THE *CONVERSATORIOS* AND THE HISTORICIZATION OF MEMORY IN CHALATENANGO

Perhaps because I could not quite reconcile what I had lived with the peasants in 1984 and learnt about the significance of their efforts to self-organize[6] in the midst of army invasions and aerial bombardments, that I could never quite leave my engagement with them to a book published in the middle of the war and never translated into Spanish. I, therefore, returned to Chalatenango in September 2014 to work with the peasants on their history. I worked with the Museum of Historical Memory, established by the peasants of Arcatao, Chalatenango, and used my book, *Promised Land*, and the photos taken by Mike Goldwater, my professional photographer companion in 1984, as a stimulus to three *Conversations*.[7]

There had been other initiatives by the peasants and from outside organizations. In Arcatao, the population had been asked to attend mental health workshops in 2003. However, many felt this was not how they wanted to address their memories. They wanted something that could be seen and was tangible. A workshop on mental health would mean they would talk to each other, which was good, Nicolás, a Committee founding member said, but:

> Something needed to be registered so that the future generations would get to know what happened…In the "guindas,"[8] I had thought this history needed to be told, I will do that. Then we also said: "But it's just a book. And if there is nothing to see?" People will say that the book is just what someone puts there and we wanted something that can be seen…Well, that's why the museum… And that's how we began. (Interview with Nicolás, September 2014, Arcatao)

The importance of tactile objects and artifacts for memory reflects the deeply emotional character of experiences that could not be captured in words, especially when the peasants themselves could not write or read them. The value of the photos taken in 1984 of themselves and their loved ones was immense, and triggered the conversations we organized together. The significance of the Museum lay in the artifacts the peasants collected from the war and which were real evidence of what they had lived. The Sanctuary which members of the Arcatao museum were building to house the remains of victims of the war who began to be exhumed around 2011/2012 was another example of the importance of making their lived experiences visible and tangible to others.

The Conversations were held in three villages of north east Chalatenango: Las Vueltas, Las Flores and Arcatao. Around 150 peasants participated altogether; given costs and logistics of travel, mostly peasants attended their nearest village Conversation. The themes which are highlighted below are a small selection from rich discussions around the detailed experience of war and its aftermath, as well as more in-depth follow-up interviews with some of the participants.

Both the dates given by historians to this war, and its nomenclature as a "war" rather than a "revolution" is contested by the peasants. These basic historical "facts" are caught between the tidy reconstructions of history and the complex subjectivities of memory. For the peasants, the war began in the 1970s, while most historians date it officially from 1980. For the historians, it was a 12-year civil war. For the peasants, it was closer to 20, and those extra years matter. For some peasants, the struggle began when they organized a peasant union, the Union of Rural Workers (UTC) in 1974, and the government and a private armed group supported by the army and landowners known as ORDEN, started to arrest, torture and kill the leaders. The role of this peasant union has not been widely recorded for history, although there is an important book on FECCAS (Christian Federation of Salvadoran Peasants), its counterpart in Aguilares (Cabarrus 1983); *Promised Land* offered an account of the UTC written in the midst of the war.[9] For many peasants, it was the reactions of the state toward union leaders which led them into support for armed struggle. Many of those leaders and anyone suspected of involvement with the growing popular movements could no longer sleep in their homes at night by the late 1970s. Many date the war from that moment, and recall vividly the time when they began to awaken to their condition, as something not "natural" or given. Julio uses the metaphor of overcoming "blindness" and articulates something of Caygill's resistant "consciousness":

> Look, at the beginning when the UTC began, I wasn't organized, because I had lived in blindness – I didn't see reality. We didn't know the things we were living, nor what those with money were doing to us. One day, a friend of mine was coming to the house and we passed on the way and he says to me: "Hi there, friend" and I said "I'm well", and he said "In what way are you well, friend? Don't you lack schools, health; do you have money, do you have food". And I said to him "No, I lack all of that" and he says to me: "So, you are not well, get organized then". And that is how I became organized. I opened my eyes, and I said to myself: "it's right what this man says, I lack all of those things"…and I organized for that reason, and principally because we worked the land and had none. The struggle was for a land reform, so that the government would give us a piece of land that we could own… and that's why we got involved because we didn't have land to cultivate.
>
> It was as if we had been blind. And when they began to propose things, it was people who were prepared who came to us, professors from the university…We began to wake up, and we began to see, that in reality we were children of the same God, and why did we live in such poverty and the rich live with such power. We began to see, ourselves, how to organize, because all of that was really strange to us. And we began and we liked it, the poor

liked the proposal. That's when we began to know things and to organize ourselves. In the *cantón* (hamlet) where I used to live, it was a big hamlet, about 90 percent got organized and about 10 percent agreed with what the government did, because they were peasants with medium sized landholdings, because they had land and money. (Interview with Julio, September 2014, Las Flores)

And Amado explains how it felt to have no access to education or medicines:

All of us who belonged to the poor class of day laborers, we had a difficult life. The most difficult was that we had no access to education; the most that there was, was first grade in the hamlets. And as there were a lot of children in the classes, you didn't learn anything. Another difficult thing, was health. In our hamlet where we lived, there was no clinic nor a pharmacy to buy medicine, absolutely nothing. So the consequences of an illness were that it attacked you more…Life, before we got organized was a difficult life. And not just in our hamlet, but for everyone in the poor class, who lived in the countryside, we suffered the same. We all had to sell our labor power to make miserable money and at the same time enable our family to survive. (Interview with Amado, September 2014)

Julio also explains how the repression forced the peasants to leave their houses:

From the moment I got organized in 1975, for me from that moment on people were persecuted by the army…at the beginning the struggle was not to make a war, but it was a struggle around demands for improvements in where we worked, in health, and, when we asked for those things, the government and the army responded with repression. That meant that at one point, we had to leave our houses because we couldn't live there, every day they would come to the house and if someone was there, they would kill them, not take them prisoner and then release them later. (Interview with Julio, September 2014, Las Flores)

The peasants shared many detailed memories of organizing and the violent response and the horrors of surviving army massacres, invasions and the moments they had to flee in collective *guindas* as they were called. And they also recalled the PPLs. The PPLs are one of the "flashes" of history. For some in the guerrilla leadership, they were part of the building of a new society in which the peasants would have a participatory role. For others, they were part of the military logics and enabled the peasants to defend themselves through their militia, when the guerrilla armies were off fighting. They also gave a propaganda advantage in framing the revolutionary struggle for a growing European solidarity movement, mobilized more easily in support of a popular movement in arms than a guerrilla army. The uneasy balance between the self-organizing logic and the military logic was always present. The true significance of the PPLs, I would argue, lies elsewhere. For the peasants, the PPLs were an experience of "real power" and they were able briefly to build the content of this power and distinguish it from all their previous experiences, as Julio expressed it with particular clarity:

> At that time, popular power was for us a real power, because the government had lost control here. It had been left a zone without control of the state. So we had to do all things that a town council had to do, like a local government. And these were our roles: defense, agriculture. We struggled to make sure there were schools. At that time we didn't have schools, but children got classes even though it was under a tree, sat on the ground or on a rock. There was no paper, only boards, like at the time of Moses, when it is said he recorded the tablets on a stone, and that's how education was done here. And we in the local government, in the local popular power, we wanted all the children to have access to education, because we hadn't had that opportunity. There were almost no schools or they were far away and we couldn't get there. Our parents didn't believe that you could live from education, they said: "You are going to live through working not the alphabet."
> ...For the State, we were always unknown, we were apart. We could never be capable of having a (government) post. But at the popular level, yes, because we brought everyone together in a place. And there were lots of candidates. From this huge number, it was those with the most votes who took on responsibilities. We, at that time, felt that we had a real power, that the people chose their activities, not like before, when they were imposed. Yes, there were elections, but the elections were imposed. They already had people who would win the posts, although supposedly we voted for them. But it wasn't true. In popular power no, it was real. People voted for the person who could respond to their needs. (Julio, September 2014, Las Flores)

The peasants were clear about the importance of remembering the war, not just to deal with trauma, but also to communicate what it was all about to new generations and also to the wider world. Their messages are against war as such, a positive learning from trauma. This is apparent in these words of Rosa, a *campesina* and founder of the Museum of Historical Memory in Arcatao, who still today can hardly read or write, who was tortured as a 16-year-old girl and whose parents were tortured to death in the civil war. She remains, nevertheless, acutely conscious of the general import of her own experiences of violence, which she wants to communicate:

> ....so that our young people see, they know what we gave for change, for the small changes that there are now in this country. And we want to leave a legacy to the next generations, so that they will continue struggling, so that what we lived, others will not have to live, and no-one else, no-one in the entire world. Because I have lived this and when I hear about wars in other countries, I live that same reality, because wars are the same, who supplies the dead, it's the civilian population, the defenseless population. And for that reason, I make an appeal to the entire world that we unite, we organize ourselves, that we join efforts to say no to war, yes to life, because that's what interests the world. (Interview with Rosa, September 2014, Arcatao)

This wider awareness of the significance of what the peasants have learnt, gives this experience its character as a form of resistance which transformed people and communities into public actors for peace and justice. In building "real power", one where they ran communities for themselves and elected the best people to lead them, the peasants turned resistance into a positive vision of the future they were struggling for and into a contingent possibility for true emancipation from poverty, exploitation and violently policed exclusion. The PPLs marked the moment when resistance briefly became the basis for a new social and political order. It was a vision which has left the peasants with insights about peace and war that go beyond what most would expect from a peripheral corner of a peripheral Central American republic. The vision did not rely on literacy, books or better educated leaders, but on a value system based on cooperation and solidarity, enhanced through cruel necessity and experience of shared suffering. Ideas from the educated played an important role, but alongside the knowledge and wisdom which peasants gained through their own experiences.

History: "An Argument About the Past"

> History is an argument about the past, as well as the record of it, and its terms are forever changing. (Samuel 1994 and 2012, 430)

This process of digging for "sparks of hope" in the past, has to justify itself not only through the validation of co-production with communities of experiential knowledge, but also to communities of disciplined and authored knowledge production, such as academic historians. This is not simply to appease the historicists, as Benjamin called those who insisted on the factual purity of history in linear "empty" time. It is because in order to be capitalized, the peasants' history needs authority, and their powerlessness in relationship to mainstream structures of power, makes it very difficult for them to communicate the authority of their lived experience as history rather than memory. Pierre Nora has eloquently summed up the challenges:

> Memory and history, far from being synonymous, appear now to be in fundamental opposition. Memory is life, borne by living societies founded in its name. It remains in permanent evolution, open to the dialectic of remembering and forgetting, unconscious of its successive deformations, vulnerable to manipulation and appropriation, susceptible to being long dormant and periodically revived. History, on the other hand, is the reconstruction, always problematic and incomplete, of what is no longer. Memory is a perpetually actual phenomenon, a bond tying us to the eternal present, history is a representation of the past...Memory is blind to all but the group it binds...History on the other hand, belongs to everyone and to no one, whence its claim to universal authority. Memory takes root in the concrete, in spaces, gestures, images and objects; history binds itself strictly to temporal continuities, to progressions and to relations between things. Memory is absolute, while history can only conceive the relative. (Nora 1989, 8–9)

Nora reminds us that there is no straightforward way to translate memory into history. Even the meaning of the PPLs, is disputed, as has been discussed. However, the first task of the *Conversatorios*, was to rescue the meaning and import of processes of resistance with the peasants themselves. It was to ensure that this "primary" source would not be lost to historians of El Salvador or of historical resistances in general. By preserving it as a primary source, historians could assess it against other sources. The *Conversatorios* were filmed and a documentary made for the Museum,[10] so that there will always be a record of the peasant's own voices and analysis.

There has been a reassertion of the value of memory in recent years and one historian has claimed it has become "one of the central preoccupations of historical scholarship", indeed there is a palpable "turn to memory" (Cubitt 2007, 1). History has also gone well beyond the historicists of the nineteenth century that Benjamin disliked. There is a much greater recognition of unpacking how understanding of the past is produced and the potential gaps between history "as written" and history as "lived" (Cubitt 2007, 28), although these are approaches that still often contest dominant historical methods. Even if one is contesting the latter, it does not exonerate the historian (in this case myself) from methodological rigor. How can these memories be fed into the histories which some Salvadorans will write? Historian Erik Ching has collected and analyzed an extraordinary collection of firsthand accounts and testimonial collections of the Salvadoran civil war (Ching 2016). These illustrate Raphael Samuel's (1994, 2012) description of history as an "argument about the past". They reveal the spectrum of competing memories and memoirs of civil war, and varied silences and claims about victimhood. Ching's "memory communities" are also "emotional communities", and his collection highlights the importance of ensuring that memorializing does not reflect the power to write and publish, but also that the historian takes on the responsibility of methodological scrutiny with all such communities.

One of the dangers some see in memory as well as testimonial and oral history is precisely the influence of emotion and personal conviction that often emerges from particular stories and which can seduce the historian or his or her reader too easily. So, clearly this kind of history requires other sources to contextualize, probe and question it. The debates on memory as individual, social, collective or public have raised many issues about the way memories mutually influence each other and how individual narratives can easily emerge unquestioned as collective truths. At the same time, the authenticity of voice is often precisely what provides clarity and power to historical events and processes. Without it, we lose the humanness behind these processes. The powerful memories of the present in this chapter which were tested against oral testimony and history of three decades earlier, collected in my book *Promised Land*. When set against the voices captured in that book, a consistent thread stands out, in how the peasants speak of their decisions to organize and why they opted to stay in a guerrilla-controlled zone (rather than flee to refugees camps in Honduras) where, despite being civilians, they and their families were targets of relentless attack. This continuity suggests that the peasants' narratives are as close as can be got to trustworthy accounts of realities that have persisted in memories, which have had little or no influence from other written accounts.

The methodology for the Conversations was developed in order not to direct discussion in any way. Promised Land was not available in Spanish, and it was the photographs that were used to trigger memories from a varied range of participants in the civil war; some who had spent the entire period in Chalatenango and others who had gone to the refugee camps in Honduras. There was also a range of ages, with many young people, who had not heard any detailed stories of that period, even from their parents and grandparents, who often kept silent about the traumas of their life. It is in this context, that this history emerges as emblematic of many such experiences of resistance, in which ordinary people have paid a huge cost in human life to defy a violent and exclusionary social and political order and to attempt to replace it with a humane one. In the emergent "argument about its past", this historiography of resistance attempts to ensure that the unwritten memories of lived experience are recognized for their immense value and insights to narratives of El Salvador's past and future.

Conclusion

The *uncounted* or sometimes *discounted* memories of violence and resistance in Latin America have allowed historical narratives of the region to dominate that tend to stress its *progress* toward democratization and economic growth. Benjamin's approach to historiography offers an alternative to apparently factual "historicism", as he calls it. It is a means through which we can rescue emancipatory lessons from the accumulated strata of rubble. This chapter is about one such effort to build history from memory *with* a community of peasants who are also resistant makers of history and a source of resistant citizenship of the present. In the example from El Salvador that this chapter is based on, Benjamin's understanding of the redemptive power of remembrance resonates powerfully. However, it is not a metaphysical story. It is a deeply real and material one. This is a story about rupture in history through the agency of the peasants, these "subjects" of memory, and at a huge personal cost to them. To some extent, it is also about my own complex role as "excavator" and how by capturing the discontinuities of history, an historiography for resistance "brushes history against the grain" (Benjamin 1940, Thesis VII, 392) and reveals its hidden treasures of defiance. Uncounted and discounted memories are part of a systematic erasure of experience and learning in Latin America about responses to violence and struggles for dignity. Benjamin proposes that we have to make these memories count again, and while he is talking about another place and time, the point is very resonant to a region where violence remains such an everyday instrument of politics. It is by taking control of a memory "as it flashes in a moment of danger", that the historian ensures that nothing is "lost to history" (Benjamin 1940, Thesis VII, 390). And when the agents of rupture in history rescue that history themselves, it is possible that *they* rather than the historian alight the "sparks of hope" in the past enabling them to realize the "historical capital" in their experiences and to gain greater influence over their present.

Notes

1. My thanks to Sami Khatib for articulating for me the real intent of this paper.
2. "The only historian capable of fanning the spark of hope in the past is the one who is firmly convinced that *even the dead* will not be safe from the enemy if he is victorious" (Benjamin 1940, 391).
3. "The concept of mankind's historical progress cannot be sundered from the concept of its progression through a homogenous, empty time. A critique of the concept of such a progression must underlie any criticism of the concept of progress itself" (Benjamin 1940, op. cit.: Thesis XIII, 295) "History is the subject of a construction whose site is not homogenous, empty time, but time filled full by now-time (Jetztzeit)" (Benjamin 1940, op. cit.: Thesis XIV, 395).
4. Deriving from the Latin stare to *come* to a stand or to *cause* to stand (Caygill 2013).
5. In Chalatenango, these were brought to the peasants by a cadre, Andres Torres of the FPL. No-one knew Torres was from the organization until his assassination in 1977. However, the ideas of these "educated" thinkers had a big impact on the peasants. In neighboring Aguilares, the story of how these messages reached peasants is told by Carlos Cabarrus (1983).
6. I have deliberately used the word self-organize here. The guerilla movement clearly played a role in enabling and promoting this process, but it was the peasants who did the organizing on the ground. This is based on my observations in 1984. However, my interpretation is disputed. Sprenkels (2014, 116) put my argument that the PPLs had power of decision making to a mid-level FPL cadre who responded that "There was a war, and it was necessary to have control". The view that the PPLs were mere instruments of the military leadership is common. There is no doubt that the military command was in charge of waging the war; but the PPLs served the needs of that war at the same time as it enabled peasants, who chose to do so, to stay in the guerila zone of control through organizing for their needs, from defense to production. In the process, my observations were that the peasants made decisions about these processes, with guidance from the FPL undoubtedly. But at that time the FPL was going through a transition following the suicide of Marcial, and there was still belief in the importance of peasant participation, although this was evidently weakening. The peasants certainly felt that they were gaining experience they could never have imagined in the past, by running their own elected local government and organizing services. This does not necessarily contradict the claim that the FPL as a political-military structure was still "in control", rather it emphasizes the significance to the peasants themselves of their own space for social and political organizing.

7. The term "Conversation" or *Conversatorio* was the title agreed with the peasants to the process of using the photographs and the book to build history with the communities of North East Chalatenango. The peasants from the Museum did not like the word "workshop". They were uncomfortable with the disempowering structure of workshops, with their facilitators and "training".
8. The word used to describe mass flights during army invasions.
9. Carlos Lara completed his doctoral thesis 'Memoria Histórica del Movimiento Campesino de Chalatenango' at the National Autonomous University of Mexico in November 2016, and this will be published by UCA Editores.
10. *The Past Is not History.* Directed by Richard Duffy and downloadable from richardnduffy.com

References

Benjamin, Walter. [1932] 2005. Excavation and Memory. In *Selected Writings*, Vol. 2, Part 2 (1931–1934), "Ibizan Sequence", 1932, ed. Marcus Paul Bullock, Michael William Jennings, Howard Eiland, and Gary Smith. Cambridge, MA: Belknap Press of Harvard University Press.

———. 1940. On the Concept of History. In *Walter Benjamin Selected Writings*, ed. Howard Eilandand and Michael William Jennings, Vol. 4, 1938–1940. Thesis V. Cambridge, MA/London: The Belknap Press of Harvard University.

Cabarrus, Carlos. 1983. *Génesis de una Revolución: Análisis del Surgimiento de la Organización Campesina en El Salvador*. México DF: Ediciones de la Casa Chata.

Caygill, Howard. 2013. *Resistance: A Philosophy of Defiance*. London: Bloomsbury.

Ching, Erick. 2016. *Stories of Civil War in El Salvador: A Battle of Memory*. Chapel Hill: University of North Carolina Press.

Cubitt, Geoffrey. 2007. *History and Memory*. Manchester: Manchester University Press.

El Faro. 2015. *Las Claves de Cinco Municipios que se Vacunaron Contra la Violencia*, May 14. www.elfaro.net. Accessed 24 June 2015.

Hamacher, Werner. 2005. 'Now': Walter Benjamin on Historical Time. In *Walter Benjamin and History*, ed. Andrew Benjamin, 38–69. London/New York: Continuum.

Insight Crime. 2015. *El Salvador Homicides Skyrocket after Gang Truce Unravels*, January 9. www.insightcrime.org. Accessed 21 June 2015.

Nora, Pierre. 1989. Between Memory and History: Les Lieux de Memoire. *Representations* 26 (Spring): 7–24.

Pearce, Jenny. 1985. *Promised Land: Peasant Rebellion in Chalatenango, El Salvador*. London: Latin America Bureau.

Salazar, Armando, and María Carmen Cruz. 2012. *CCR: Organización y Lucha Popular en Chalatenango*. San Salvador: Asociación de Comunidades para el Desarrollo de Chalatenango.

Samuel, Raphael. 1994. *Theatres of Memory*, 2012. London: Verso.

Silber, Irina Carlota. 2004. Not Revolutionary Enough? Community Rebuilding in Postwar Chalatenango. In *Landscapes of Struggle: Politics, Society and Community in El Salvador*, ed. Aldo Lauria-Santiago and Leigh Binford, 166–186. Pittsburgh: University of Pittsburgh Press.

———. 2011. *Everyday Revolutionaries: Gender Violence, and Disillusionment in Postwar El Salvador*. New Brunswick: Rutgers University Press.

Sprenkels, Ralph. 2014. Revolution and Accommodation. Post-Insurgency in El Salvador. Unpublished Ph.D. Thesis, University of Utrecht Netherlands, Utrecht.

Todd, Molly. 2010. *Beyond Displacement: Campesinos, Refugees, and Collective Action in the Salvadoran Civil War*. Wisconsin: University of Wisconsin Press.

Traverso, Enzo. 2016. Memoria y Historia del Siglo XXI. In *Archivos y Memoria de la Represión en América Latina (1973–1990)*, ed. María Graciela Acuna et al., 17–29. Santiago de Chile: LOM ediciones/FASIC.

Tumblety, Joan. 2013. Introduction: Working on Memory as Source and Subject. In *Memory and History: Understanding Memory as Source and Subject*, ed. Joan Tumblety, 1–16. London: Routledge.

Van der Borgh, Chris. 2003. *Cooperación Externa, Gobierno Local y Reconstrucción Posguerra: La Experiencia de Chalatenango, El Salvador*. Amsterdam: Rozenberg.

CHAPTER 5

Protesting Against Torture in Pinochet's Chile: Movimiento Contra la Tortura Sebastián Acevedo

Morna Macleod

Introduction

On 14 September 1983, a decade after the military coup that overthrew Salvador Allende's socialist government, a group of priests, nuns, grassroots Christian communities, and laypersons carried out a lightning protest in front of Borgoño 1470, a notorious torture center in the heart of Santiago. A group of women and men interrupted the traffic, stretched out a wide banner: "A man is being tortured here". They chanted slogans and sang "I name you Freedom" a resistance song[1] against torture, in front of the astonished gaze—and turning away—of passersby. This five-minute intrepid action was the first time torture was publicly named and shamed under military rule. Police fired a rubber bullet, lightly wounding one of the priests, and then started arresting several protestors. The others flocked into the police van as willing detainees (Parissi 2005 in Tyndale 2006, 140). The Movement Against Torture assumed the name Sebastián Acevedo (MCTSA) two months later, after Acevedo in desperation burned himself alive in front of the cathedral in Concepción, as his daughter and his son were being held and tortured in a secret detention center.

M. Macleod (✉)
Autonomous Morelos State University, Morelos, Mexico

© The Author(s) 2018
M. Macleod, N. De Marinis (eds.), *Resisting Violence*,
https://doi.org/10.1007/978-3-319-66317-3_5

On 21 November 1983, over a hundred people gathered in front of Chile's right-wing newspaper *El Mercurio* cutting off the traffic and occupying the crossroads in central Santiago. They stood behind a long banner: "In Chile there's torture and the Mercurio remains silent", handed in a letter to the newspaper's editor, Agustín Edwards, and chanted the names of people who had died under torture. The police reaction was fast and brutal: *guanacos* (water-cannon trucks) forcefully jetted out water and police fired tear gas straight at the protestors. Some shielded their faces with scarves; others passed limes around to soothe their smarting eyes. But rather than flee, the demonstrators stood fast. They knelt down, locking arms together, becoming a single body or mass, intoned the Lord's Prayer and sang their freedom anthem. The police wacked one youth with his baton and fractured his arm. No one reacted violently. Eighteen-year-old architect student Ana Cristina remembers this as her first participation in the movement:

> It was powerful, forceful, very united and had tremendous energy. It lasted about 20 minutes, the *guanaco* arrived and spurted water at us. We didn't flee, we embraced each other more tightly. Pepe [Father José Aldunate, S.J.] began intoning "Our Father who art in heaven", and everyone, believers and non-believers joined in the Lord's Prayer. It was potent, my baptism by fire, I was very young. Clothes and shoes flew everywhere. Afterwards we met up [at an accorded site] to evaluate the action, this was as important as the action itself… to make sure no-one was missing, that we were all there and in good shape, that no-one had been arrested or left on his own. (Interview with Ana Cristina, October 2015, Santiago de Chile)[2]

One of the largest and most compelling MCTSA actions was on Santiago's verdurous main avenue, the *Alameda*, near the San Francisco church. Blocking the traffic on all sides, dozens of non-violent protestors lay down on the street. The large banner read: "It wasn't war, it was slaughter", and a liturgy followed, one person after another on the ground lifting up small banners naming particular cases of collective killings: *Mulchen wasn't war, it was slaughter; Pisagua wasn't war, it was slaughter; Laja wasn't war, it was slaughter; Paine wasn't war, it was slaughter….* Crowds gathered, and suddenly from the passersby began a slow, steady, rhythmic, prolonged applause. Emotions circulated, binding protestors and bystanders together. People joined in the song for freedom from the sidelines, while the protestors, nuns, university students, shantytown dwellers, priests, young and old, backs to the traffic, ignored the police. This is the moment, caught on tape,[3] when most pedestrians approached the scene and joined in. From the first action described above, where bystanders looked on amazed, or turned away their gaze in fear, the action on the Alameda years later clearly resonated with large number of citizens who had shed their fear, at least temporarily. In contrast to the 1983 action when Chile was still in the grips of terror, this theatrical performance took place when the military regime was clearly beginning to crumble.[4]This chapter digs up the "flashes of memory" (Benjamin 2006) of a group of ordinary women and men, inspired by the progressive Catholic church, who sought through Gandhian active non-violence to denounce torture as a systematic practice during Chile's military dictatorship. I first analyze the place of torture in Pinochet's Chile and the creation of the MCTSA to denounce torture. Then I reflect on the notion of emotional communities in this particular context, understanding them as manifold and diverse. These can be momentary or ephemeral, through performative actions that create an impact on unsuspecting passersby witnessing a protest action and on people watching videos on the movement. They can also involve *processes* between group members, sympathizers directly and indirectly involved with the movement, through memories and over decades. Lynn Stephen (2017) refers to the latter as "strategic emotional communities", including empathetic listeners and those willing to take risks to reveal and denounce torture. While "emotional communities" would have had no coinage during the 1980s either for movement militants or for academics then theorizing human rights abuses, the notion resonates with movement members I interviewed in 2014, 2015 and 2016. In this way, I argue that "emotional communities" have a versatility and elasticity during and over time. These flow with "inside/outside" positionalities (Rappaport 2005) of a variety of actors who take part in diverse ways at different moments of time.

The chapter also aims to help visibilize the MCTSA's place in Chile's recent history of resistance to bloody military dictatorship, through appealing to ethical values, the arousal of strong emotions, and dealing with fear and terror through collective action. It highlights two curious paradoxes about the movement: first, its highly charged emotional nature at a moment when militant social politics did not allow for the expression of emotions. Second, the movement prioritized performance and high visibility actions; at the same time, it resorted to almost clandestine forms of organizing to ensure the safety of its members.

I followed the MCTSA intently through close friends deeply involved in the *Sebastián* and wrote about the movement (Macleod 1987, and once under the pseudonym Marianne Howland 1985),[5] but I was never in Chile when an action took place. The Chilean coup literarily changed my life, impelling me to become a human rights worker. But when the Movement Against Torture carried out its first action in Chile, my relationship was from afar: I had already left London and the Chile Committee for Human Rights, and was doing similar work with Guatemala from Mexico at the time of the massacres (Macleod 1988). This illustrates the idiosyncratic nature of emotional communities that not only bring together groups of people from different walks of life but also women and men who never personally meet. Rather, what joins them together are emotional, political and ethical bonds, produced both discursively and through public actions.

Torture Under Military Rule

Torture against real or simply suspected opponents formed the backbone of Chile's military dictatorship from 11 September 1973 until 11 March 1990: "torture is the cornerstone of the entire repressive system" (Orellana 2015, 33). This conclusion is shared by many human rights activists and scholars. However, its centrality was overlooked in Chile's National Commission for Truth and Reconciliation set up by President Aylwin's transitional government immediately after the return to civilian rule. The commission, presided over by lawyer and politician Raúl Rettig worked for nine arduous months. The February 1991 *Retting Report*[6] as its findings are known documented 2,279 killed or forcefully disappeared persons particularly during the early years of General Pinochet's dictatorship. However, nothing was said about the far greater numbers of people who were arrested, tortured, or forced into exile. The discontent created by this omission preempted another government-sponsored truth commission: the National Commission on Political Imprisonment and Torture, presided over by Monsignor Sergio Valech. The *Valech Report* (18 August 2011), documented 40,018 victims, including 3,065 dead and disappeared.[7]

However, the *Valech Reports* (I and II) included a clause that had not been announced, still less agreed upon, with the more than 60,000 who gave testimony: that the information would remain secret for 50 years. Not even victims could have access to their testimonies. People were outraged. A legal process ensued and still continues, with small gains, to allow free access to the Valech Commissions' digital data base for survivors, their organizations and the judiciary to enhance their work in bringing torturers to trial.[8] It is ironic that a Truth Commission has contributed so blatantly to impunity. This is an extreme example of the way truth commissions can actively reduce political projects for justice (Castillejo 2007), prioritizing "political stability" over ethical issues and rule of law.

Professor and researcher Patricio Orellana, a recognized Allende Popular Unity supporter, was expelled from Chile's National University after the military coup; he spent the next 20 years documenting human rights abuses. Using rigorous procedures and statistics from a variety of sources, Orellana concludes that while it is clearly impossible to ascertain precise figures (given the vast percentage of unreported cases), the estimate probably closest to reality is 114,000 cases of torture during the military dictatorship (Orellana 2015, 97). The author sets out a classification of 66 varieties of 15 types of torture—ranging various forms of sexual violence, electric shock treatment, hanging and near-drowning, psychological torture, signing declarations under duress and other forms of mistreatment, all aimed at gleaning information, incriminating and degrading human beings. Very few judges and courts dared or wanted to take up torture cases, and those that did, such as judge René García Villegas (1990) was removed from office. The MCTSA carried out various activities in support of Judge García and his court cases brought against secret police[9] use of torture.

Jesuit priest José Aldunate, one of the founders and clearly the MCTSA's spiritual leader, reflected on the implications of torture and its effect upon societies. In his 2001 European Economic Community prize speech in Brussels, Aldunate affirms:

> Torture is perhaps the most sinister instrument that the force of evil has used to destroy us. It is sinister because it disintegrates and dehumanizes society. Used systematically it creates an environment of fear, distrust, silence and even complicity. It tends to convert us all into tortured or torturers… or both things at once: tortured by fear, we become accomplices of torture through our silence. (Aldunate 2004, 33)

It is this indignation and horror of torture, the feeling of colluding through silence and ethical and political values that give rise to the Sebastian Acevedo Movement Against Torture.

A Note of Caution: History and Memory

During their seven years of official existence,[10] the MCTSA carried out 180 public actions. However, surprisingly little has been written academically about the Sebastian Acevedo Movement Against Torture, save a doctoral dissertation that became a book (Vidal 1986), a couple of BA theses (Torres and Vega 2010; Bastidas et al. 2013), a chapter by MCTSA member Rosa Parissi (in Tyndale 2006), short articles in journals and press (Macleod 1987 among others) and passing mentions in human rights documents (Orellana 2015). Reference is made to the movement in founding founder members' essays (Aldunate 2004) and memoires (Bolton 2010), and the courageous judge who was removed from office for taking up torture cases (Villegas 1990). Most national radio and foreign television coverage of the movement was ephemeral. Videos are probably the most important source of documentation, as they continue to circulate on Internet, bearing individual and collective witness. As Lynn Stephen reflects, these are "Strategies of representation… presented in the physical speech act of testimony, its codification in text and audio and on video" (2017, 95), thus emphasizing the ways that testimony travels. In the 1980s, MCTSA videos circulated abroad—even on television—and among small circles of mainly human rights activists and grassroots Christian communities in Chile. Decades later, several videos are available on Internet. This highlights the non-linear spatial and time-frames that movement actions and emotional communities can have. Bhaskar and Walker's analysis of videos on Internet sheds particular light on the way the MCTSA has persisted and traveled over time; testimonial videos are archives with ethical vocation, "the act of speaking truth to power… for both present and future purposes" (Bhaskar and Walker 2010, 6). The MCTSA videos allow us to understand the performative nature of the protests: body stances, gestures, linking arms and theatrics—as in the case of lying down on Santiago's main avenue-, as well as the movement's anthem, litanies, slogans and banners. These performative aspects tend to be flattened out in movement reports and academic texts.

While video has been the most widespread way of archiving and disseminating MCTSA action, only a small corner of Santiago's Memory and Human Rights Museum is dedicated to the movement. Many Chileans, even progressive leftists, have never heard of the *Sebastián Acevedo*. The risk of falling into oblivion inspires me to dig up the "flashes of memory" (Benjamin 2006) and help secure a place for the movement in Chile's recent history, as an exemplary form of active non-violent resistance to the cruel and degrading practice of torture.

However, a need of caution is in place on events and methodology used in the chapter. One of the difficulties I encountered in gathering information is the unreliability surrounding figures. The number of people participating in the movement's first action is illustrative: while Vidal's PhD dissertation-cum-book (1986) speaks of 70 protestors, the published memoires of a founding member who participated in the action Father Robert Bolton (2010, 297) refers to 15 or 17, all of whom were detained save Jesuit priest José Aldunate who tried unsuccessfully to be arrested. In another interview, a nun says no one was detained during the first action, and another woman interviewed spoke of everyone being arrested. Nor do MCTSA's reports and lists of activities mention the numbers of demonstrators. MCTSA member Rosa Parissi (telephone call 20 April 2017) reminded me that as the movements' actions were so secretive for security reasons, many newcomers were unaware of or had not assimilated previous activities, and considered their own first experience as the movement's first. This was further complicated by various activities being carried out in the same place, as in the case of Borgoño 1470. This illustrates how memories vary. Pilar Calveiro (2006, 378) sees collective experience giving way to "many distinct, contradictory, ambivalent narratives" as something positive, as memory should not be reduced to a single homogeneous account. But discrepancies between differing accounts of the same event also demand the contrasting and verification of information whenever possible. The inability to validate figures obliged me to discern between memory writing and recent history based on strict verification methods (Hobsbawm 1997), compelling me to turn instead to "new perspectives on historical writing" (Burke 1991), with a more anthropological approach and to rely on memory work, with a logic of its own. Halbwachs, as far back as 1950 wrote about the importance of affective communities, where collective memories are shared notions and reconstructions of events, gathered together piecemeal rather than being the sum of individual memories. Collective memory thus allows people to appropriate experiences not lived directly.

Enzo Traverso (2016) reminds us about the clash in the intersection between recent history and memory. This is particularly so as the twentieth century has become history:

But it's a lived, recent history: a past that still leaves traces in the present. This has the effect that the 20th century as an object of history forcefully makes claims on the historian's own subjectivity: often implicated in his research subject, he is called upon as actor and witness. That is, he carries out research [on themes] he knows well as he experienced them, he was an actor in some of the events he studies and analyzes. (Traverso 2016, 19)

The women and men I interviewed were actors in the movement; their memories are at once individual and collective: they confirm, add to and contradict each other in the smaller details. This made me realize the salience of Walter Benjamin's insight: "Articulating the past historically does not mean recognizing it 'the way it really was'. It means appropriating a memory as it flashes up in a moment of danger" (Benjamin 2006, 392). Memory work with Sebastian Acevedo activists requires setting the record straight for the movement to go down in history, but at the same time requires a memory work approach, as historical methods are simply not appropriate or possible when speaking to activists imbued with vivid and poignant memories that still mark their friendships and daily lives.

My methodological route in this chapter was to use my own archive collected over time, access all literature available on Internet and at in the Memory and Human Rights Museum's archives in Santiago; however, I fundamentally rely on the six interviews I carried out in October 2015 one in December 2014 and another in December 2016, as well as videos. I also consulted with key MCTSA member, friend and colleague, Rosa Parissi[11] throughout the process. Much of the description and analysis is based on my interviews, though I have omitted naming these, save the longer citations, to enhance the reading flow. In this sense, the text is indeed collective, though I assume full responsibility for any mistakes and for my own personal views. This attempt to work collectively responds to MCTSA principles and tradition. As José Aldunate said in Brussels in 2001: "I speak in plural as nothing I've achieved have I done alone. I have participated in collective action to which I bear witness. The true protagonists are the Chilean people: a suffering and oppressed people, at once admirable for their resistance and hope" (Aldunate 2004, 31).

Taking to the Streets to Protest Against Torture

In this section, I hope to highlight two paradoxes. One is that to achieve performative high visibility, the movement had to recur to almost clandestine forms of organization. Another is that in the midst of an historical context where emotions were frowned upon, feminized and hidden, the very thing that brought the MCTSA together were emotions: an ethical indignation against torture, the love and empathy for tortured bodies and acute fear, overcome through collective public performance and protest.

The movement formed to reject torture "…we had a general idea about this issue, but not of its cruelty, its brutality, its savagery, its means and methods… We were perplexed. It was not enough, nor could we let this remain as simple information, an analysis or a study. We had to do something" (Bolton 2010, 296). The decision to take to the streets was applauded by the Episcopate Committee Against Torture, dedicated solely with a growing sense of impotency to research and identifying cases of torture and political repression. The trust placed in the movement by people in the know and different human rights organizations meant immediate and reliable access to information concerning human rights abuses (Fig. 5.1).

Fig. 5.1 The Sebastián Acevedo Movement Against torture. Photograph by Rosa Parissi

The MCTSA was very active during its official seven years' existence, with an average of 25 actions per year, 2 per month. The most common were lightening activities usually lasting 5–10 minutes in front of key places: secret police torture centers, police stations, mass media headquarters, courts, the iconic *Moneda* where former presidential palace where Salvador Allende lost his life, the *Alameda*, Santiago's city center, places politically implicated and as public and filled with people as possible. Their highly performative actions create reactions in their unsuspecting publics—passersby: some scared, others frankly antagonistic to their cause,[12] and increasingly, many sympathetic:

> I was always moved by people's reactions to our activities: some were scared, others joined in, people stayed and clapped. They didn't say anything as they didn't dare, but there really was an amazing solidarity among the standers-by. I feel that this gave us the courage to carry on; it also strengthened camaraderie between us and the will to continue ... Few people reacted negatively, most supported us by stopping and watching, clapping when the protest came to a close; that was the reaction we normally encountered. (Interview with Sara, October 2015, Santiago de Chile)

Joining the MCTSA was very difficult; these were dangerous times, and the movement sought at all costs to avoid infiltration. Thus, individuals were personally invited by a member who knew and trusted them. This explains why the MCTSA could never grow into a mass movement, why some human rights activists felt excluded, but it also accounts for its efficiency, precision and the military's incapacity to infiltrate. In this sense, it operated like a clandestine political cell:

> Usually there was someone coordinating from a university: for example the Catholic University. The person in charge invited others they could trust and committed to condemning the horror we were living. There were various groups from different areas, including popular organizations. Most people came from different universities, vicariates, the *Vicaría de la Solidaridad*, the Group of Relatives of the Disappeared, and other human rights organizations. (Interview with Rosa and Erika, December 2014, Santiago de Chile)

There were even several upper-class women who participated in movement actions, including the wife of a military man. The movement started with a handful of people, mainly members of religious orders and grassroots Christian communities; it grew to around 600. There was a smaller permanent core, and others participating for differing periods of time.

Initially, the MCTSA's aim was to put an end to the practice of torture in Chile. While this may seem self-evident to human rights workers, shantytown dwellers and opponents to military rule, given national censorship as well as right-wing ideology, it was surprising to movement members that so many people simply did not know—or did not believe—that torture was commonplace in Chile. Founding member Elena Bergen, known to all as "Pocho" describes the process of becoming more realistic about the movement's aims: "Originally we thought our actions were going to influence widespread public opinion, obliging the government to put an end to torture. Over time we realized this was naïve, that the most we could aspire to was raising awareness of the existence of torture in Santiago and nationally."[13] And this they did, albeit not massively.

MCTSA submitted reports with advocacy aims to international organizations and delegations, the first Truth Commission (in 1990), and critical media. It also carried out various awareness-raising activities, giving talks, organizing forums, projecting videos and going to talk to church congregations. The movement received two international prizes, one from the European Community and the other from the Latin American Human Rights Association (ALDHU), based in Ecuador.

In contrast to other experiences, where the victims themselves give testimony, the *Sebastián Acevedo* assumed the role to testify, as the tortured, disappeared and imprisoned could not. Felman (2000) synthesizes this action by reminding the reader of Zola's "*J'accuse*", the accusatory finger that the MCTSA pointed at those guilty or colluding with torture. At the same time, Gandhian active non-violence required putting oneself at risk in the public sphere for their shared moral cause; if one person was arrested, the rest would follow. The policemen were disconcerted, as they were used to protesters resisting or fighting back aggressively.

> I'll never forget the face of a policeman, after furiously and relentlessly beating one of our young members with his baton, when the latter serenely asked: "why are you hitting me?" The policeman turned pale and walked away. And the strength of our young friend Oswaldo Ulloa during a sit-in protest on the street in front of the Justice Tribunals, arms linked. The police approached to unlock the group's arms, and thrashed Ulloa's, breaking his elbow. Ulloa did not let go of the circle he'd formed with his companions. (Bolton 2010, 312)

Many police reacted by attacking the protestors more viciously: commentators were astonished by the level of violence used against peaceful demonstrators, though deference was often shown to priests and nuns (Bolton 2010) and some members of the upper class. The unprecedented levels of police brutality were put down to the fact that the non-violent protests were aimed at the secret and formal police themselves, denouncing their systematic use of torture. As an active non-violent movement, reacting aggressively to the police was strictly forbidden; when one viciously beaten young man fought back, he was expelled. A few policemen were metaphorically disarmed and shamed, others reacted with fury.

But precautions were taken; this was not an exercise in martyrdom. Thus, with growing experience of police brutality, teargas, water cannons, even acid in dirty water that burned protestors' hair and skin, and short-term arrests, MTCSA core-organizers increasingly refined and sophisticated their methods to avoid police brutality and detentions. Activities were planned out with militant efficiency: the number of minutes the action would last, strict timing and punctuality. Protestors would mill about, pretending to be passersby and suddenly spring into action at the set time: "while we were getting ready, if I saw you, I pretended not to know you, so that everything would appear normal. It was a whole strategy. We'd walk around, sniffing the newspaper, and suddenly, at the given moment, we'd all punctually join together" (Interview with Sister Margarita, October 2015, Santiago de Chile).

Organizers carefully worked out the most important and precise message to get across in each action, synthesized in the banner, the litanies or slogans and always the song. They also sought ingenious ways of slowing down the police's arrival: getting sympathizers to use their cars to block the way, seeking the busiest streets and times of day, never publicizing the event beforehand, and taking precautionary measures to invite only their allies in the media.

Organizers also relied on confidential sources for immediate and reliable information. For example, within hours of receiving the news, the MCTSA was protesting outside the police station where Juan Antonio Ballesteros was being tortured in September 1984.[14] This was possible due to the moral confidence deposited in persons like José Aldunate, and because the MTCSA could take to the streets while others could not.

One of the movement's greatest virtues was its diversity and capacity to bring together people from very different walks of life, political ideologies and militancy, religious orders, believers and atheists. All shared one common purpose: to name and put an end to torture.

We were very different, from differing social backgrounds, political ideologies, and dissimilar life histories. Some had heavy backpacks [militancy], others lighter. The *Sebastián Acevedo* brought us together, it was such a profound militancy it marked me deeply. Facing repression, receiving blows, being arrested was very intense, it left me life-long friends as a result. The *Sebastián* had a huge impact on me, not only politically, but on my entire life, I think on all our lives. (Interview with Ana Cristina, October 2015, Santiago de Chile)

MCTSA militancy also included political beliefs and ways of doing things of its times. Contradictorily, emotions in movement members and actions abounded. In practice, these were frowned upon, as Rosa Parissi points out:

In politics, when people wanted to destroy women, they'd say "so-and-so is emotional, she does everything emotionally"… So you had to always show coldness, and when you put forward your argument, it needed to be politically correct, based on Marxist analysis. References had to be very objective, and you couldn't show your emotions. If you did, you were frowned upon. (Interview with Rosa, December 2016, Santiago de Chile)

This is one of the MCTSA's central paradoxes. On the one hand, Rosa describes with precision how emotions were deprecated in general, particularly on the left, and at the same time, the movement was rife with emotions and caring for one another: "Rosita saved a friend of mine who was left practically blind, people helped each other, passing lime or salt, there was a lot of caring for others, no 'saving my own skin.' Caring was not planned, it was not talked about; it simply emerged among the group. And it was lovely, there is heroism in this as well" (Interview with Sister Margarita, October 2015, Santiago de Chile). Father José Aldunate speaks of love: "In a practice like ours, a force arises from truth. It is the force of love: love for the tortured bodies. And solidarity unites us all, over and above our differences, shaping a new society" (2004, 34). However, this greater good did not allow for personal feelings of weakness. In contrast, in the interviews I carried out decades later, mention of fear, and overcoming fear, abounds. Sara remembers the first movement action in front of the Borgoño Street secret police center: "we were scared, the night before we did everything as if we were going to die, it was intense. My hair stands on end just remembering it" (Interview with Sara, October 2015, Santiago de Chile).

Movement leaders realized that *fear* was an emotion that had to be dealt with. They invited Dr. Fanny Pollarolo, a psychiatrist and experienced human rights practitioner in work with torture victims to give MCTSA members a workshop.

> Fanny Pollarolo came to teach us how to place ourselves, how not to be scared. In the group we all had butterflies in our stomachs, but once we were there, and we began to sing, it was so lovely, so wonderful. We created friendships with people we didn't know. There were about 300 of us, all very supportive. It was a good cause. If we had to do it again, it would be worth it. (Interview with Sister Margarita, October 2015, Santiago de Chile)

Elena Bergen sums up the movement's coherency and ethics; this included: "a high degree of discipline in each action, strong bonds, group trust and solidarity. This enhanced action effectiveness and helped members to not respond aggressively to repression" (Personal correspondence with Elena Bergen, September 2015). It was this capacity to overcome fear, engage in active non-violence dependent on trusting others that not only produced deep bonds between people—who often did not even know each other—but that also created the force of public resistance under military rule.

Emotional Communities and the MCTSA

The Sebastian Acevedo Movement Against Torture defies current perspectives on emotional communities.[15] Myriam Jimeno's concept, that "through testimonies of suffering, a reciprocal socio-affective link is forged and projected onto social and citizen action" (Jimeno et al. 2011, 275) resonates, though the link is established not between victims and academics, but those denouncing the plight of victims, collaborators on the "outer circles", and unsuspecting audiences. Many university professors, researchers and students *joined* rather than *accompanied* the movement. In their place, emotional links and practical support described by Jimeno and her team (2015) were created with the sympathetic press—mainly local radio, foreign correspondents, progressive magazine journalists and alternative media, especially video-makers. These also took risks covering movement events; at least one, video-maker Pablo Salas, was arrested. These members of the media were clearly motivated by a sense of commitment to the movement's ideals and ethics, indignation and the search for justice.

There is greater similarity between Kitek Kiwe's annual commemorations, where memories are performed and enacted, and MCTSA's privileged use of performance and theatrics as central to their organizational strategies. There is "a mise-en-scène and the construction of a public narrative"... "that produces a process of narrating lived suffering to others, testifying to others. This enables others to identify with this suffering through an account, a narrative" (Jimeno and Macleod 2014, 2).

Norman Denzin refers to this kind of performance as "a form of public pedagogy. It uses the aesthetic to foreground cultural meanings and to teach these meanings to performers and audience members alike" (2003, 6). The public pedagogy to raise consciousness about torture in Chile is primarily achieved through what Baz Kershaw (1997: 256) refers to as "the performative *in* the political" replacing the previous school of Brechtian and others' political theater. He insightfully adds that "...while the performativity of protest may always evade the closure of interpretation, the analysis of protest as performance may reveal dimensions to the action which are relatively opaque to other approaches" (Kershaw 1997, 260). Very little has been written exploring the performative nature of the MCTSA, and yet it is precisely in the way protests are designed, staged and risks consciously taken that account for the movement's impact and ability to arouse strong emotions. The *Sebastian's* endeavors of the performative *in* the political are pioneer; these gain growing coinage in more recent decades.

The lack of attention to the performative quality of MCTSA actions illustrates scholars' and practitioners' lack of interest or difficulty to explore embodied expressions and performance as an episteme (Taylor 2003). This was less the case during Allende's Popular Unity government, with the flourishing of music, murals and other forms of audiovisual arts, though demonstrations relied on slogans and speeches. Military rule curtailed artistic expression, and just taking to the streets represented an act of defiance. In that sense, the MCTSA combined traditional militant techniques with performance and affect; and as Jimeno reminds us, such emotions are deeply rooted in the political.

In his writing about Canada's Truth and Reconciliation Commission on Indian Residential Schools, Ronald Niezen (2013) points out that public sympathy—or consciousness—becomes the interim goal when the judicial system is not taking up and punishing grave human rights abuses. His exploration of emotions surrounding quasi-legal truth commissions is relevant for understanding the circulation of emotions aroused by performative protests against torture. The author insightfully points out that "the sense of injustice or indignation is clearly set in motion by simultaneous feelings of love, loyalty, and compassion" (Niezen 2013, 14). In MCTSA actions and interviews, there is moral indignation based on love and the uncompromising belief in the right to human dignity.

The performative plays a crucial role in creating MCTSA emotional communities, opening up a multilayered panorama of intertwining emotions—indignation, acute fear, courage, empathy, solidarity, trust and the intensity of intentionally placing oneself in life-threatening situations. Multilayered, as there is—if not recognized as such at the time—a profound emotional coming together of MCTSA members during their risk-taking practice of protest.

Momentary and lasting emotional communities take place during the actions themselves and during evaluation meetings, though most MCTSA members did not even know each other's names, for security reasons. However, decades after the MCTSA officially ended, an intense sense of community continues: members gather to celebrate movement anniversaries, or give support and condolence when participants die. Emotional communities were not created between committed researchers and movement activists, as eloquently described by Jimeno et al. (2015), given the secrecy shrouding their lightening protests. In their place are foreign and national press and video-makers, such as Pablo Salas and Chaskel Benkel, who were also exposed to police brutality.

Paradoxically, from an "outsider" position (Rappaport 2005), I was deeply involved in the movement. Rappaport's use of the metaphors "inside" and "outside" identifies the complexity of different forms of positioning and collaboration, in this case between the movement, the sympathetic alternative national and foreign press, activists and intellectuals. There is an intensity to human rights work that I lived experiencing firsthand the inspiration of people who put their lives at risk to defend their principles or their loved ones (Macleod 1981); as a human rights worker in my mid-twenties it was devastating when several friends and acquaintances were killed in Chile. Lynn Stephen's notion of *strategic emotional political communities* illustrates this sense of belonging.

Although I did not live this personally, I resonate with the depth of Sara' words when 25 years later she says: "There's a very special kind of bond when I see people from the *Sebastián*, a deep sense of fraternity, it's as if they are my brothers and sisters… this happens when you have put your life in your brothers' hands, and you know, you trust, that they will accompany and care for you" (Interview with Sara, October 2015,

Santiago de Chile). Here the memory and recent history of the movement combine, defying a lineal sense of time.

The singularities of the movement give rise to a series of reflections about the nature of emotional communities, and question their boundaries in time and space. I see a collage of interrelated emotional communities: some ephemeral—passersby who are moved and empathize with a movement action. Here the performativity of the MCTSA's actions as well as participants' courage are key factors conducive to creating bonds—or fear or rejection—in their unwitting audiences. Among those who are moved by indignation and the courage of the protesters join a momentary kind of emotional community, we have no evidence to evaluate whether this impact is fleeting or long-lasting, motivating some to join other organizations. Ex-MCTSA members, on the other hand, recognize how they took their experience and inspiration to other more recent movements:

> It was wonderful, I couldn't believe it was happening… a load of people who don't know each other, but who question and feel the same suffering and are able to abandon personal positions to join a common cause. It was wonderful because it provided a space to collectively surmount fear, a fear that perhaps one can't face alone, but holding hands, singing together, one can overcome. I learned a lot, and have replicated these active non-violence techniques later on in *"Color Mapuche."* (Interview with Claudio, October 2015, Santiago de Chile)

Ana Cristina, the young Catholic University architect student inspired by the movement and its ideals, did her thesis on a project to convert the notorious secret police torture and detention center *Villa Grimaldi* into a peace park. She met with great resistance from her tutors, but was finally able to convince them. This thesis was then used to work with ex political prisoners and people in the neighborhood to create *Villa Grimaldi* as a site of memory, which opened as a peace park in March 1997.[16] Others simply carry the movement in their minds and bodies, a trace, an indelible, profound mark on their lives.

Final Reflections

Analyzing the MCTSA through the lens of emotional communities provides various insights into the intensity and depth of the experience of resisting violence under military dictatorship. The chapter also highlights the non-linear quality of emotional communities in terms of time and space, and illustrates the versatility of the notion itself. Appraising this process, one of the MCTSA founder members, Elena Bergen, wrote the following:

> The Movement was my school of life in the deepest and broadest sense of the term. I learned to know and test myself, to see how artificial or how solid I was, and the values and principles that guided me. I came to recognize what I truly believed in, what kind of God I trust in, and if I was up to putting my life on the line for something or someone. (Personal communication with Elena Bergen, 27 September 2017)

Movement members—whether participants from the start or those joining later—share the intensity of experience of risking their well-being for what they believed in. This has deeply marked their lives.

Also, different kinds of emotional communities emerge: these can be momentary and ephemeral—the passerby who happened to be present when a lightning action took place, and empathized by clapping or joining in the Freedom song. There continue to be deep and enduring friendships between some MCTSA members, whose future participation in the struggle for social justice is marked by their experience in the movement. Personally, I discovered that even as a sympathetic outsider, one can belong to a strategic emotional community. The MCTSA synthesized all that had motivated me to change my life and become involved in human rights work: the ethical imperative to do something to put an end to torture in Chile.[17] This questioned my understanding of emotional and political involvement and drew me toward Rappaport's (2005) inside/outside metaphors.

The insight, then, is that there are moments, organizations and social processes that crystallize and condense years of lived experience, accompaniment and emotions perhaps not recognized at the time. This non-linear relationship—rather than a quantitative approach to time and direct experience—has to do with the intensity of emotions that surface in political and ethical contexts. Feelings of awe, inspiration and indignation still well up in me when I watch MCTSA videos on Internet: fragile bodies outstretched on streets with looming potentially crushing vehicles behind; police officers viciously attacking peaceful demonstrators, emotions circulating and binding bodies. There is hope and inspiration in the locking together of arms and singing, chanting litanies: emotions circulate among them, turning them into one collective self, strong and able to resist police brutality.

In my experience, emotional communities can condense in particular events and moments, as well as through accompanying social movement and organizational processes, or when acting as a public intellectual. A kind of emotional community can emerge even in the classroom, when university students empathize with the experience of victims and realize that social engagement is not antagonistic to academia.

Another finding are the paradoxes. First, the important place that emotions played in the movement's performative actions: acute fear beforehand, placing one's life in the hands of others, the strength of union, solidarity and caring for one another. All this, at a time in recent history when emotions were regarded as "feminine" and denoted weakness. Emotions of love, indignation and ethical values motivated and drove the movement. These emotions are clearly political, grounded in a sense of justice, human dignity and caring for others. And yet there was scarcely space at that political moment in recent history to acknowledge, still less write about emotional implications.

Another paradox emerges around MCTSA's high-profile performative resistance actions at the same time as perfecting clandestine organizing methods to minimize police reprisals. Many movement members did not know each other's names, though faces became familiar and emotions shared; others pretended not to know each other before an action, and suddenly joined together as the action began. Very few people knew about the MCTSA inside Chile (or some had heard about them but not seen them in action); more people were familiar with the movement particularly in Europe, through news coverage and solidarity committees. The MCTSA is more visible and accessible in the twenty-first century through videos on the Internet than it was during its official seven years existence. This also raises issues and questions assumptions about the nature of visibility in time and space, and the way videos and testimony assume a life of their own (Stephen 2017).

Thus, videos on the net have contributed to perpetuating Benjamin's "flashes of memory", and become an important source, together with photographs, documents and other written texts to create a public place for the movement in recent history and collective memory. In different ways, movement members still create strategic emotional communities that inspire others through their example in fighting for human dignity, ethical values and social justice.

Notes

1. *For the caged bird*
   For the fish in the fishbowl
   For my friend who's imprisoned
   For saying what he thinks
   For the uprooted flowers
   For the trampled grass
   For the shorn trees
   For the tortured bodies
   I name you Freedom....

   Yo te nombro/I name you, by Gian Franco Pagliaro, based on Éluard's poem "Liberté", MCTSA anthem.

2. All interviews and publications in Spanish are my translations.
3. https://www.youtube.com/watch?v=fH8_Kp6ab48
4. Unfortunately the action "It wasn't war, it was massacre" does not appear in the Movement's reports and lists of actions so its exact date was not recorded.
5. I ask myself now why on earth I used a pseudonym, and can only conclude that being in Chile under state of siege in 1985, immediately after the "*3 degollados*", men whose throats were slit, one a human rights worker I knew, and marching to denounce the killing of the "*2 cabros del MIR*" (2 brothers from a leftwing organization) had drenched me with fear.
6. http://www.gob.cl/informe-rettig/
7. http://bibliotecadigital.indh.cl/handle/123456789/455
8. *La base de datos digital que esconde el secreto Valech*, 17 abril de 2017, http://www.biobiochile.cl/noticias/opinion/tu-voz/2017/04/17/la-base-de-datos-digital-que-esconde-el-secreto-valech.shtml
9. The CNI (*Central Nacional de Investigaciones*, 1977–1990) replaced the notorious DINA (*Dirección de Inteligencia Nacional*, 1973–1977) after international outcry over its flagrant human rights abuses.
10. I say "official" as there was a conflict within the movement, some wanting the MCTSA to carry on, as torture and impunity continued, while others—including movement founders and leaders of weight, such as José Aldunate, s.j., considered the MCTSA had fulfilled its purpose once democratic transition had taken place. A group continued carrying out actions for many years, and Father Aldunate participated in the protest against General

Pinochet becoming a life-long senator, an action that met with fierce police brutality.
11. Rosa Parissi organized my first trip to Chile in December 1980 when I was in charge of the Chile Committee for Human Rights based in London. It is thanks to her that I was able to write "Pinochet's Chile: An Eyewitness Account" (1981), as a result of that intense, emotionally charged, eye-opening visit.
12. In two interviews and a video, shock was expressed at the hatred some Movement members encountered when they visited churches and talked to church-goers. While this strategy was well-met in shantytowns, in Santiago's richest neighborhoods, particularly upper-class women virulently verbally mistreated Movement women who were denouncing torture.
13. Video *El camino de la no violencia*, https://www.youtube.com/watch?v=fH8_Kp6ab48
14. Ballesteros was forcefully disappeared and his body was subsequently found. The MCTSA carried out three actions to save and then mourn his life.
15. Barbara Rosenwein's (2010, 11) notion of emotional communities as "largely the same as social communities—families, neighborhoods, syndicates, academic institutions, monasteries, factories, platoons, princely courts" refers more clearly to other contexts.
16. http://villagrimaldi.cl/
17. This entailed coordinating the adoption of Chilean political prisoners, commuting their sentences to exile in Britain; advocacy and urgent actions; organizing defense lawyer and victim tours; and giving endless talks around England and Scotland.

References

Aldunate, José. 2004. *Signos de los Tiempos. Crónicas de una década de dictadura*. Santiago de Chile: LOM Ediciones.

Bastidas Urrea, Bárbara et al. 2013. *Memorias de resistencia en la dictadura militar chilena: El caso de Sebastián Acevedo*. B.A. Dissertation, Concepción University.

Benjamin, Walter. 2006. [1940] On the Concept of History. In *Walter Benjamin, Selected Writings Volume 4, 1938–1940*, ed. Howard Eiland and Michael W. Jennings, 389–400. Cambridge MA/London: Harvard University Press.

Bhaskar, Sarkar, and Janet Walker, eds. 2010. *Documentary Testimonies. Global Archives of Suffering*. New York: Routledge.

Bolton García, Roberto. 2010. In *Testigo soy; memorias del Rvdo. Roberto Bolton García*, ed. Rosa Parissi. Santiago de Chile: IGD.

Burke, Peter, ed. 1991. *New Perspectives on Historical Writing*. Oxford: Polity Press.

Calveiro, Pilar. 2006. Los usos políticos de la memoria. In *Sujetos sociales y nuevas formas de protesta en la historia reciente de América Latina*, ed. Gerardo Caetano, 359–382. Buenos Aires: Clacso.

Castillejo Cuellar, Alejandro. 2007. La globalización del testimonio: Historia, silencio endémico y los usos de la palabra. *Antípoda* 4, enero – junio 2007, pp. 76–99.

Denzin, Norman K. 2003. The Call to Performance. In *Performance Ethnography*, ed. Norman Denzin, 1–24. California/London/New Delhi: Sage.

Felman, Shoshona. 2000. Theaters of Justice: Arendt in Jerusalem, the Eichmann Trial, and the Redefinition of Legal Meaning in the Wake of the Holocaust. *Theoretical Inquiries in Law 1.2* 1: 465–507.

García Villegas, René. 1990. *Soy testigo. Dictadura, tortura, injusticia*. Santiago: Editorial Amerinda.

Halbwachs, Maurice. 1950. *La mémoire collective*. Paris: Les Presses universitaires de France.

Hobsbawm, Eric J. 1997. *On History*. London: Weidenfeld and Nicholson.

Howland, Marianne. 1985. Exactly What Is a 'State of Seige'? *Encuentro, The Mexico City New Political Supplement* 90: 7.

Jimeno, Myriam, and Morna Macleod. 2014. *Interview with Myriam Jimeno*, November 2014. Available at http://mornamacleod.net/?p=767

Jimeno, Myriam, Daniel Varela, and Ángela Castillo. 2011. Experiencias de violencia: etnografía y recomposición social en Colombia. *Sociedade e Cultura* 14 (2): 275–285.

Jimeno, Myriam, Daniel Varela, and Angeles Castillo. 2015. *Después de la masacre, emociones y política en el Cauca Indio*. Bogotá: ICANH y CES: Universidad Nacional de Colombia.

Kershaw, Baz. 1997. Fighting in the Streets: Dramaturgies of Popular Protest, 1968–1989. *New Theatre Quarterly* 13: 255–276.

Macleod, Morna. 1981. *Pinochet's Chile: An Eyewitness Report*. London: Chile Committee for Human Rights.

———. 1987. La no violencia en Chile. In La aventura de la no violencia, Revista Casa del Tiempo, número 72, volumen VIII, July–August 1987, 76–78.

———. 1988. *Un Estudio Comparativo de la Represión en Chile y Guatemala*. MA Dissertation, National Autonomous University of Mexico (UNAM), Mexico.

Niezen, Ronald. 2013. *Truth and Indignation. Canada's Truth and Reconciliation Commission on Indian Residential Schools*. Toronto: University of Toronto Press.

Orellana Vargas, Patricio. 2015 [2008]. *La represión en Chile 1973–1989*. Serie CODEHS. Stockholm: Editorial Senda.

Parissi, Rosa. 2006. Sebastián Acevedo Movement Against Torture: A Project for the Dignity of Life. In *Visions of Development, Faith-Based Initiatives*, ed. Wendy Tyndale, 137–144. Hampshire: Ashgate.

Rappaport, Joanne. 2005. *Intercultural Utopias: Public Intellectuals, Cultural Experimentation, and Ethnic Pluralism in Colombia*. Durham: Duke University Press.
Rosenwein, Barbara H. 2010. Problems and Methods in the History of Emotions. *Passions in Context I: Journal of the History and the Philosophy of the Emotions* 1 (1): 1–32.
Stephen, Lynn. 2017. Bearing Witness: Testimony in Latin American Anthropology and Related Fields. *The Journal of Latin American and Caribbean Anthropology* 22 (1): 85–109.
Taylor, Diana. 2003. *The Archive and the Repertoire: Performing Cultural Memories in the Americas*. Durham: Duke University Press.
Torres Bruna, Aliro, and Sebastián Vega Morales. 2010. *Testimonio y no violencia: la historia del Movimiento Contra la Tortura Sebastián Acevedo*. B.A. Dissertation in Journalism, Academy of Christian Humanism, Santiago de Chile.
Traverso, Enzo. 2016. Memoria e historia del siglo XX en Acuña. In *Archivos y memorias de la represión en América Latina*, ed. María Patricia Flier, Miriam González Vera, et al., 17–29. Santiago de Chile: LOM Ediciones-FASIC.
Vidal, Hernán. 1986. *El Movimiento Contra la Tortura "Sebastián Acevedo": Derechos Humanos y la Producción de Símbolos Nacionales Bajo el Fascismo Chileno*. Edina: Institute for the Study of Ideologies and Literature, Society for the Study of Contemporary Hispanic and Lusophone Revolutionary Literatures.

Key Videos

El camino de la no violencia (Claudio Escobar, Prensa Opal). https://www.youtube.com/watch?v=fH8_Kp6ab48
Por la vida, (Movimiento contra la Tortura Sebastián Acevedo), Peter Chaskel Benko and Pablo Salas. Published 19 Aug 2016, Filmed in 1987. https://www.youtube.com/watch?v=U2ZUzYcK0bY

CHAPTER 6

Emotions, Experiences, and Communities: The Return of the Guatemalan Refugees

Angela Ixkic Bastian Duarte

INTRODUCTION

In April 1995, around 100,000 Guatemalan *campesinos* returned to their country after having received refuge in Mexico for 14 years. Some 35 buses and several United Nations vans, non-governmental organizations (NGOs), and other entities crossed the jungle of northern Guatemala for a four-day journey, during which rallies were held, Catholic mass was celebrated, and welcoming ceremonies were observed. I was especially moved by the Mayan ceremony celebrated in Tikal, among the majestic pre-Columbian structures surrounded by luxuriant and millennial jungle, as priests purified the memories of war in a ritual fire and opened new horizons for rebuilding. I am aware that, 22 years later, having accompanied that caravan deeply influenced my understanding of the world.

The scenario of the return, the movement of the population itself, displayed both the drama of being uprooted and the refugee community's role as a political subject. The setting was the department of Petén: tourist destination, center of illegal goods trafficking, territory of confrontations, and site of untold slaughter during the war.[1] By their act of returning, through poignant silence and inspirational speech, with their presence, the refugees narrated their history of forced displacement. They told their story to those waiting impromptu along the streets and plazas of Petén:

A.I. Bastian Duarte (✉)
Autonomous Morelos State University, Morelos, Mexico

Before being forced to flee to Mexico by the Guatemalan government's counterinsurgent policies, they had been internal migrants in search of land, temporary workers, semi-enslaved laborers in the coffee, cotton, and sugar cane plantations, but also members of cooperatives. During their time as refugees, they trained in different areas, such as health and education. They told their listeners of plans to foster local and regional development and share what they learned with neighboring communities.

Among other experiences, the refugees' return spoke of the multiethnic nature of the communities yet to be built; of the deep and complicated organizing efforts they implemented during their asylum; and of new political actors who arose within the communities, many of them women.[2]

Those of us observing the event were also members of Guatemalan and Mexican NGOs, of offices of the Guatemalan government, such as the Special Commission for Attention to Refugees (CEAR) and their Mexican counterparts, such as the Mexican Commission for Attention to Refugees (COMAR), as well as the United Nations High Commissioner for Refugees (UNHCR). Among us were internationalists in solidarity, students, aid agency workers, trade-union members, civil servants, political advisors of the Revolutionary National Guatemalan Unity (URNG), Catholic priests, and evangelical pastors. We were there to safeguard the returnees, resolve logistical issues, offer emotional support, and cover the event for news outlets. Some people had spent years working with the refugees in the lead-up to the return; others came from abroad to accompany the move. I had spent three years with the refugees, initially working at the office of the Permanent Commissions of Guatemalan Refugees (CCPP) in Mexico City and later as a member of an NGO called Meso-American Office for Development and Peace (COMADEP), in a popular education project in the Mexican states of Campeche, Quintana Roo, and Chiapas. After the first return to Petén, I stayed on for another year in the department as part of a team that published the *El Porvenir* community newspaper.

Guatemala's acute crisis during the 1980s drew worldwide attention. During the time of the internal armed conflict, 17% of the country's population was forcibly displaced from their communities as they fled from the Army's counterinsurgency operations (Coello et al. 2008). Most took refuge in Mexico. This chapter focuses on the refugees' collective return to the department of Petén, not in view of the success or failure of their political or developmental objectives, but rather as an event that the refugees transformed into an educational opportunity that transformed the social imaginary of sectors of Guatemalan society.

It is my belief that an emotional community was constructed around the return of the refugees whose bonds, even today, more than 20 years later, are galvanized at certain moments and continue to be significant for those involved at that time. As conceptualized by Myriam Jimeno (2010; Jimeno et al. 2015), emotional communities are affective, rather than geographical; they arise in response to events that connect and network actors who may be very diverse and, when witnessing injustice, are able to transcend their indignation by channeling their efforts toward political action.

The emotional community I analyze herein is inhabited by the returnees and by those of us who accompanied the return and reintegration process; yet, the division between observers and the directly affected population is not always clear; connections exist between both populations. There are also different ways of carrying out the role of observer or defining oneself as a displaced person. Clearly, the distances between *acompañantes* [accompanying volunteers] and the returning population are defined by having experienced (or not) persecution and refuge, but they are also an expression of power relationships.

Times of Violence

Manolo Vela (2014, 66) defines the genocide in Guatemala as the response of a totalitarian government to a rebellion by "those from below," in the form of a preventive massacre in the face of what could have become a revolution. The counterinsurgency policy implemented by the Guatemalan state during the late 1970s and most of the 1980s[3] aimed at eradicating the social base of the guerrilla movement and preventing the *campesino* and indigenous communities from becoming autonomous social subjects with agency and their own programs. Counterinsurgency was the reason that entire communities were internally displaced and thousands of persons sought refuge in Mexico, Belize, and Honduras.

The Army and paramilitary forces committed more than 626 massacres, thousands of civilians were murdered or "disappeared," more than a million people were internally displaced, while another 200,000 fled the country (CEH 1999). Mass displacements occurred in the departments of Huehuetenango, El Quiché, Chimaltenango, and Alta Verapaz. Approximately 80% of the inhabitants of these areas abandoned their communities, equivalent to a population of 1.3 million (Mack et al. 1990).

Tens of thousands of Guatemalan men and women struggled to survive by hiding in the mountainous regions, fleeing from one location to another. The internally displaced and the refugees were able to survive due to their knowledge of the terrain and the strict discipline they followed in response to harsh conditions and communal organization.

Francisco (interviewed by Teresa Coello and Rolando Duarte in Guatemala 2007), like so many others, survived for two years by hiding in the mountains:

> In many places in the mountains, the Army surprised groups of refugees at night. Sometimes, the Army would set traps in the cornfields, where people would go to find a bit of food. They were massacred. They killed everyone: men, women, children, and the elderly (Francisco, interviewed by Teresa Coello and Rolando Duarte, 2007, Guatemala)

Guards posted around the camp kept a constant vigil in order to sound an alarm when the military approached:

> We always had to be ready to pick everything up and move elsewhere. Sometimes we were warned or heard the Army [approach]. No time to think. Just run. The elderly had to flee first because they were the slowest. In the end, everyone in my community survived. It's a miracle (Francisco, interviewed by Teresa Coello and Rolando Duarte, 2007, Guatemala)

In Mexico, the UNHCR recognized 40,000 refugees, although the [Catholic] Church in Chiapas and non-governmental institutions verified another 160,000 lacking papers to back them as refugees. Even Mexican authorities estimated that the figure was not below 200,000.

The peace accord signed between the URNG and the government halted 36 years of armed conflict but left deep wounds. The neoliberal model implemented in parallel with a process of "pacification" deepened inequality, making the entire Central American region more economically insecure. Other factors that influenced events include renewed regional security policies and strategies, expanding militarized violence, and the growth of organized crime.

Within a Cold War Framework

The Guatemalan armed conflict should be understood as part of the Cold War, that is, a war within another global war. To claim success in this world confrontation, the United States had to deactivate any plan that clashed with it hegemony in the Americas (Calveiro 2006; Traverso 2016).

In Central America, this implied controlling and limiting the expansion of guerrilla activity. In Guatemala, escaping families encountered different fates. They took to the most isolated mountain locations and tried to survive by eating the frequently scarce undergrowth.

The most vulnerable, the elderly and children, perished. The military located some displaced groups; others, exhausted and ill, turned themselves in to authorities. Turned over to the military, they underwent indoctrination and some returned to their homes under strict supervision, while others were forced to move to Development Hubs.[4] Displaced populations who successfully avoided military control formed Communities of Populations in Resistance (CPR),[5] complete with their own government and authorities or, alternatively, chose to leave the country as refugees.

Within the country, the displacement of one million persons (Coello et al. 2008) from the central, western, and northwest highlands failed to have an impact on public opinion. It stirred trade-union members, students, and human rights groups, but the Cold War mindset prevented the population from mobilizing. As part of this low-intensity strategy, the military exercised strict control over information, mobilization, and organization. In these circumstances, the plight and exodus of so many families failed to make an impression on the imagination and awareness of the greater population until many years later.

Guatemala: Emotions and Memories

My paternal grandmother lost two of her five children in this internal armed conflict. Both uncles were wonderful accomplices of my childhood adventures, almost magical beings who filled my first five years with laughter and enchanting stories. When I wanted to talk to my grandmother, as a child still, about my beloved *Tato* and *Coy*, she answered evasively and even scolded me. In contrast to other women in the Mutual Support Group (GAM),[6] she chose not to seek out other mothers to share her pain or search for justice, nor did she give her testimony to the UN truth commission, the Historical Clarification Commission (CEH). When an official from the peace verification United Nations Mission to Guatemala (MINUGUA) knocked at her door to take her testimony, my grandmother maintained that she preferred to keep that part of history silent and carry it to her grave. Bitterness grew; it consumed her physical self and her affections. I was unable to fathom her sadness; my world as a young girl, and hers, fell apart simultaneously, and we lost the opportunity to accompany one another.

In 1980, when I was seven, my mother and I left Guatemala for Havana, Cuba, where she started a "creative community" for children who were unable to be with their parents due to the war.

Many years passed before I could return to Guatemala. To explain the effects of the war on my own childhood, I told myself an epic and heroic story in which protest songs, revolutionary leaflets, and fragments of adult conversations were intertwined.

Accompanying the refugees in 1995 during their return to Guatemala and their first year of reintegration helped me to lift the romantic veil from the revolutionary saga and see the experience of others. Guatemala, as an image of lost childhood, turned into a flood of entangled and contradictory emotions in which nostalgia prevails at times and, at other moments, rage holds sway.

Testimony

As Lynn Stephan (2015) explains, testimony, as an *incarnated act of speaking*, has the power to contradict official versions, by offering alternative narratives for social memory. The history told by refugees with their bodies and their words heightened the awareness of many Guatemalans and led to a better understanding of the country's recent history, in contrast to the official version that hid or diminished the importance of being displaced.

Among the wide audience listening to their testimonies, some of us recognized each other, bonded by the indignation, pain, and hope of the returnees. To be a listener of a narrative that leads to the creation of emotional communities implies accepting how very deeply the story of the uprooted population touches us; further, listening to their narratives gave us the intuition that from then on, their paths would connect to our own in different ways. To be a witness for days, months, or years shaped many observers' political identity and encouraged questions that have become more complicated in the diverse venues where we currently find ourselves, 20 years after accompanying the returning population to Petén.

The emotional community I mention was shaped by the experience of pain and struggle of the returnees and consists of the latter and those of us who accompanied the journey as sundry volunteers and witnesses. Below, I retrace the important moments in the returnees' story and examine some of the memories of the accompanying volunteers. It seems important to query why people joined as witnesses, what motivated them, and what commitments they made. Equally worthwhile are my own self-reflections about these same questions and an examination of the kind of spectator and *acompañante* I have been.

The Refugees

The collective, organized, and voluntary return, as refugee leaders systematically defined it, was a turning point in the history of the communities involved. If placed on a timeline, the event was a milestone from which we could analyze the past and future.[7] Nonetheless, the story of poverty, migration, organization, and struggle of those who have now resettled began a long time ago. For generations, the people who in the 1980s fled violence and crossed into Mexico had been *campesinos* in an environment of social tensions produced by the Guatemalan agrarian structure. During the 1950s and 1960s, a growing population and a lack of access to land or other sources of income for the highland *campesinos* turned Guatemala into one of the poorest and most divided nations in the Americas. The boom in export agriculture along the southern coast attracted hundreds of thousands of migrants from the highlands to the coffee, cotton, and sugar plantations, where they spent three or four months a year in extremely difficult working conditions. When they returned to the cold mountain regions, they continued life as *campesinos* on tiny plots of land (Coello et al. 2008).

Before the repression, many of those who currently inhabit the returnee communities in Petén were members of the five cooperatives organized by US, Spanish, and Belgian priests at the beginning of the 1970s in Petén and Ixcán: Mayalán, Xalbal, Pueblo Nuevo, Los Ángeles, and Cuarto Pueblo. The priests, in unison with the local Catholic Church, encouraged migration to the (then practically uninhabited) jungle regions of Ixcán and Petén and purchased federal lands to distribute among poor *campesinos* and landless workers organized in cooperatives (Coello et al. 2008).

Most of those who in the 1970s migrated to Ixcán came from the indigenous highland areas, in Huehuetenango and Quiché, and belonged to distinct, mostly monolingual, ethnic groups, principally Mam, Q'anjob'al, Popti' and Chuj. Those who migrated to Petén were generally from the impoverished eastern regions of the country, that is, Zacapa and Jutiapa. This makeup changed during their refuge: The communities that returned to Petén were composed of an indigenous majority with some *mestizos*.

The effort to colonize Ixcán and Petén was a unique possibility to begin life anew with dignity and escape poverty and exploitation (Falla 1992;

Stolen 2001). The refugees' experience of working in cooperatives and organizing to survive while fleeing played an important role two decades later in building a notion of development based on ideals of equality and justice that took shape as they planned the process of returning to Guatemala.

Francisco Coc Teul, currently a cooperative member of the returnee community of La Esmeralda in Petén and ex-coop member in Ixcán, shared his experience from the 1970s:

> I lived in Ixcán, Quiché, in western Guatemala. At that time, people began organizing to be stronger. The Catholic Church held courses and workshops and helped people obtain medicines. In those years, cooperatives began to proliferate. People worked together. It was wonderful. We built schools and inaugurated the first cattle project. In just two years, we had 200 cows. (Francisco, interviewed by Rolando Duarte and Tere Coello, 2007, Guatemala)

In spite of the difficult initial years in Ixcán and Petén, the budding coop members had expectations of building a better future. Their story as cooperative members occurred at a time when diverse sectors of Guatemalan society were organizing feverishly to question the powers that be during the 1970s and searching for new alternatives to old problems. Simultaneously, a non-indigenous sector of Guatemalan society began to question the liberal idea stemming from the 1944 revolution of "taking modernity" to the indigenous peoples, opting instead to strengthen the communities' abilities to build a future of their own.

Non-campesino Displaced Peoples

The emotional community that concerns me here did not initiate during the return phase. It began much earlier, when the refugees fled to Mexico and began weaving together solidarity networks and obtaining commitments from different actors. Some of their ties date from earlier years. Theirs was a web of commitments and affinities that had been pieced together over decades.

Alberto Colorado, founder and director of COMADEP, left Guatemala due to state violence, like the other refugees. During the 1970s, he participated in founding and developing the Ixcán cooperatives. There, this future NGO director established his first friendships and work connections with coop members.

Alberto arrived in Chiapas (Mexico) in February 1982 and met many of the families he had worked with in Ixcán. The communities were then in an emergency, even as the Catholic Church and a Mexican solidarity committee channeled humanitarian aid. He joined their efforts, working in solidarity with the dioceses of San Cristóbal de Las Casas and Bishop Samuel Ruiz. Alberto remembers: "There was a humanitarian crisis with no political strategy established to respond. The refugees made known their immediate felt needs and those of us who could, did what we could. International solidarity began to grow. Initially, nothing was planned; it was spontaneous aid" (Interview with Alberto, 2007, Guatemala).

There were many humanitarian, developmental, and organizational needs, so the refugees were approached about creating an office charged with helping to satisfy those requirements. An advisory committee of around 40 men and women leaders discussed the proposal and then took the information to their constituents. After some time, the response was positive: Grassroots members agreed to undertake systematic efforts to address refugees' needs, but their main concern centered on working with others to set in motion a project to return to Guatemala (Coello et al. 2008).

Political Conditions for the Return Process

In 1986, a civilian was elected president of Guatemala, a fact that helped lay solid groundwork for discussing a return. The refugees and COMADEP jointly began developing strategies and implementing practical projects to further this end. Six years later, on October 8, 1992, the government and the CCPP signed an agreement outlining the conditions for a collective, organized, and dignified return. At that point, there were two versions of the process: One, set out by the CCPP and called a "return," took into account the refugees' organizational structure and conceived of moving an entire community to a venue it selected, centered on a holistic proposal of alternative development. The government's version, called "repatriation," referred to the movement of families, not communities, to sites chosen by the government, with no follow-up plan of its own.[8]

On January 20, 1993, the first return was carried out and the community settled at *Polígono 14* in Ixcán. The people involved in this initial and subsequent returns suffered great hardships. Returnees had to bid farewell to relatives and friends who remained in Mexico and forgo the lifestyle in camps that were equipped with electricity, transportation, roads, drinking water, and houses with cement floors. Returning to Guatemala meant beginning from scratch and overcoming the fears arising from the memory of repression and their original flight; fears were heightened when a massacre occurred in Xamán in October 1995.[9]

The Emergency Phase

The initial months in Guatemala were difficult and painful for the returning population. Medicines were scarce; the food sent by the international community and the government was insufficient and often arrived spoiled. In the case of those returning to *La Quetzal*,[10] the first leg took them to Petén, where the lack of a highway and the terrible roads (where they existed), complicated conditions even further. Clearing the fields and building homes and communal structures, such as the clinic or the cooperative store, went on continuously (Van der Varen 2000). This initial return was especially difficult: Five people died due to difficulties involving the emergency phase (Bastian 1998).

The emergency phase was forecast to last one year but it surpassed the deadline; governmental institutions often created obstacles. The following activities should have concluded during this phase: layout of the urban sector, building of temporary homes and sanitation facilities, layout of family plots for planting crops for self-consumption during the emergency, installation of drinking water facilities, roads where required, health services, education for children, and installation of corn-dough mills. Yet several communities lived in rudimentary sheds for quite some time, family plots were not laid out, drinking water was not installed, nor was the road completed on time. These goals took three or four years to finish. Requirements that did not depend on outside factors, such as health and education, were covered by promoters and implemented as planned.

National and International Volunteers

Accompaniment During the Return Journey

Following displacement due to armed conflicts, the presence of international observers and accompanying volunteers in areas designated as destinations helps to assure a more sustainable return and reintegration process (Rogge and Lipman 2004; Chamorro 2014). Guatemalan refugees were able to weave together a wide network of solidarity to cover this facet of their return. Internationalists of every age and nationality came.

I remember meeting Mexican, Austrian, Dutch, German, Spanish, Belgian, French, British, Canadian, and American volunteers. Some remained solely for the return journey; others stayed months, a few for years.

The volunteers' main objective in accompanying the return—established in the October 8th Agreement and signed in 1992 by the CCPP and the Guatemalan government—was to guarantee that the initial reintegration process would proceed free of military violence and that human rights would be permanently observed. Strictly speaking, the area was still at war, since the peace accords were signed after the initial return journeys.

Sonja arrived into this scenario in Petén, in April 1995. We met during the return journey to *La Quetzal*. I was coming from Mexico on the same plane as the refugees, while she awaited the arrival of the returning families, together with a numerous and diverse group of people at the Flores airport.

Both accompanying observers and returning Guatemalans faced the same risk of being targeted for attacks by paramilitary or military groups. During the return journey, this danger was perhaps the factor that united observers with returnees: the willingness to face identical circumstances.

Sonja, an Austrian, came by way of the organization *Guatemala Solidarität Wien* (Vienna in Solidarity with Guatemala). Accompanying the returning families led her to choose a path:

> I decided to make the defense of human rights my life's work. There (accompanying the returning families in Petén), I matured and became an adult; my adolescence was over. That was my first contact with a reality outside Europe, being with the people and listening to their testimonies shaped me profoundly. It was a major shock [to confront] the reality that I knew solely through written accounts and my life took on a much more serious meaning (Interview via Skype with Sonja, June 2017).

Sonja explains that hers was not a unique experience and speaks about the contacts she has maintained since that experience: "Those of us who accompanied the returning families made up a community; we were tied together by that experience." Sonja stayed two decades in Guatemala, working at different institutions to clarify the crimes committed during the armed conflict. "After what we learned, many of us returned to live or work in Guatemala or we continued being activists in other countries." The refugees knew how to display the wounds of contemporary Guatemalan history and convene a community that worked to heal them.

As Myriam Jimeno explains—in an interview with Morna Macleod (Jimeno and Macleod 2014)—the relationships established during observation are also human relations, and emotional ties are created during those interactions. When witnesses, such as Sonja, listened to the accounts of pain and suffering, a bond of identification was established that can change how we understand the world and redefine what paths our lives will take.[11]

Long-Term Accompaniment

A number of international accompanying volunteers worked with the refugees in Mexico and stayed several years in the new communities in Guatemala, often becoming involved with development projects. They were generally affiliated to international organizations, such as Oxfam, Hivos, or the Canadian University Service Overseas (CUSO), and coordinated their work with local NGOs such as COMADEP or the Association for the Development of Central America (ADEPAC).

In spite of their many differences, volunteers concurred that the origin of the exodus had to do with unjust socioeconomic structures and other social conditions in Guatemala, militarism, and an economic stranglehold that impoverished Guatemalans (Coello et al. 2008). They also agreed that long-range strategies ought to build a democracy "from below," while short-term strategies should cover emergency needs while maintaining the underlying objective of furthering structural change.

The accompanying volunteers offered their knowledge (agricultural, organizational, gender-related, information and communications technology, etc.) and integrated popular-education strategies in the many training courses they imparted. They conceived of their work not just as humanitarian but also as part of a search for social transformation. In essence, they shared the communities' history, experiences, suffering, and aspirations.

David, an accompanying volunteer who remained in Petén for eight years, recalls the following process:

> At first, I thought I was part of the communities, totally, just another one of the returning *compañeros*. Of course, I was not, I was a white Canadian, not a *campesino*; I worked for an institution and could leave the jungle whenever I chose to do so. They could not. But this doesn't dispute the fact that many of us became deeply and genuinely involved in the life of the communities and in transforming Guatemala. (Interview via Skype with David, June 2017)

David went to Petén through CUSO. His activities included working with young people who had been especially affected by the return and organizing workshops on cooperatives, ecology, and Include Pierre topics. He explained in our interview, "The years I spent in Guatemala had an enormous impact on my life. So much so that I'm surprised that I didn't continue working on the problems of the country." He currently focuses on *campesino* communities in India, Bangladesh, and the Philippines through the Canadian organization Inter Pares-Globalize Equality. "But I continue working for social and economic justice and the world of international development… even though I don't like the term." He says that having worked with the Guatemalan *campesino* communities helped him better understand Asian *campesinos*: "Although there are, obviously, many differences, they share many things; my experience with the returnees taught me how best to contribute to other communities' efforts" (Interview via Skype with David, June 2017).

I remember many discussions on how the work of NGOs encouraged relationships of dependency because, in communities in extreme poverty, the NGOs were financing activities, workshops, assemblies. The genuine solidarity of the accompanying volunteers does not erase the colonialist implications of some of those practices. In our diversity as accompanying volunteers, are we able to listen and build, collectively, with the returnees? (See Crosby, Lykes and Doiron in this volume).

This complex and vivid reflection was a learning experience for many of us. Pierre Van der Varen, a Belgian agronomist who volunteered for six years in the camps in both Mexico and Petén, said, "We accompanying volunteers had many differences between us, as there were between the returnees and the volunteers. But we were united by the utopia that the *campesino* communities once resettled could escape poverty and reintegrate with dignity. The return made that utopia tangible." (Interview via Skype with Pierre, June 2017).

Pierre arrived at the refugee camps in Mexico through a program of the Belgium government that substituted for military service. He stayed seven years as an Oxfam-Belgium aid worker in charge of several projects involving land management, development planning, and agricultural production. He commented in our most recent conversation, "Twenty years after the first return processes to Petén, the memory of that experience is so strong that I can't get over the emotion. It's a feeling that is alive in me and I know it will accompany me for the rest of my life. It's an enormous privilege to have experienced that moment" (Interview via Skype with Pierre, June 2017).

Widening the Experience, Widening History

Although most inhabitants in returnee communities in Petén belong to different Mayan ethnicities, the meaning of being indigenous and the ways this multicultural coexistence played out was not touched upon during the return process. At least not in public debates, even though there were bicultural families, linguistic loan words, and some revival of Mayan rituals.

Perhaps part of the reason for this lacunae is because the wider return process to the north of Guatemala had ties to a political-military organization, the Rebel Armed Forces (FAR, a member of the URNG), that had analyzed the indigenous question less deeply.[12] Nonetheless, the identities were present and expressed themselves in everyday activities and organizing processes.

Alma López, a Guatemalan Mayan K'iche' social worker, was also a member of COMADEP in Petén. Her work supported Ixmucané, an organization of returnee women. That is where we met. She was born and raised in Quetzaltenango, popularly known as "Xelajú", a city largely unaffected by the war. Her first contact with the returnee communities occurred during the emergency phase in *La Quetzal*. Even though she stayed in the camps for just a year, her experiences made a deep impact:

> I encountered a very painful part of my country's history. To see the war up-close, through their (the returnees') experience taught me to identify as indigenous and as a woman, to strengthen my overall awareness. I learned how important it is to work horizontally and about solidarity systems. I was amazed at the impressive level of organization in these communities. (Interview with Alma López, 2001, Guatemala)[13]

Although being *K'iche'* is a fundamental aspect in Alma's identitary definition, she understood when leaving her family to work alongside the returnees that "being indigenous in Guatemala (often) has to do with being poor, illiterate, and without access to the same opportunities as *ladinos*... the strength of the organizational process of the indigenous peoples has to do with their history and the solidarity that emanates as a result" (Interview with Alma López, 2001, Guatemala).

Alma came to know an important part of recent Guatemalan history through the experience of the returnees and thus strengthened her own identity when challenged by other ways of being Mayan. The return of the refugees and the dissemination of her testimony helped to reshape imaginaries and profoundly change perceptions.

Conclusions

Those of us who worked together during those years often said, "The accompanying volunteers received much more from the returnees than we could ever give back." It is a sentiment that underlies the testimonies of the volunteers cited herein. My work in Petén ended in 1996, yet the experience continues to be a personal reference point. In the following years, I visited La Quetzal and La Esperanza a number of times, the first in 1998, to share my undergraduate degree thesis, a journalistic account of the process based on my work as a grassroots communicator. The last visit was in 2007, as part of a consulting contract in the returnee communities.

During their initial years in Guatemala, the communities I witnessed made considerable improvements on their preliminary living situation. Roads and schools were built, services and projects were implemented, and good relationships were forged with neighboring communities. Yet poverty persisted, investments were wanting, and insecurity and crime grew in the department (Coello et al. 2008).

Furthermore, during the first few years, the returnee communities suffered serious internal conflicts that severely hindered development projects. Migration was another factor that weakened returnees' continuing organization: Not only were there absences but also remittances fostered great economic inequality within the communities. More than a few resettled residents had to sell their plots of land to those within the community who could afford the purchase; people who had once shared the same experience of fleeing and seeking refuge were now divided: Some became small landholders and others continued to be the eternally dispossessed. Other situations worsened their plight: the returnees were abandoned politically by political parties and former allies; NGOs withdrew or began downsizing their work as funding agencies reappraised their priorities vis-à-vis the communities.

In this chapter, I have posited the idea that the return of the Guatemalan refugees led to the creation of an emotional community made up of returnees and their *acompañantes*. Notwithstanding their diversity, the bonds within this community are still active and meaningful for the actors involved. For some, the experience of "having accompanied" provided new signifiers and meanings to their own lives, while deepening their understanding of social and human relationships. The deep solidarity and bonding displayed by volunteers toward the returnees did not erase differences between these groups, but it did lead to questions about hierarchical positions and dependencies that are seemingly a part of the relationships between *campesino* populations and outside volunteers.

This emotional community has deep historic roots. The first contacts among some members occurred a decade before the outbreak of violence that forced both indigenous *campesinos* and many urban *mestizos* involved in the struggle for social transformation to leave Guatemala.

The entire process involved an accompaniment that went beyond witnessing. Although it was evident to everyone that the "commitment" of the "outsiders" could not substitute for the experience of having been uprooted, taking refuge, and then returning, there were volunteers who, within their particular status, took on a leading role in this historic event. Their presence went beyond humanitarian aid and became a critique of the structural reasons for Guatemala's inequality.

During their return process, the returnees filled the plazas along the way and told their story in each town where a stop was made. This contact allowed some sectors of Guatemalan society that had remained aloof from the violence of the internal armed conflict to recast their thinking about the country's recent history and open their perceptions about new actors (Stephen 2015). During the return process and over the years that it took to be reintegrated, the returnees' testimonies allowed a wider "historical truth" and its oft-excluded actors to gain legitimacy in the eyes of many. Their political and emotional resources (Jimeno 2010) allowed the depth of that experience to be disseminated.

Perhaps at any other time other than during the return process, the discourse of the refugees would not have had the same impact. The families and the communities gave witness with their presence, and very different institutions, such as the United Nations, NGOs, and other offices, were on hand to validate the experience. The refugee community took on visibility and spoke about their experience to others untouched by the same misfortunes. These activities helped to neutralize the Army's campaign of disparagement before the returnees' arrival.

The impact of the returnees' testimonies was not limited to the route of return. They also articulated the experiences shared during the emergency phase in the returnee communities.

Diana Taylor (2003) asserts that we learn and transmit knowledge through actions and corporal representations, demonstrating agency and the ability to make decisions. Although the return was not a staged representation, its testimonial content was strengthened by strategically focusing on the stories of pain and resistance, as part of a wider struggle. Thus, the return, both the movement of people itself and the founding of new communities, functioned as an educational opportunity, as a way of transmitting memory and knowledge.

Notes

1. For information on the nature of violence in the department of Petén during the internal armed conflict, see Vela Castañeda (2014). Los pelotones de la muerte. La construcción de los perpetradores del genocidio guatemalteco, México, El Colegio de México.
2. For more information regarding the organization of returning women, see Alison Crosby (2000).
3. Manolo Vela Castañeda (2008) finds that most of the violence occurred between late 1981 and early 1983 as part of a military counteroffensive that destroyed the population base of the insurgency.
4. Communities subject to the Army's counterinsurgency plans. Residents had to join the paramilitary Civil Self-Defense Patrols (PAC) and condition their agricultural activities to the needs and orders of the Army. The PAC, the so-called Development Hubs, and the Model Villages were key parts of the Army's (and government's) counterinsurgency strategy during the internal armed conflict.
5. The Communities of Populations in Resistance (CPR) were composed of displaced people who chose not to seek refuge and opted to hide from the Army and the paramilitary in wilderness areas that would protect them.
6. A group of relatives of the disappeared that emerged in 1984, during General Mejía Víctores' military regime.
7. In her chapter in this volume, Gisela Espinosa reflects on and proposes a definition for "turning point" (*parteaguas* in Spanish).
8. For further information, see: Manz (1987), Mack (1992) and Messmacher et al. (1986).
9. On October 5, 1995, members of a Civil Self-Defense Patrol (PAC) murdered 10 members of the Aurora 8 returnee community, injuring an additional 18, at the Xamán agricultural settlement in the municipality of Chisec, department of Alta Verapaz. The returnees had gathered to plan the anniversary of their return to Guatemala. This tragic event discouraged the organization of communities in Mexico that were preparing to return to Guatemala.
10. La Quetzal is the name of the first community that returned to Petén. The lands currently inhabited are called El Quetzal.
11. Morna Macleod's chapter in this volume also mentions the potential of emotional communities.

12. For more information regarding the Guatemalan guerrilla organizations' perceptions regarding the indigenous world, see Macleod (2017).
13. This 2001 interview I had with Alma was published in 2002. The reference is Angela Ixkic Bastian Duarte (2002).

References

Bastian Duarte, Angela. 1998. *Refugiados fuimos. Reportaje sobre el retorno de los refugiados guatemaltecos*. BA Thesis, Facultad de Ciencias Políticas y Sociales, UNAM, Mexico.

———. 2002. Conversación con Alma López, Autoridad Guatemalteca. La Doble Mirada del Género y la Etnicidad. *Estudios Latinoamericanos* 18: 175–183.

Calveiro, Pilar. 2006. Los usos políticos de la memoria. In *Sujetos sociales y nuevas formas de protesta en la historia reciente de América Latina*, ed. Gerardo Caetano, 259–382. Buenos Aires: CLACSO.

CEH-III (Historical Clarification Commission). 1999. Las violaciones a los derechos humanos y los hechos de violencia. In *Guatemala memoria del silencio, Tomo III*, ed. CEH. Guatemala: UNOPS (Oficina de Servicios para Proyectos de las Naciones Unidas).

Chamorro, Soren. 2014. Acercamiento al proceso de Desarme, Desmovilización y Reinserción (DDR) en Nicaragua después de 28 años de la firma de los acuerdos de Esquipulas II. *Cultura de Paz* 21 (65): 14–26.

Coello, Teresa, Rolando Duarte, e Ixkic Bastian. 2008. *Sistematización de la experiencia de la Cooperación Mesoamericana para el Desarrollo y la Paz*. COMADEP – in México and Guatemala 1986–2007. Unpublished.

Crosby, Alison. 2000. Return to the Nation: The Organizational Challenges Confronted by Guatemalan Refugee Women. *Canada's Journal on Refugees* 19 (3): 32–37.

Falla, Ricardo. 1992. *Masacres de la Selva: Ixcán, Guatemala 1975–1982* [Massacres in the Jungle, Guatemala 1975–1982]. Ciudad de Guatemala: Editorial Universitaria, Universidad de San Carlos.

Jimeno, Myriam. 2010. Emocoes e política: A vitima e a construcao de comunidades emocionais. *Revista Mana* 16 (1): 99–121.

Jimeno, Myriam, and Morna Macleod. 2014. Interview with Myriam Jimeno, November 2014. Available at http://mornamacleod.net/?p=767

Jimeno, Myriam, Daniel Varela, y Ángela Castillo. 2015. *Después de la masacre: emociones y política en el Cauca indio*. Bogotá: Universidad Nacional de Colombia, Instituto Colombiano de Antropología e Historia.

Mack, Myrna. 1992. ¿Dónde está el futuro? Procesos de reintegración en comunidades de retornados, Guatemala. *AVANCSO, Cuadernos de Investigación* 8: 266.

Mack, Myrna, Paula Worby, and Helvi Mendizabal. 1990. Política institucional hacia el desplazado interno en Guatemala, Guatemala. *AVANCSO Cuadernos de Investigación* 6: 29.

Macleod, Morna. 2017. Ri Ajxokon, ri Amaq'i' Chi Iximulew. Organizaciones revolucionarias, indianistas y pueblos indígenas en el conflicto armado – Análisis y debates. Guatemala: Editorial Maya' Wuj, Chi Iximulew.

Manz, Beatriz. 1987. *Refugees of a Hidden War: Aftermath of Counterinsurgency in Guatemala*. New York: University of New York Press.

Messmacher, Miguel, Santiago Genovés, Margarita Nolasco, et al. 1986. *Dinámica maya. Los refugiados guatemaltecos*. México: Fondo de Cultura Económica.

Rogge, John, and Betsy Lippman. 2004. Haciendo que el retorno y la reinserción sean sostenibles, transparentes y participativos. *Forced Migration Review* 21: 4–5.

Stephen, Lynn. 2015. Ser testigo presencial—Acompañando, presenciando, actuando, LASA/Oxfam Martin Diskin Lectureship/Award, LASA 2015, San Juan Puerto Rico. *LASA Forum Summer* 46 (3): 4–14.

Stolen, Kristi Anne. 2001. Experiencias de retornados guatemaltecos en el Petén. *Amérique Latine Histoire et Mémoire* 2. Available at http://alhim.revues.org/587

Taylor, Diana. 2003. *The Archive and the Repertoire: Performing Cultural Memory in the Americas*. Durkham: Duke University Press.

Traverso, Enzo. 2016. Memoria e historia del siglo XX. In *Archivos y memorias de la represión en América Latina*, ed. María Acuña, Patricia Flier, Miriam González Vera, et al., 17–29. Santiago de Chile: LOM Ediciones-FASIC.

Van der Varen, Pierre. 2000. *Perdidos en la selva. Un estudio del proceso de re-arraigo y de desarrollo de la Comunidad-Cooperativa Unión Maya Itzá, formada por campesinos guatemaltecos, antiguos refugiados, reasentamiento en el departamento de El Petén*. Guatemala: Thela-Thesis.

Vela Castañeda, Manolo. 2008. Notas para el estudio de las relaciones entre la rebelión y el genocidio en Guatemala. *Espacios políticos* 0: 21–29.

———. 2014. *Los pelotones de la muerte. La construcción de los perpetradores del genocidio guatemalteco*. México: El Colegio de México.

CHAPTER 7

Political-Affective Intersections: Testimonial Traces Among Forcibly Displaced Indigenous People of Oaxaca, Mexico

Natalia De Marinis

INTRODUCTION

In this chapter, I shall reflect on research in contexts that are immersed in terror and human rights violations, on our role in the testimonial traces that are created as we approach to study these settings, and on how emotions circulate through victims' testimonies and public denouncements. My reflections are based on my research with the Triqui indigenous people who in 2010 were forcibly displaced from their town San Juan Copala, in the state of Oaxaca.[1]

In the past few years in Mexico, due to the growing levels of violence in the country, there has been increasing interest in examining the phenomenon of violence from a number of analytic perspectives. These range from current protests against the war on narcotics-trafficking—that increased rather than curtailed violence—to analytically situating them on an historical continuum of violence stemming from weak institutions and high levels of marginalization and poverty among a wide sector of the population (Azaola 2012; Maldonado 2013). The growing number of studies on the subject generates concern as to how violence is addressed theoretically and

N. De Marinis (✉)
Center for Research and Postgraduate Studies
in Social Anthropology, Veracruz, Mexico

© The Author(s) 2018
M. Macleod, N. De Marinis (eds.), *Resisting Violence*,
https://doi.org/10.1007/978-3-319-66317-3_7

analytically, involving numerous challenges due to its polysemic, productive, and performative nature (Scheper-Hughes and Bourgois 2004).

The productive capacity of violence to generate silence, bewilderment, and sudden readjustments crosscuts our own research, while defining possibilities and limits of cooperation, approaching, and establishing possibilities of dialog with the victims. For a number of decades, critical reflections have surfaced regarding the "what for" of our researchers in these contexts, which added important contributions regarding the ethical-political commitment of research, particularly where myriad forms of violence, dispossession, and human rights violations predominate (Espinosa, this volume; Rappaport 2008; Speed 2006; Mora 2015; Robledo 2016).

The notion of *situated knowledge* (Haraway 1988; Rosaldo 1993; Hernández 2016) is the point of departure for this chapter, since it allows me to delve into the place of emotions—those of the victims and researchers—to understand more fully how pain, joy, and sadness are emotions that do not belong to a particular subject, as part of an individual essence that is projected outward, or to a social structure with defined corporal/structural limits. Rather, as Sarah Ahmed (2004) and Veena Das (1997) have suggested, these emotions flow beyond the limits of the body.

Rather than being fixed categories, emotions are part of an affection through which we can understand the porous and permeable limits of bodies and spaces (Navaro-Yashin 2012; Clough and Halley 2007). I argue that the performative scenarios of victims' testimonies and public denouncements create an affective social fabric in which victims, researchers, and the public play differentiated but intertwined roles. This is what Jimeno and her team conceptualized as "emotional communities" (see Introduction and Jimeno et al. this volume), which allows us to recognize closeness and care, empathy, complicity, and the ethics of cooperation, in the construction of affective and political ties in the search for justice (Jimeno et al. 2012).

I am interested in addressing this notion that intersects the political and the emotional based on my research experience with displaced Triqui men and women. I shall do so in three dimensions: The affections provoked by terror where I confronted my collaborative research; the testimonial traces created in the organizational space of displaced people; and the way in which emotions that circulated in this space and among people displaced to various communities made it possible for them to acknowledge their humanity and dignity and construct new narratives, based on their own knowledge, memories, and narratives of pain, amid a dehumanizing context of terror and forced displacement.

Submersion in Terror

The territorial and political control in the Triqui region has historically involved armed confrontations between communities linked to the Institutional Revolutionary Party (PRI) or to leftist movements in Mexico, as well as hierarchical-political and violent rule within communities since the 1970s (De Marinis 2013, 2015). The organizations traditionally in conflict and that control more than 30 communities in the region—the leftist Movement of Unification and Struggle of Triqui People (MULT) and the PRI organization Unity for Social Welfare of the Triqui Region (UBISORT)—were responsible for an armed conflict that led to the murder of hundreds of people and displacement of a large part of the population. In the midst of this conflict, in 2007, a group of communities declared San Juan Copala an autonomous municipality.[2] Their main complaints centered on the violence that had become the main mechanism for controlling roads, public resources, and bodies. This political domination was based on a significant increase in forced marriages, control of the dowry, heavy fines if the orders of the organizations were not followed, and extortion of large sums of money from migrants in exchange for protecting their families. Further, the autonomy movement criticized changes in the attacks on "enemies" that often involved the murder of entire families and, beginning around the year 2000, the staggering increase in sexual violence against women committed by PRI followers and the leftist movements.

My research in the Triqui region began in 2008 in San Juan Copala. Even though it was not my objective to focus on an analysis of violence, unexpectedly, violence permeated my fieldwork experience. The central strategies of my initial period in the town involved documenting the fears, silences, and the particular ways this autonomy was conceived in a highly conflictive and violent context. Autonomy had brought a period of peace for the people, but, also, a wider solidarity network (of organizations and researchers who, like me, helped carry out different projects) underpinned the peaceful moment.[3]

As I was finishing my first field stay in the region, Triqui leaders linked to the PRI began returning from the United States, intent on reestablishing party ties in the town. Without immediately recognizing the prelude of the massacre that occurred sometime later, I was able to identify once again the fear that people had spoken to me about before the times of peace they associated with autonomy. Shootouts increased, as did people's silence. Their openness was ending. As the power of these returnees grew based on

PRI handouts, the community radio station, "The Voice that Breaks the Silence," was finding it increasingly difficult to broadcast. Two of the station's announcers, Teresa Bautista and Felicitas Martínez, were murdered in April 2007, in a clear attack against the autonomy movement.

I visited the town for the last time in October 2009. The scenario of terror had worsened: People from the surrounding hills murdered a young man. His sister, who had been arranging soft drinks, was wounded. I called on Libertad, a young woman who lived two houses away from the murder victim and worked at the radio station. I was surprised to see her left arm bandaged. A "stray" bullet had perforated her arm as she arrived in San Juan Copala from the town of Juxtlahuaca accompanied by her three-year-old niece. "If the bullet hadn't hit my arm, it would have struck the girl in the head... Oh Lord!" Libertad recalled that, apparently, they had not intended to shoot, but a bullet "went off." In a flash, she saw the bullet strike a car window but felt nothing. She was oblivious until she realized she could not move her arm. There was blood everywhere and her arm "was dead." The shooters were only fined, since there was no intention of injuring her. With the money, she was treated at the hospital and began therapy. Libertad felt very afraid and no longer left her house. While she recounted the events, we admired through the windows how green the hills looked after a long rainy spell. "Have you seen how pretty Copala is?" she asked after a pause. Without much conviction, I answered that I had, still surprised by how serene she was as she recalled the events. "Yes. But we can no longer live here," she said, lost in thought.

I felt as if I were in the uncertainty that Michael Taussig narrated in his field notebooks, later published in "Law in Lawless Land: Diary of a *Limpieza* in Colombia" (2003). As I drew closer to it, this reality turned out to be more complex and chaotic. I had entered an environment of suspicion, impunity, lawlessness, where there is no "outside," because the boundary between the state and the paramilitaries is roughly drawn, there is no clear line, the paramilitaries are at once part of, and opposed to, the state. As Green (1995) suggests, the limits imposed by terror can be so invisible that we are blind to them until we cross them, and then it is too late. Yet, hewing to the signs that people give you became a valuable source of protection, such as when they avoid saying outright, because of the responsibility and the risk involved, that it is time for you to leave. Clearly, the time I lived there and the confidence I was able to build allowed me to recognize and interiorize those signals in order to know exactly when I had to leave, and if perhaps I could not quite strike a balance, I had a better possibility of separating irrational fear from real insecurity. The stories of terror I had recorded during the period of peace, when people would tell me of their fear, before the autonomous municipality was established, of the "damned bullets," of the signals they had to read, the silence, the disorientation, were now materializing, and I was experiencing them for the first time in my own body. I chose to leave, much before I had planned. A few days later, the PRI leaders organized one of the fiercest attacks recorded in the region. Some logs blocking the only road into town prevented people from leaving. The permanent siege that began that day lasted until October 2010. Some 30 people were murdered, including three women and a child, dozens of women were injured with firearms and raped, and close to 600 people were forced to relocate.

Forced Displacement and Testimonial Traces

I learned from diverse sources of the escalation of violence that began with the armed blockade and the massacre in town. During the initial months of 2010, I received numerous phone calls from the young women at the community radio station telling me of the profound terror they felt and the ongoing threats they received. The loudspeakers on top of the municipal building broadcast threats against men and women; they were to be hanged, murdered, women were going to be raped. They told me of their fear and their refusal to leave home. The calls were brief but reoccurring. Even though words failed me at times, I tried to calm them. They asked me to do something. So I sent emails describing the situation and called people who could write something in the press. People who for years had accompanied the independent movements in the region[4] said there was little to be done beyond disseminating information. Solidarity networks were reactivated in a context of impunity in the state of Oaxaca, where it seemed nothing could be done to guarantee people's rights. Rumors and distrust factored into this helplessness. The Triqui people had lived with violence for so long that a very powerful stigma, linking their culture to violence, arose and took hold at that moment in different settings, including the government, academia, and the press.

I met the displaced people during the initial months of 2010 when I moved to the city of Oaxaca. People from San Juan Copala were fleeing homicides, kidnappings, sexual violence, and assaults on homes when residents walked the paths in the hills in search of food. I began documenting their testimonies in response to people's requests. They wanted to talk about their experiences and give meaning to what they had survived. Our meetings were the opportunity and a space for emotional accompaniment.

My collaborative work of documenting testimonies began in August 2010, after a group of displaced women, joined by organizations in solidarity, decided to denounce the situation by setting up a permanent sit-in at the doors of the government palace in the center of the city of Oaxaca. In addition, some people were displaced to other communities. I visited both settings over several months in 2010 and 2011. During my fieldwork lasting over a year, I recorded the testimonies of terror and violence in both spaces.[5] Just as the violence at San Juan Copala had unexpectedly permeated my research, I had not foreseen people's requests to record their testimonies. Giving testimony was a response to the need to denounce. Perhaps my presence would lend the credibility to their experiences that they were unable to find in the halls of the justice system where they originally took their accusations. I had not planned it, but I became a witness to the terror, uncertainty, fear, sadness, and lack of trust that had taken hold of everyone in San Juan Copala.

I too experienced those same emotions. The loneliness, bewilderment, and mistrust that people projected were increasingly overcoming me. During the initial testimonies at the sit-in and in the communities, links would be drawn connecting what had happened to some offense. Some people thought they deserved the violence, such as having their property looted after escaping from town. If his property was sacked, it was because "he left," "because he hadn't endured sufficient pain." In other cases, especially those involving sexual violence, blame was placed because "she's a single woman," "what was she doing wandering in the hills at that hour?", "we told her not to return to town but she did anyway. Just plain stubborn." People who left town and began protesting or undertaking public actions were subject to rumors that questioned their political ties or the supposed amounts of money they received; the rumors even began linking protesters with assailants.

I tried to focus on the fragmentation that terror generates, on how each person had saved his or her life, even though "saving" their lives in this context had made them the butt of unceasing suspicion. Certainties also faded in my case, especially when I was unaware of how to act and protect myself in this environment and the significance my research could have. Castillejo Cuéllar (2009) suggests that our research in contexts of terror should be subject to numerous reflections, especially in light of the parade of "trauma experts" who were keen on bearing witness and gathering painful testimonies without concern for ethical considerations. In this regard, Scheper-Hughes and Bourgois (2004) maintain that one of the major challenges for those of us writing about violence is to avoid making it into theater or a "pornography of violence," creating an opposite effect to the criticism of the injustice and suffering we wanted to address in our work. Furthermore, in many institutional settings, a critique has arisen regarding testimonial work with victims of violence that refers to the racialized moral hierarchies that are constructed between people who are forced to give their testimony and those located in the moral place of listening (Crosby and Lykes 2011; Theidon 2009).

The Circularity of Affects and the Construction of a "We"

Forced displacement implies a threshold situation involving transition that Liisa Malkki (1995) aptly analyzed in the case of forced displacement of the Hutus in Tanzania. Malkki revisited the concept of *liminality* that Victor Turner (1969) coined to describe the rituals of the Ndembu. She suggests that a status of marginality that implies a generational or power transition in the community for the Ndembu can be observed in the displaced by a sudden dispossession of the identifying categories linked to territory, community status, and identity, which are set by the framework of the nation state. This threshold moment denotes ruptures to the structure and construction of a status of marginality, where subjects are stripped of their identifying categories, thus losing the meanings that ordered their world. Nonetheless, the power of the threshold concept lies both in describing the dispossession and in establishing the possibility of reconstruction based on a shared experience of marginality. A *communitas* is created, a temporary construction within marginality, where community is experienced by all those that live in a state of *liminality*, a sense of shared spirituality, unity, and equity.

The Triquis sought to find their place in this situation of loss of physical and mental control over space and their lives, characterized by arbitrary lines that in some cases meant violent death. The testimonies that I registered were based on building new narratives that would transmit what the Triquis had lived and from where they could cobble together a vague idea of a "we" and thus some type of certainty and protection for their lives. This construction of a "we," or *communitas*, was experienced differently in accordance with the places families were displaced to. Explanations of experiences changed, and so did the affections and the ties of solidarity that emerged in different contexts.

For the women of the sit-in, the rage, indignation, and pain were emotions that allowed them to deal with a public political struggle. Unable to locate their narratives within a specific, logical framework, given women's historical exclusion from political activities in the community, women's emotions welled up even stronger. "Emotions" became a possible way to express oneself. As one of the women told me some time after: "We began to let out all the rancor we had pent up and so both my *compañeras* and I began to speak, to say things, and, from that point on, we were no longer ashamed and we said what we were feeling inside because no one told us what we were going to say" (Interview with Reyna, April 22, 2011, Oaxaca).

For the displaced people at the sit-in, the "we" became linked mainly to an acknowledgment as victims of a greater structure and to an understanding of violence as a response to the struggle for indigenous autonomy that they had defended for years. The recognition of their struggle as something wider and the structures of racism and exclusion that indigenous people in Mexico experience helped them build another possibility of the communal, linking their lived experiences and violence as women and men, within a greater violence orchestrated by paramilitary strategies in several indigenous territories. Likewise, these connections made it possible to begin a process of removing the blame they felt as women, many of whom had suffered sexual violence and armed attacks (De Marinis 2015). I saw that these explanations made it possible for them to shift their focus away from the victim, or turn aside explanations regarding what a particular woman did, or did not do, before being attacked, in order to refocus on denouncements regarding the paramilitary apparatus that orchestrated the dispossession.

The solidarity networks that sprung up around the sit-in, where we were joined by activists and reporters, created a circle of support for the women, yet it also allowed them to coordinate other knowledge and actions aimed at generating a wider social effect. The testimonies we gathered, many of them videotaped, were made public at screenings held at specific activities. The individuality of the testimonies was blurred in public spaces and became part of a "we." Recurring demonstrations, their presence at the doors of the government palace, and a public wake for three men murdered in the communities were scenarios where not only the "we the displaced" gained momentum, but so did a wider "we," encompassing people in solidarity, passersby, who, by approaching with empathy, were able to connect with the displaced people's emotions and memories recounted in their own narrative forms.

The documentation work I began with them had been surprising insofar as "to speak" of violence had always been a very difficult topic to access during my previous research. So too during my first encounters at the sit-in. Asking about their experiences could have meant a re-victimization that I wanted to avoid. During the first few weeks, I limited myself to taking food, helping them with handicraft sales, downloading Triqui music from the internet so that they could listen to stories in their language, and showing videos of San Juan Copala that I had filmed during my stay. When they asked me to document their testimonies, almost all women wanted to participate in filming and translations. The women reviewed and often edited the published materials produced from the interviews.[6]

Some women decided not to talk and everyone respected their wishes; other women preferred not to be filmed and still others only wanted to speak in a group setting. As in other collaborative work that involved the use of testimony in contexts of conflict and post-conflict, their impact came through in this production. One of the effects was the possibility of overcoming personal trauma by sharing with others, of discovering one's own injuries in collective injuries and one's body within structural violence. This is a far cry from a pathological condition stemming from being a "victim." From documented testimonies, it became possible to build a "we," which in turn allowed the women to order and understand their experiences de-individualizing pain by sharing it with others.

These narratives, however, did not necessarily involve the spoken word. Political actions that involved silence and individual ways of processing grief were also present at the sit-in, where we had gathered as witnesses. One of these actions at the sit-in was the wake for the three men murdered in August 2011.

"So They Will Know What the Odor of Death Is Like That We Have to Smell Constantly"

The wake for three murdered men who belonged to the Movement for Autonomy was held August 7, 2011, at the entrance to the palace of government in the city of Oaxaca. When people at the sit-in heard about the murder of Álvaro Cruz, Francisco Ramírez, and José Ramírez, between 20 and 40 years old, they decided to transport the bodies and hold a wake for them right there. "To show that we aren't lying: The governor says we are at peace but they continue killing us. Here they are: We're not lying," said Luz, who was nervous about the decision, continuously talking into her cell phone, awaiting the arrival of the remains. They were told their decision could mean legal problems: It is against the law for individuals to move bodies, even if they are on a public road. It had probably been their relatives' decision to move them and, after a seven-hour journey without being stopped by the police, they arrived at the government palace (see Fig. 7.1).

At two in the morning, the coffins were lowered from a red pickup truck, the kind usually used for carrying passengers in the region. They were carried off, one by one, as the murdered men's relatives and other family members from the community stepped out of other vehicles. The widows were with their children. I greeted a number of them as they cried when they saw the setting, and they asked me how I felt about what they were doing. One woman from a community told me, "We can't take anymore!"

Fig. 7.1 The wake for three murdered men at the Government Palace, Oaxaca city, August 2011. Photograph by Natalia De Marinis

After a half hour, the three coffins were placed opposite to the grand old iron door of the government palace. Working swiftly, the women from the sit-in mounted the setting. The relatives stood at the head of the coffins, and the smallest tortillas sold in the Oaxaca market were placed to the sides, together with candles and bouquets of flowers. There were no cigarettes, beer, musical groups, or dancing as stipulated by community tradition. The silence, crying, and camera clicks at this wake lent another meaning to farewell. A call for justice rang out as the posters, in Spanish and English, were affixed in front of the coffins and on the columns of the palace.

As is custom in the communities, women at the sit-in prepared food for those of us who had gathered. The first plates of food were placed next to the coffins. Then they served those attending. Some women walked about with copal, spreading the smoke about the coffins and the family members in circular movements. In due time, they opened the coffins' small viewing windows and we could see the men's disfigured faces from being shot in the head. Their open mouths signaled a violent death; dried blood spotted the white lace muslin.

More pickup trucks arrived that morning with men, women, and children from the communities that dot the region. There were about 100 people, plus a significant number of journalists and passersby who approached. Some asked why the wake was held there, others took photos and were perplexed to see the bodies laid out on the cold palace floor, their faces disfigured, amid the smell of flowers, copal, and the food now more than 12 hours old. Behind the coffins were crosses with the names of murdered men and women. More than 20 crosses were placed along the palace doors; observers kept a generalized silence, interrupted by the expression of horror of those who approached to see what was happening. Some people approached the women to offer their solidarity, hear their stories, and embrace them.

Death laid out at the municipal palace doors immediately got the attention of the Oaxaca health authorities. They refused to approach, but they summoned Luz, the woman in charge, to pressure her to remove the bodies, given the epidemics they could cause and the "illegality" of placing them on a public street. Several of us gathered to hear the discussion. Luz told the authorities that the *campesinos* had been murdered, the government claimed that peace had come to San Juan Copala, and so the women wanted to show that it was not true. If the authorities were so worried about health issues, Luz continued, the women had been at the sit-in for a year, unable to return home, and no one had approached to ask about the conditions they were living in. The authorities were left speechless but Luz promised that at two in the afternoon the bodies would be taken away. She said that they would not let the bodies decay out of respect for the dead, not because of the authorities' orders. The authorities took their leave.

At two in the afternoon, several men from the communities, shouting demands for justice and peace in the Triqui region, carried the bodies to the pickup truck parked a half block from the palace. When the women were returning to the sit-in, also demanding justice and holding crosses and flowers, they were intercepted by a group of heavy-set men, many of them over 1.70 m, dressed in civilian clothing or wearing the uniform of the state police. They stopped the women from returning to the sit-in. The women were leading the group, many holding babies in their arms, the rest of us accompanying behind. They were confronted with a long line of state police. Some of the women were injured and one of the men grabbed a four-year-old girl by the ears. After ten minutes of pushing and shoving, the men let the women through, who shouted as they passed alongside the police, "You are killing us! Enough! We want justice."

I met up with Aurelia, who was crying by one of the columns at the palace, where for almost a year she had lived with her family. Indignant, her face etched with rage, fists clenched, she said with a choked cry of anguish, "I want to die and may my body rot here! So they will know what the odor of death is like that we have to smell constantly."

Performance, Witnesses, and Building Political-Affective Communities

As a body-centered action, performance incorporates emotions, linking those who stage it with the wider public. Diana Taylor (2003) suggests, that perfomance is a way of generating and transmitting knowledge by including others bearing the emotional impact of the grievance and the act of transmitting it to others. Similarly, Das (1997) maintains that if terror has the ability to annihilate all possibilities of language, then words and denouncements are starting points, an invitation to fuse into a single body, so that the pain can be experienced by other bodies as well.

Testimony as a narrative includes words, but also actions and silences. It assumes that there are witnesses, including necessarily a relationship between the person that survived violence and the person listening, but those observing are also witnesses. The testimonial moment is even wider, encompassing other observers and listeners at other moments. Jelin (2002) characterizes this range of testimony as *testimonial traces*, referring to all those who are involved in listening and remembering. The survivors, Primo Levi says, are the only witnesses who are delegated to speak for those who have lost the human ability to do so, either due to death or due to their bodily death through the annihilation of their human condition (Levi 1989).

Lynn Stephen (2017), in her work with testimonies of victims of repression during the Popular Assembly of the Peoples of Oaxaca (APPO) movement in Oaxaca, and in her role as "expert witness" in cases of political asylum requests of Mexican indigenous peoples in the United States, critically reflects on this complex relationship between witness and the victim-witness. If, for Primo Levi, the victims' ability to observe has been annihilated by suffering and incomprehension, and only survivors can reconstruct memory based on testimony, in the re-victimizing spaces of justice there is also an annihilation of the truth of the testimony of those who have suffered violence, particularly of actors who have been historically marginalized from the halls of justice, which is precisely the case of indigenous peoples. According to these re-victimizing constructs, it is the academic "expert" who is granted the possibility of speaking from an "objective vision" and "accredited position," who accompanies the testimony and gathers evidence and theoretical backing (Stephen 2017).

The wake, then, became a narrative, a testimony of displaced Triqui men and women based on the deposition of victims and making death visible in a public space. The emotional impact of this action made it possible to accompany and translate. We all became witnesses and, in this sense, part of what was happening, the family's sorrow, and the indignation hovered around the doors of the government palace. The action sought to translate trauma, permanently discredited in the halls of justice where indigenous peoples have been excluded and where, at that moment, suspicion regarding their experience with violence permeated the environment.

Myriam Jimeno and her team (Jimeno et al. 2015) suggest that sharing personal trauma in some form of organized action involves creating "political-affective communities," which in itself, in contexts of extreme violence and impunity, is a fountainhead for recovery.[7] This empowering and healing aspect of the word, the action, and the emotions that permeate the environment of shared actions create an idea of "we" that allowed the Triquis to face the stigma that they have been subjected to historically, which had implied considering themselves as individual victims and without agency in the cracks of the official justice system. It is a struggle to humanize and dignify life in the face of the dehumanization brought by fear and terror.

In turn, the rebuilding of "we" involved a need to distance oneself from the *abject*, not involving so much the public display of the human in connection with others, but rather in dehumanizing the other, the assailants, experiences, the space and the time of lived terror. Theidon (2004) also analyzed this in narratives of the pain of conflict in Ayacucho, Peru: the explanation of how a relative, neighbor, fellow man had been able to murder someone close to him had to do with reference to evils, the madness that possessed their bodies, the lack of a conscience—the Triqui women linked this to insanity—and a dehumanization translated into animality, into inertness. The assailants could not be human, they were "rocks," "madmen," but likewise they were relatives who had become something different due to the evil that possessed the town. The testimony of a grandmother had the following reflection:

> I think the reason is that they're thieves. Because good people, men or women who are relatives of somebody, how were they going to do that, leaving homes completely empty? Nobody would do that, good people wouldn't do that. They shot women, men, and children, dogs. Because they don't shoot particular people, their enemies, they shoot everybody [...] How do they do that to us if we are all persons? I don't know if they are insane, drunk, they aren't normal people, because I've lived many years in Copala and nobody has ever done anything like that to their relatives. (Interview with Teresa, February 2011, Triqui region)

For Elvira, another displaced grandmother, "they are stones and very soon grass will sprout under them." For Marta, "they are the devil incarnate." Martina shared with me her belief that they were not human because "they have no heart" (the heart is a Triqui synonym for soul). Dehumanizing the enemy, due to the dehumanization that the assailants exercised on them, demonstrates the change of codes in the exercise of violence occurring in the region. The first step they took was to dehumanize the assailants as a way perhaps of humanizing themselves, to trace out new lines, while they escaped through the hills, running to avoid being hit by bullets, stripped of any semblance of dignity and humanity. To flee from the abject, filth, sordid, and impure allowed them to define an otherness in order to save oneself. Yet, for the displaced women and men, the "abject" they tried to define in their narratives had also seized control of their bodies and their surroundings.[8]

Affection, such as the ability to affect and be affected that both Clough and Halley (2007) and Navaro-Yashin (2012) analyze from the Spinozian standpoint of affection, was translated in the case of the displaced Triquis, not only in specific emotions but also in wider collective affectations that involved the human and the non-human. This included living in the ruins of a destroyed town under siege, seeking refuge in other people's homes, or grounded on the street in a sit-in, touching things that do not belong to them. These things generated a sort of normalization of abjection that materialized in their bodies, that is, skin and respiratory ailments, but above all a profound state of sadness, expressed in the Triqui language as "Ni' aj má," loss of a part of the soul. For the displaced women, an individual and collective recovery and the construction of a *communitas* far from evil meant rebuilding a sense of humanity and dignity. This wider focus of affectivity allows me to revisit the notion of *political-affective communities*, based on an analysis of shared emotions and affectations.

Final Reflections

The building of the communal/*communitas* in a history of marginality and dispossession that was part of the displaced Triquis' experience of terror involved explanations, narratives, and expressions of solidarity that were interwoven in the process of reconstructing their memory and their truth, a setting in which emotions played an important role. Yet, to speak of them creates the challenge of removing them from the limits of individuality or social entity where they were placed by academic thought, in order to revisit the emotional fabric from which pain is not only experienced and narrated but also shared by others. The insight of the so-called affective turn rethinks the analysis of affect as affection, in which the human and non-human affect individuals and connect us in different ways, based on different emotions, but which also become part of the shared fabric.

This insight of affectivity also allows me to rethink the notion of testimonial traces, insofar as it widens the notion of testimony as an individual narrative, solely that of the victim, and situates it in a framework of an interaction with several witnesses-actors. Testimony necessarily involves interaction, but so too bearing witness of the experience of those whose human ability to express their pain has been stripped from them.

Initially, many displaced women, the first to establish the sit-in in Oaxaca, were embarrassed by the fact that emotions played a part in their political actions. Their historic exclusion from the political actions in a region fighting for people's territory and autonomy led them to think that emotions could not be part of political activity, discourse, and search for justice. It was almost as if, inevitably, the emotional aspect arose uncontrollably, in spite of their efforts to frame their experience from specific subject-position formats. It was the emotional strength of pain, fear, sadness, and rejection that caused such a singular impact on those of us who approached this setting.

Affectivity and politics intersected in the women's testimonies by articulating words, but also silences and concrete actions in their search for justice. The notion of political-affective communities allowed me to understand that those emotions that went beyond the limits of the body also went beyond spatial limits and the objectives of *being there*. The narratives, performative acts, and memories of displaced men and women projected onto scenarios where traditionally they had been excluded.

Notes

1. The Triqui region is located in the northeast area of the state of Oaxaca, in the Mixtec region. Its three divisions are the Upper Triqui, centered in Chicahuaxtla, Middle Triqui, centered in Itunyoso, and the Lower Triqui, centered in San Juan Copala. The Lower Triqui has a population of around 13,000 people living in more than 30 communities.
2. The building of autonomous municipalities began in Chiapas with the armed uprising and repossession of territory launched by an indigenous movement that in 1994 coalesced into the Zapatista Army of National Liberation (EZLN). These self-defined autonomous municipalities are part of the demands of indigenous people to the right to organize following ways of governing and imparting justice decided by the people. For this reason, the autonomy movement does not recognize the official municipalities whose political and governmental administration is controlled by the state.
3. With a team of researchers and students from the Universidad Autónoma Metropolitana-Xochimilco campus, we gave a short course on autonomy to the bilingual primary schoolteachers in San Juan Copala. We also lent support to the "Voice that Breaks the Silence" community radio station, together with the CACTUS civil organization, led by Beatriz Cariño, who was murdered in San Juan Copala in April 2010.
4. Following the advent of the MULT in the early 1980s, a number of outside actors, including activists, lawyers, and others, undertook solidarity activities in the region. Many activists, coming from left-leaning movements and

organizations of victims of state repression, sympathized with the budding autonomy movement in 2006.
5. The ethnographical work occurred in two spaces. In the beginning, it focused on the voices and political acts of the women at the sit-in in the city of Oaxaca held by displaced families. I worked there continuously from August to December 2010 and sporadically during the first seven months of 2011. In 2010, I also undertook visits to displaced families in other communities in the region and then took up permanent residence in the communities from January to July 2011.
6. Fifteen testimonies in audio-visual format were gathered at the sit-in in the city of Oaxaca and from people displaced to communities surrounding Copala. Many transcribed testimonies figured in the case before the Inter-American Human Rights Commission (IAHRC) and were published in the book "A solas contra el enemigo" [Alone Against the Enemy] (2011). Marisa Villarreal and David Cilia, human rights activists, helped to gather testimonies. Meztli Yoalli Aguilera was in charge of post-production of the audio-visual material. These became important materials for purposes of denouncement and dissemination, to seek precautionary measures from the IAHRC, and for presentation to Mexico's National Human Rights Commission (CNDH). An example of the responses to the women's demands before these bodies was the granting of precautionary measures by the IAHRC and subsequent follow-up. Similarly, the CNDH issued a statement with recommendations for pertinent government offices in May 2011. Available at http://www.cndh.org.mx/sites/all/fuentes/documentos/Recomendaciones/2011/REC_2011_026.pdf. Last accessed: January 2017.
7. Jimeno explores the notion of political-affective communities (2007) and emotional communities in several articles reviewed for this chapter (2011, 2015). I am particularly interested in showing the interweaving between the political dimensions and the affections; for this reason I use the notion of political-affective communities.
8. The idea of Ruin and Abjection in the work of anthropologist Navaro-Yashin (2012) is highly suggestive in understanding how incorporating what is disgusting in daily life creates deep affective transformations in the displaced. I explored these ideas in De Marinis (2017).

References

Ahmed, Sara. 2004. *The Cultural Politics of Emotions*. London: Routledge.
Azaola, Elena. 2012. La violencia hoy, las violencias de siempre. *Desacatos 40*, September–December, pp. 13–32.

Castillejo Cuellar, Alejandro. 2009. *Archivos del dolor: ensayos sobre la violencia y el recuerdo en la Sudáfrica contemporánea.* Bogotá: Universidad de los Andes.
Clough, Patricia, and Jean Halley, eds. 2007. *The Affective Turn: Theorizing the Social.* Durham: Duke University Press.
Crosby, Alison, and Brinton Lykes. 2011. Mayan Women Survivors Speak: The Gendered Relations of Truth Telling in Postwar Guatemala. *The International Journal of Transitional Justice* 5 (3): 456–476.
Das, Veena. 1997. *Critical Events: An anthropological Perspective on Contemporary Indian.* Oxford: Oxford University Press.
De Marinis, Natalia. 2013. Indigenous Rights and Violent State Construction: The struggle of Triqui Women of Oaxaca, Mexico. In *Gender Justice and Legal Pluralities: Latin American and African Perspectives,* ed. Rachel Sieder and John-Andrew McNeish, 156–179. London: Routledge.
———. 2015. Nombrar la violencia de Estado: El testimonio como herramienta política de mujeres triquis de Oaxaca. In *Desposesión: Género, Territorios y Luchas por la Autonomía,* ed. Marisa Belausteguigotia and María Josefina Saldaña, 57–78. PUEG-UNAM: México.
———. 2017. Despojo, materialidad y afectos: la experiencia del desplazamiento forzado entre mujeres triquis. *Desacatos* 53: 98–113.
Green, Linda. 1995. Living in a State of Fear. In *Fieldwork Under Fire: Contemporary Studies of Violence and Survival,* ed. Antonius Robben and Carolynn Nordstrom, 105–127. Berkeley/Los Angeles: Columbia University Press.
Haraway, Donna. 1988. Situated Knowledges: The Science Question in Feminism and the Privilege of Partial Perspective. *Feminist Studies* 14 (3): 575–599.
Hernández Castillo, R. Aída. 2016. *Multiple Injustices: Indigenous Women, Law and Political Struggle in Latin America.* Arizona: The Arizona of University Press.
Jelin, Elizabeth. 2002. *Los trabajos de la memoria.* Buenos Aires: Siglo XXI.
Jimeno, Myriam. 2007. Cuerpo personal y cuerpo politico: violencia, cultura y ciudadanía neoliberal. *Universitas Humanísticas* 63: 15–34.
———. 2011. Después de la massacre: la memoria como conocimiento histórico. *Cuaderno de Antropología Social* 33: 39–52.
Jimeno, Myriam, Sandra Liliana Murillo, and Marco Julián Martínez, eds. 2012. *Etnografías contemporáneas: Trabajo de campo.* Bogotá: Universidad Nacional de Colombia, Centro de Estudios Sociales.
Jimeno, Myriam, Daniel Varela, and Angeles Castillo. 2015. *Después de la masacre, emociones y política en el Cauca Indio.* Bogotá: Universidad Nacional de Colombia.
Levi, Primo. 1989. *Los hundidos y los salvados.* Madrid: El Aleph Editores.
Maldonado, Salvador. 2013. Desafíos etnográficos en el estudio de la violencia Experiencia de una investigación. *Avá Revista de Antropología* 22: 123–144.

Malkki, Liisa. 1995. *Purity and Exile: Violence, Memory and National Cosmology Among Hutus Refugees in Tanzania.* Chicago: The University of Chicago Press.

Mora, Mariana. 2015. Ayotzinapa, violencia y sentido del agravio colectivo: Reflexiones para el trabajo antropológico. *Ichan Tecolotl* 25 (293): 8–10.

Navaro-Yashin, Yael. 2012. *The Make Believe Space: Affective Geography in a Postwar Polity.* Durham: Duke University Press.

Rappaport, Joanne. 2008. *Utopías interculturales. Intelectuales públicos, experimentos con la cultura y pluralismo étnico en Colombia.* Bogotá: Universidad del Rosario.

Robledo Silvestre, Carolina. 2016. Itinerarios de búsqueda ¿Estamos preparados para encontrar? *Opción* 36: 24–34. Available at http://opcion.itam.mx/?cat=807. Accessed 16 Apr 2017.

Rosaldo, Renato. 1993. *Culture and Truth: The Remarking of Social Analysis.* Boston: Beacon Press.

Scheper-Hughes, Nancy, and Philipe I. Bourgois, eds. 2004. *Violence in War and Peace: An Anthology.* Maldem: Blackwell Publishing.

Speed, Shannon. 2006. Entre la antropología y los derechos humanos. Hacia una investigación activista y comprometida críticamente. *Alteridades* 16 (31): 73–85.

Stephen, Lynn. 2017. Bearing Witness: Testimony in Latin American Anthropology and Related Fields. *The Journal of Latin American and Caribbean Anthropology* 22 (1): 85–109.

Taussig, Michael. 2003. *Law in Lawless Land. Diary of a Limpieza in Colombia.* Chicago: The University of Chicago Press.

Taylor, Diana. 2003. *The Archive and the Repertoire: Performing Cultural Memories in the Americas.* Durham: Duke University Press.

Theidon, Kimberly. 2004. *Entre prójimos: el conflicto armado interno y la política de reconciliación en Perú.* Lima: Instituto de Estudios Peruanos.

———. 2009. La teta asustada: Una teoría sobre la violencia de la memoria. *Ideele Revista del Instituto de Defensa Legal* 191: 56–63.

Turner, Víctor. 1969. *The Ritual Process: Structure and Anti-structure.* London: Routledge.

CHAPTER 8

Affective Contestations: Engaging Emotion Through the Sepur Zarco Trial

Alison Crosby, M. Brinton Lykes, and Fabienne Doiron

INTRODUCTION

We felt happy that the court allowed us in, listened to us, especially us women, because we never thought that they would grant us that right or give us that space. We thank the judges who listened to us… Then I felt calm and at the same time I cried from the effort. I remembered those of us who were sitting, watching and listening. When we rejoiced the most is when the judge issued the ruling, because we fulfilled our struggle and I felt calmer because I heard how many years the culprits were sentenced to serve in jail. Because before they were sentenced we were not calm, but when we heard it or when I heard it I felt calmer knowing that they will pay for what they did to us. (Interview with Demecia Yat, plaintiff in the Sepur Zarco case, Impunity Watch and the Alliance 2017, 46)

A. Crosby (✉)
School of Gender, Sexuality and Women's Studies,
York University, Toronto, ON, Canada

M. B. Lykes
Lynch School of Education and Center for Human Rights
and International Justice, Boston College, Boston, MA, USA

F. Doiron
Graduate Program in Gender, Feminist and Women's Studies,
York University, Toronto, ON, Canada

© The Author(s) 2018
M. Macleod, N. De Marinis (eds.), *Resisting Violence*,
https://doi.org/10.1007/978-3-319-66317-3_8

The process of documenting human rights violations is paradoxical in that violence is often represented in order for it to be resisted. But are violent representations necessary for the construction of social and legal recognition? What forms of empathetic engagement are constituted as solutions to violence, and what are the limits of such forms? ... I use the term *crisis of witnessing* to refer to the risks of representing trauma and violence, to ruptures of identification, and to the impossibility of empathetic merging between witness and testifier. (Hesford 2011, 99)

On February 26, 2016, three judges from High Risk Court "A" in Guatemala City convicted Esteelmer Francisco Reyes Girón, former second lieutenant of the Sepur Zarco military outpost, and Heriberto Valdez Asig, a former area military commissioner, of crimes against humanity in the form of sexual violence and domestic and sexual slavery, which were committed against 15 Maya Q'eqchi' women during the 1980s at the height of Guatemala's 36-year armed conflict. Reyes Girón was found guilty of the murder of Dominga Coc and her two daughters, and Valdéz Asig was convicted of the forced disappearances of seven of the plaintiffs' husbands. They were sentenced to 120 and 240 years in prison, respectively. At a reparations hearing the following week, the Guatemalan state was tasked with enacting 16 measures addressing health care, education, land, memory, and the (re)training of the military. Reyes Girón was ordered to pay Q5.5 million (US$732,700) to the plaintiffs, and Valdéz Asig was ordered to pay Q1.7 million (US$226,500) to the families of the seven men who had been disappeared.

This chapter explores the possible contributions of what Lynn Stephen (this volume), drawing on Myriam Jimeno's foundational work (2010), refers to as a "strategic emotional community," in thinking about and making meaning of the Sepur Zarco trial. Stephen argues that a strategic emotional community can be formed between direct survivors of violence and "empathetic listeners who are non-sufferers, but who are willing to act and take risks to bring tragic and horrific events to light and work to prevent their recurrence." We suggest that the Sepur Zarco trial was a performance of Q'eqchi' women's protagonism[1] emergent at the intersection of multiple strategic emotional communities that were formed among Mayan women survivors of sexual violence, and between these protagonists and the diverse set of intermediaries (Merry 2006) who have accompanied them in their long struggle for redress.

We ground this chapter within the heartfelt recognition and acknowledgement of what has been accomplished by the protagonists and those who have accompanied them, against tremendous odds, at high personal risk, and in the context of ongoing unfettered military and oligarchic power. As described by those involved in the case, "the verdict is undoubtedly a result of the resistance, resilience and courage of the Q'eqchi' women" (Impunity Watch and the Alliance 2017, 5). However, we are mindful of how the judicial realm spectacularizes sexual harm and circulations of power dispossess those historically oppressed in ways that affect survivors' subjectivity and agency, which can perhaps rupture the potentiality of a strategic emotional community. As cited above, Wendy Hesford (2011) flags the "impossibility of empathetic merging between witness and testifier" and the "crisis of witnessing" inherent to (re)presentations of violence (99). From our own positionality as white Western feminists from the settler colonial contexts of Canada and the United States, we are cognizant of how relationships between protagonists and ourselves as empathetic listeners, and our (re)presentations of the meanings we co-construct with them, are forged within the fissured landscape of ongoing colonial structures and practices.

We frame our analysis of particular affective moments during the trial within the context of our own eight-year engagement with 54 Mayan women survivors of sexual violence during Guatemala's genocidal armed conflict, including the 15 Q'eqchi' plaintiffs in the Sepur Zarco trial, and the intermediaries, that is, the Mayan and feminist activists, interpreters, lawyers, and psychologists, who have accompanied them in their search for redress. In 2009, we formed a partnership with the National Union of Guatemalan Women (UNAMG, for its Spanish name) to document and conduct research alongside these processes and, in particular, to explore what reparation meant from the standpoint of the 54 Mayan women protagonists (Crosby et al. 2016).[2]

We worked alongside UNAMG in the design of a feminist participatory action research (PAR) process through which we facilitated workshops with protagonists and intermediaries, together and separately, using creative resources such as drawing, dramatization, and "image theater" (Boal 1985), as well as beliefs and practices from the Mayan cosmovision (Grupo de Mujeres Mayas Kaqla 2014). We sought to elicit multifaceted and non-linear narratives about how Mayan women have navigated their everyday lives in their families and communities and with each other in post-genocide contexts of ongoing violence and impoverishment resistance, and contestation. From the onset protagonists made clear they were not interested in continuously retelling singular stories of sexualized harm. This was partly because they were too painful. It was also because they had other stories they wanted to tell; protagonists have continuously resisted being reduced to "the raped woman" (Buss 2009). As Mayan women they locate themselves as part of the indigenous collectivity that emphasizes autonomy and self-determination, as opposed to as Westernized subjects of individuated rights (Grupo de Mujeres Mayas Kaqla 2014; Eng 2011).

We begin by situating ourselves as researchers to "probe how we are in relation with the contexts we study and with our informants" (Fine 1994, 72). We then turn to the protagonists, situating the 15 Sepur Zarco plaintiffs vis-à-vis the larger group of 54, and include some of the relevant antecedents to the trial. We identify multiple hypothesized strategic emotional communities performed through protagonists' relationships to intermediaries, and interrogate some of the potential risks attendant to them. We center our analysis of the trial on the (dis)ruptures in "ocular epistemology" (Hesford 2011, 29), that is, "seeing is believing," that occurred in the courtroom space, through the plaintiffs' decision to conceal their identities and not testify live, and as such resist the spectacle. We explore the multiple mediations of relationality that occur in judicial space, through the continued translation, interpretation, and (re)presentation by judges, lawyers, expert witnesses, and audiences of indigenous women's experiences of violence into the language of the hegemon. We conclude with a brief reflection on Gloria Andalzúa's concept of *nos-otras* as a way to think through relations of empathetic engagement within not outside of colonized time and space.

SITUATING OURSELVES: INTERMEDIARY RESEARCHER REFLEXIVITY

> Self and Other are knottily entangled. ... Despite denials, qualitative researchers are always implicated at the hyphen. When we opt... simply to write *about* those who have been Othered, we deny the hyphen. ... By *working the hyphen*, I mean to suggest that researchers probe how we are in relation with the contexts we study and with our informants.... Working the hyphen means creating occasions for researchers and informants to discuss what is, and is not, "happening between." (Fine 1994, 72; emphasis in original)

As suggested in the introduction to this volume, each chapter takes up ways in which emotions and affect inform, facilitate, and constrain the relationships among multiply positioned women and men struggling for a better world, including those activist scholars like ourselves who accompany

Mayan protagonists' meaning making and knowledge construction "from the bottom up." We recognize and identify the researcher's positionality as integral to the co-construction of knowledge(s) performed through iterative action-reflection processes through which we understood Mayan, *mestiza*, and *ladina* protagonism in the search for redress in post-genocidal Guatemala. Feminist action research is constructivist and participatory, generating, interpreting, and reporting multiple creative processes that facilitate the constitution of "data" and are the basis for new knowledge(s). Although regularly noted by action researchers who have embraced the interpretivist turn in social scientific research, relatively few research reports discuss researchers' reflexivity, including their positionalities and performances as co-constructors of knowledge. Leeat Granek (2013), extending the work of Michelle Fine cited above, urges researchers to engage an "epistemology of the hyphen," that is, a recognition of the ways in which the researcher-participant is not a hyphenated dichotomous positionality but rather reflects intersubjectivity, wherein "Self and Other are not on opposite ends of the pulsing line, but ... in a constant process of co-creating each other in the research dynamic, and therefore, are fundamentally dependent on one another" (180). Such positioning acknowledges that all knowing is dialogical (Crosby and Lykes forthcoming), while making explicit the all too often unspoken power of the intermediary in naming the experiences of those whose stories she seeks to narrate or (re)present. Granek (2013) identifies a second set of relationships between the researcher and the audience, one to which we return below vis-à-vis the multiple audiences engaged in and through the Sepur Zarco trial. She characterizes this intersubjective relationship as "a different type of line or hyphen [that is] co-created, one that moves from the researcher/researched dynamic into the researcher/audience realm, but that carries with it all the assumptions of interconnection, intersubjectivity, and mutual vulnerability, empathy, and care that characterize the self/other relationship in qualitative research" (Granek 2013, 151).

Shaw (2010) argues that reflexivity is a methodological resource through which she as a researcher "proactively manage[s] my self in my interactions with my participants and the world and to actively explore how these encounters impact my pre-existing beliefs and knowledge—my fore-understandings—in order to understand afresh the phenomenon I am studying" (241). It is critical that researcher reflexivity not become the center, sustaining and reproducing researcher fore-knowledge rather than the knowledge(s) of participants co-constructed at and through the relational hyphen described above. Thus, Shaw (2010) cautions that these reflexive efforts not inadvertently displace the participants', or in our case the protagonists', narrative, which is perhaps more likely in unconscious performances of researcher power. The hypothesis here—that is, that dialogic knowledge(s) constructed within these accompaniment processes are embodied and performed through affective and emotional processes—further complexifies possible circulations of power that displace or reframe rather than center protagonists' experiences. Thus, we note where we are situated at the intersection of gender, "race," social class, nationality, language, and education, which are some of the identities and positionalities through which power circulates in our partnerships and which risk, despite or perhaps because of these strategic emotional communities, reproducing the colonial and hegemonic power relationships that we seek to critique and redress.

Each of us has worked as an intermediary with indigenous communities in Guatemala and beyond. Yet we are each "outsiders" not only to their lived realities as indigenous women but also to the particularities of the experiences of the 54 Mayan women protagonists who survived racialized gendered violence during Guatemala's armed conflict. Alison Crosby is white, upper middle class, Scottish and Canadian, trained as a sociologist in the UK and Canada. She has been engaged as a researcher and activist in Guatemala since the early 1990s. Before taking up an academic position in 2007, she worked for six years for the Canadian social justice organization Inter Pares, accompanying social movements in Latin America, including the initial work with the 54 Mayan women protagonists in Guatemala that began in 2003. Brinton Lykes is a white, upper middle class Unitedstatesian born, and raised in New Orleans, Louisiana. She studied in Paris during the 1968 student movement and completed a MDiv degree in liberation theology prior to completing a PhD in community-cultural psychology. She is an activist scholar who has drawn on the creative arts and local beliefs and practices in accompaniment of Mayan women and children in the rural town and villages of Chajul, El Quiché, Guatemala and in refuge in Mexico and the United States since the early 1980s. Fabienne Doiron is a white, upper middle class Canadian whose interdisciplinary graduate work has focused on gender and post-conflict issues in Guatemala. Her continued involvement in and understanding of social justice struggles have been shaped since 2005 by her participation in the Maritimes-Guatemala Breaking the Silence Network, which has worked with grassroots groups in Guatemala based on relationships of mutuality and solidarity since 1988. She is currently completing her PhD dissertation on femi(ni)cide and gendered and racialized violence in Guatemala. We are all Spanish speakers, although Spanish is a second or third language for each of us and none of us dominate any of the Mayan languages. As privileged people who are white and from the north, we benefit from the legacies of colonialism that permeate the social fabric of Guatemala and the dynamics of racism that oppress and marginalize indigenous populations from many social and political spaces. Moreover, we are citizens of countries that were deeply implicated in Guatemala's genocidal violence and/or have controlling economic interests in the extractive industries that continue to push Mayan communities off their ancestral lands and perpetuate gendered racialized violence (Solano 2013). These shared and not so shared intersectional identities and circulations of power informed, facilitated, constrained, and also contributed to disruptions within the hypothesized strategic emotional communities discussed in this chapter.

BUILDING A STRATEGIC EMOTIONAL COMMUNITY AROUND SEXUAL HARM

In the wake of the finalization of the peace accords in 1996 after 36 years of devastating armed conflict, the report released by the UN-sponsored Historical Clarification Commission (CEH) in 1999 found that during the war over 200,000 people were killed, over 45,000 people were disappeared, and 1.5 million people were internally displaced, with another 150,000 having to flee the country (CEH 1999). The violence was directed in particular against the indigenous population, with 626 massacres occurring in rural Mayan communities. The CEH found that at the height of the counterinsurgency scorched earth policies of the early 1980s during the Ríos Montt regime, genocide was committed against specific Mayan groups. Violence was gendered and sexualized as well as racialized and classed, with poor rural Mayan women the targets of sexual harm; the CEH concluded that sexual violence was used as a weapon of genocide.

The CEH report identified 1465 cases of sexual violence, and 88.7% of the victims were Mayan women (CEH 1999, Volume 3, 23). The report acknowledged that these cases were just a fraction of what was known to have been a widespread and systematic occurrence. In 2003, 54 Mayan women who had experienced sexual violence during the war came together in mutual support groups, accompanied by the Actors for Change Consortium (heretofore, "the Consortium"), which was comprised of two organizations, UNAMG and the Community Studies and Psychosocial Action Team (ECAP), and several independent feminist activists. The 54 Mayan protagonists came from three different regions of the country: 21 Q'eqchi' women from Alta Verapaz (who included the 15 protagonists in what would become the Sepur Zarco case), 14 Kaqchikel women from Chimaltenango, and 7 Mam, 6 Chuj, and 6 returnee women (who were in refuge in Mexico during the war, and do not identify by ethnic group) from Huehuetenango. Most had not yet formally "told" their families, friends, and neighbors what had happened to them; they were sometimes referred to by community members as "the soldiers' wives," and the perpetrators often still lived in their communities or in the surrounding areas (Fulchiron et al. 2009). Protagonists' experiences of sexual and other forms of violence during the war, as well as their strategies of everyday resistance and struggle, were multifaceted and context specific, according to the particularities of the war in their region. As such the meaning and significance of harm, its effects, and impact is not fixed or homogeneous.

Violence is of course deeply embodied (Taylor 2003), and as such, workshops facilitated by the Consortium with protagonists between 2003 and 2008 engaged the body and the emotions held within, which complemented the more orally based psychosocial support groups that were also organized (Fulchiron et al. 2009). Techniques such as massage and dance were used to develop trust among protagonists and help them become more comfortable with each other's bodies and with their own. Fulchiron et al. (2009) suggest that the women were slow to embrace these embodied approaches, and interpreters and Mayan healers who accompanied them sought to respect their hesitancies while adopting multiple strategies that would introduce them to the embodied pain they carried within them.

In one workshop we facilitated in June 2013, participants reflected on their experiences of coming together in the participatory processes facilitated by intermediaries over several years. One protagonist noted that: "Now we feel happy. Before we were ashamed to give opinions and talk but not now." Others described the relationships of trust that they had built among themselves as women in their communities: "It is necessary to give support to other women. I am not going to stay with my arms crossed if I see another woman's suffering." They experienced this affective relationship as dialogical, "when other women help, it makes us happy." Thus, despite many differences, including ethno-linguistic (often having to communicate with one another through several interpreters), experiences of internal or external exile during and after the armed conflict, returning to their communities of origin or being forced to resettle on often non-productive land, and/or receiving a single or multiple reparation payments, they offered and received accompaniment of mutuality. They spoke about and heard from each other that they were not alone in having experienced sexual violence or the loss of husband, children, animals, and home. As one Kaqchikel protagonist stated, looking back on her participation in the workshops facilitated by multiple intermediaries, including ourselves,

> When I went there my problems were still guarded in my heart. I didn't trust enough to tell my stories from the war; we each had different problems. But when I started talking in the group I saw I was not alone, not the only one. … It was in these workshops that I have come to understand that I am a woman. I have rights, that after everything, my life can recover.

What became clear to us as the feminist PAR progressed was the importance of protagonists' relationships with one another as direct survivors, discovering that what had happened to them had happened to many other indigenous women in other parts of the country, that it was not their fault, and that the state was responsible. We suggest that this represents the first of what we argue are multiple intersecting strategic emotional communities or what we have referred to elsewhere as a "community of women" among Mayan protagonists (Lykes and Crosby 2015).

These workshops and broader organizational processes also created spaces wherein protagonists and intermediaries came together, establishing what Patricia Maguire (1987) refers to as "just enough trust," and facilitating affective relationships that reflect "outsiders'" accompaniment of protagonists in their struggles for justice and redress for harm suffered. The iterative action-reflection processes of feminist PAR facilitated opportunities through which intermediaries participated within and across their professional identities, (re)presenting their individual and shared imaginaries of hegemonic masculinities, sexual violence, truth-seeking and reparations, and the meaning of justice, among other issues (Crosby and Lykes forthcoming). Within and across these experiences protagonists critically interrogated and engaged in dialogic reflections about intermediaries' creative representations and vice versa, forming what we hypothesize here to be a second strategic emotional community, one built through varying experiences of trust among intermediaries and between intermediaries and protagonists.

Indigenous scholars have critiqued the tendency of outsider researchers such as ourselves to pathologize harm as the singular experience of indigeneity, and instead urge the centering of resilience, survivance (Vizenor 2008), desire, "the hope, the visions, the wisdom of lived lives and communities" (Tuck 2009, 417). These critical insights are particularly significant when working in the aftermath of genocidal violence, wherein the mechanisms of transitional justice rely heavily on testimonies of harm. Feminist PAR facilitated multiple relational processes toward constructing dialogic understanding through which protagonists talked not only about their pain and "carrying the heavy load" of impoverishment, which they identified as a key aspect of "violence against women" (Crosby et al. 2016), but also about a wider range of emotions, including loss and grief, anger at perpetrators, and indignation at the duplicity and complicity of the Guatemalan state in harm suffered and responses therein. We also heard continuous assertions of agency, resilience, hope, and liberation. As a Chuj protagonist told us as she described her emotional journey, "[I am] old, without suffering, without fear and without shame. Today I am capable of doing all that I can. I am like a bird. I can fly with large wings."

Yet, as Hesford (2011) argues, relationships of identification between direct survivors and empathetic listeners are continuously ruptured within processes that seek to document human rights violations. As such, these relationships are necessarily and inherently troubled, and, as suggested above in our own reflexive self-positionings, are shaped by the very structures and conditions of violence that caused the harm in the first place. The struggles for gender justice and redress in which we were individually and collectively engaged are also structured by and through broader international rights regimes, which are themselves informed by "Western subjectivity and conceptions of the human" (Eng 2011, 580). While the participatory accompaniment processes described herein sought to disrupt the authorial privilege of asking protagonists to (re)tell narratives of pain and trauma, judicial prosecutions and reparations programs in which these same intermediaries accompanied the protagonists rely upon these narratives. This is the dilemma Hesford (2011) refers to when she talks about the "crisis of witnessing" brought about by the imperative within the human rights paradigm to (re)present violence in order to stop it. Such (re) representations, including those facilitated through feminist PAR, come up against the impossibility of ever being able to know the pain of others (Das 2007); and, when violations are rooted in colonial oppression, the assumption that one can is a colonial act in and of itself; the self once again asserted at the expense of the other; the pain is really *mine* (Hartman 1997).

"Gender" itself as a universalized point of identification among women, and the assumption that all women are equally vulnerable to rape (Brownmiller 1986), has also been critiqued for its tendency to occlude—and at the same time center—colonial privilege and the implication of white Western women therein, at the expense, erasure, and objectification of indigenous, black, and other ways of knowing and being (Jaleel 2013).

The legal domain has a particular capacity to spectacularize sexual harm and produce racialized gendered abjection or the figure of "the raped woman" for the consumption of predominantly white Western audiences (Kapur 2002). And as Nicola Henry (2009) argues in her analysis of international war crimes trials, "rape is an identity-producing practice. Subjectivity is often contingent on narratives of injury and victimization" (131). But Henry (2009) also cautions us against assuming that women are acted upon within judicial processes; rather, they act intentionally as agents and are resilient. In our analysis of the emotional and affective components of the Sepur Zarco trial, we are challenged to refuse binary readings of judicial processes as "good" or "bad," but instead to explore the multiple hyphens of relationality; that is, the complexities emergent within and among direct survivors, empathetic listeners and intermediaries, and broader audiences. Our analyses of the hyphenated relationships emergent in the multiple strategic emotional communities performed in and through the Sepur Zarco trial draw on our own field notes from the trial, as well as a report analyzing the trial and its impact recently produced by the Alliance in coordination with the international organization Impunity Watch (Impunity Watch and the Alliance 2017).

JUDICIALIZING SEXUAL HARM: THE SEPUR ZARCO TRIAL

In 2008, when the Consortium came to an end, UNAMG and ECAP began working with the group of feminist lawyers Women Transforming the World (MTM) on a multifaceted strategy to support protagonists' struggles for reparations and justice, and hence the Alliance to Break the Silence and Impunity (heretofore "the Alliance") was born. To lay the groundwork for a potential legal case, in 2010 the Alliance organized a Tribunal of Conscience for Women Survivors of Sexual Violence, during which seven protagonists testified about their experiences to an international panel of honorary judges and over 800 Guatemalan and international audience members (Crosby and Lykes 2011). In the follow-up to the Tribunal, 15 Q'eqchi' women from Sepur Zarco decided to participate in a legal case. These women had been subjected to systematic sexual violence and forced labor at the Sepur Zarco outpost following the kidnapping, torture, and disappearances of their husbands, who had been involved in a struggle for the legalization of their lands. The Alliance accompanied the Q'eqchi' women in preparation of the case, providing psychosocial and legal support, and acted as joint prosecutor during the trial, which took place in Guatemala City in February 2016 (Fig. 8.1).

Fig. 8.1 Alliance to Break the Silence and Impunity banner: "Justice for sexual violence and sexual slavery." March commemorating the International Day for the Elimination of Violence against Women, Guatemala City, November 25, 2014. Photograph by Lisa Pauline Rankin

The four weeks of trial proceedings included the video testimonies by the 15 women plaintiffs from a 2012 preliminary hearing (so they would not have to re-testify), 28 witness testimonies, and 18 expert witness reports (historical, medical, psychiatric, psychosocial, forensic, cultural, linguistic, among others), and with eight witnesses for the defense (out of an original 48 who were supposed to be called to testify). In reading the ruling that found the perpetrators guilty, presiding judge Barrios outlined the violence the women had suffered, drawing extensively on the testimonies from witnesses and experts, explaining the evidence that showed that the accused had command responsibility for the violence perpetrated, and emphasizing the women's innocence. She stated that, "the judges of this tribunal firmly believe the testimonies of the women who were sexually violated in Sepur Zarco."

As the quote at the beginning of the chapter from one of the plaintiffs, Demecia Yat, emphasized, protagonists were happy that they had been heard by the court system. Being heard, and most importantly, being believed and having their truths affirmed, was reflected in their multiple affective statements about their engagement in the judicial process; as another plaintiff put it, "I feel happy because we are telling the truth, we are not lying. We suffered" (Impunity Watch and the Alliance 2017, 20). The presence and successful prosecution of the perpetrators instilled a sense of calm and relief. These affective responses to the trial remind us again of the relationality of these processes; the importance of protagonists' engagement with their interlocutors, the relationship between survivors and witnesses, and between survivors and other intermediaries and audiences, the form and content of which we unpack in more detail in the following section.

SEEING IS BELIEVING? AFFECTIVE DISRUPTIONS

As they had done in the 2010 Tribunal of Conscience and the 2012 preliminary hearing, the plaintiffs concealed their identities during the trial, using colorful shawls. Their disruption of "ocular epistemology" (Hesford 2011, 29) provoked an interesting array of emotional responses—most commonly, disbelief and discomfort—from the diverse sets of audiences for this trial. Within some feminist circles who constituted one of the strategic emotional communities described above and were audience members in the 2010 Tribunal and in the trial, the concealing of identity signified an inability to overcome victimhood, and indeed, a succumbing to "a judicial system that needs victims instead of people. The more beaten, weak, and vulnerable you appear to the judges, the better" (Hernandez 2016, as cited in Impunity Watch and the Alliance 2017, 48; see also Crosby and Lykes 2011). Audience responses—both positive and negative—are an example of the "crisis in witnessing" and ruptures in identification within human rights documentation processes that Hesford points to. The plaintiffs themselves highlighted this rupture, and the impossibility of "empathetic merging" between survivor and audience. Their experience, and their agency, can never be ours and can never be fully understood. As Demecia Yat stated:

> One of the reasons for using the shawl, for covering our faces, is for our safety. When we arrive back in our community, we do not know who will be there around us. When we are here in the city, we know that the organizations are here, supporting us. But when we get back home, the organizations are not there. We will be alone in our houses. We come from the communities, and I have the right to decide whether to cover my face. (Impunity Watch and the Alliance 2017, 33)

As mentioned above, the plaintiffs did not testify live; their video testimonies from 2012 were used as evidence in the trial instead, as a way to avoid them having to retell yet again these narratives of harm and violence. Such a strategy subverts the spectacle of the racialized gendered other providing stories of pain for the pleasure of an audience whose selfhood becomes affirmed in these (re)presentations of the "ghastly and the terrible" (Hartman 1997, 7). However, the use of video testimonies can also have a distancing and flattening effect on the audience; appearing on a screen, they can seem less "real" than the embodied victims sitting in the courtroom. And it meant that those who did testify live—the eye witnesses and the expert witnesses as well as the lawyers themselves—took center stage, as interlocutors between the plaintiffs and audience.

The courtroom dynamic and hierarchy only served to exacerbate this flattening and decentering of the 15 women plaintiffs' voices. Since procedural rules require "live" testimony to be prioritized and heard ahead of other forms of evidence, the women's video testimonies were heard separately and at seemingly random times; that is, when witnesses who had been scheduled to appear did not show, or when the court otherwise had time to fill. The trial therefore opened with testimony from a number of Q'eqchi' men who had been forced to work at the Sepur Zarco outpost where they had witnessed some of the violations at issue in the trial at the same time as they themselves suffered abuses. Listening to the testimonies of Q'eqchi' men about their experiences of gendered racialized violence at Sepur Zarco and other military outposts in the region challenged the association of victimhood with femininity, and the feminization of emotion, although it is also important to emphasize that indigenous and racialized bodies are often feminized and read as "emotional" regardless of gender (Ahmed 2015). Like many of the eye witnesses—most of whom were men—they were testifying for the first time in public space about their experiences of violence and harm, and these testimonies were emotionally embodied. As Fabienne described in her field notes from the first day of the trial (February 1, 2016), with one witness,

> it almost seemed like he was about to burst. His body mimicked his rising and falling voice, his hands moving up and coming into a half standing, crouching position over his chair before sitting back down. At one point, while he was talking about being taken to the military camp, he stood up and lifted his shirt almost over his head, energetically pointing to different places on his chest, showing the scars of where he had been beaten and had his bones broken, not pausing to let the interpreter translate. When asked if he could identify "Don Canche" (Valdez Asig), he stared him down, he seemed to be telling him off.

Sitting in the courtroom, Fabienne noted that the emotion and agitation with which this witness recounted the violence he experienced several decades before stood in stark contrast to the "flattened" (re)presentation of the 15 women plaintiffs' testimony, projected on the courtroom wall above the heads of the judges. While the plaintiffs were in fact present in the courtroom, sitting behind the prosecution lawyers, their presence was silent and veiled.

Even before all of the plaintiffs' video declarations had been heard, the court started listening to the mediation and verification of these testimonies by the 18 expert witnesses. While many of the expert witnesses had interviewed the plaintiffs in preparing their reports, a few had had long-standing relationships with them as intermediaries in the context of the Alliance's work, namely the psychologist Mónica Pinzón who had worked for ECAP for many years, and the Maya K'iche' anthropologist Irma Alicia Velásquez Nimatuj who had accompanied the work of the Alliance for several years, including participating in the 2010 Tribunal of Conscience. As such, these expert witnesses' reports were framed within relationships built over time with protagonists, and in some ways, the strategic emotional community that they had formed with these women was reflected in their reports at the same time as it was ruptured by the courtroom hierarchy.

In her expert witness report, Velásquez (2016) discussed the plaintiffs' relationships to their disappeared husbands, as mediated through her reporting of the interviews she had with them in Sepur Zarco. She discussed the vivid dreams that most of the Q'eqchi' plaintiffs reported having in which their lost husbands appeared to them "as if he were alive" (31) and engaged in conversation with them. In their interviews, Velásquez and the protagonists co-constructed socio-emotional meanings through which protagonists were able to verbalize these losses and their multiple emotional and physical responses to the absent-presence of their life partners. This strategic emotional community was developed through Velásquez' visits with the women in their communities but had to be reframed due to the demands of the judicialization process which required a public performance before the court and the multiple audiences who observed, thus rupturing the intimacy through which the knowledge(s) presented had been co-constructed.

In the context of the courtroom hierarchy, expert witnesses play a role of translation and validation: they are expected to apply their professional training and knowledge in their particular area of expertise to the task of interpreting the witnesses' testimonies and other evidence for the court. They are given, in a sense, the power to pronounce whether plaintiffs' experiences are in fact "true." While many expert witnesses, including those participating in the Sepur Zarco trial, understand their role as advocates and intermediaries, and are sometimes able to "disrupt," as Stephen (2017) argues, dominant and prejudicial constructions of "race"/ethnicity or gender, for instance, it remains that "in this frame, the 'story,' 'declaration,' or 'affidavit' of the defendant is not necessarily validated on its own terms—either for the specific life experience or information it contains, or for the system of knowledge it represents" (100). Indeed, in field notes written during the trial, Fabienne reflected on the fact that the evidence being presented was very much "for the court"—a story shaped by and for that space—leading us to wonder what effect this performance of expertise has on the plaintiffs themselves, to have so many other people present themselves as "experts" on their pain and suffering, and discussing this in often inaccessible language. As Fabienne commented at the time, this felt especially intense when the forensic psychiatrist expert witness, Karen Peña Juárez, testified that the women would never recover from some of the harms caused by the violence they experienced and that this harm was "permanent." She was giving this testimony in front of the plaintiffs, but in Spanish, so it was not at all clear that they heard or understood what she had said. Relief that they might not have heard this prognosis was accompanied by outrage that the audience or public might have more information about the protagonists' health than they themselves had. This particular moment, as well as the lack of interpretation both for the plaintiffs and for other indigenous audience members throughout the trial, highlighted the divides within the audience itself in terms of who had access to what knowledge or understanding of the judicial process.

Rights-based frameworks of trials have immediate effects and affects for indigenous victims, and are but one component of the broader systemic process of (Westernized) judicialization of indigenous life. Indigenous communities that have been violated and ruptured must then be rescued and "healed" (Million 2013) from the effects of these violations by the very colonial regime responsible, a process that erases (or assimilates) indigeneity itself. And "gender" becomes integral to the narrative of colonial rescue (Ahmed 2000). We were struck by the predominant representation of the Sepur Zarco trial as a struggle for gender justice but not indigenous justice, despite the fact that the plaintiffs themselves locate their experience within collective histories of dispossession as indigenous people. Indeed, although the joint prosecutors made concerted efforts throughout the trial to highlight how land theft was central to the harm experienced, indigeneity, racism, and continuing colonization were continuously erased from analyses of the trial and audience responses. For example, the media analysis below that claims protagonists as "the strong ones" does not name the colonial landscape that produces dispossession and privilege:

> Their colourful shawls, like beautiful flowers, accompanied them in demanding an acknowledgement that this should never happen to anyone, ever, to ensure that these crimes will not remain in impunity. They are the strong ones, and we, the broken and fragile Guatemala that still has not figured out how to look at itself and recognize itself, to accept itself and begin to heal... They have bequeathed to us dignity instead of silence. (Cosenza, March 1, 2016; as cited in Impunity Watch and the Alliance 2017, 49)

This is further emphasized in the statement from Nobel Laureate Jody Williams, an attendee at the trial, on behalf of the Nobel Women's Initiative: "These 15 women bravely told their stories to ensure that future generations of Guatemalans will have access to justice... Around the world, women are watching because wars are still being fought on women's bodies. This case is an important step in ending the nearly complete impunity for such horrible crimes" (Impunity Watch and the Alliance 2017, 50).

As the transnational audience for these public performances of harm, we are not required to engage with indigenous ways of knowing and being—or of emotion and embodiment. The Western language of affect and emotion and the hypothesized strategic emotional communities between protagonists and multiple audiences privilege and are constructed through eliciting individuated stories of pain and trauma—as well as resistance or resilience—over collective ones that emphasize an integration between the land and its peoples and point to structural dispossession and impoverishment as "violence against women." As discussed earlier in this chapter, the initial work with protagonists that began in 2003 took place outside of their local indigenous communities—a "community of women" was forged instead. However, the trial has also opened up the space for strengthening local relationships within the Sepur Zarco community and its surrounding areas.

The plaintiffs formed their own organization, Jalok U (which means "transformation" or "change" in Q'eqchi'), to act as a joint prosecutor in the case (represented by their own lawyer in court) alongside UNAMG and MTM, and which now has a membership of over 70 women and men, who together are working to ensure community-based reparations in the aftermath of the trial. During the trial, a network of 41 relatives of the plaintiffs (mostly sons and daughters), "created through emotional and family bonds," was formed as a primary security network (Impunity Watch and the Alliance 2017, 26). The plaintiffs and the Alliance also worked with community authorities, other women survivors in the region as well as in other parts of the country, and young people, to build a broader community of support for the trial and its aftermath. The community of Sepur Zarco welcomed the plaintiffs back after the trial with a community festival, and held another one a year later. Demecia Yat described the response of other women who had also survived violence, "how great that you are all organized, how great that you had the strength to go and ask for justice, how great that those men are in jail now" (Impunity Watch and the Alliance 2017, 29). Young people are using theater as a means to raise awareness and support within the community for the issue of sexual violence. The greatest desire on the part of protagonists, and motivation in their community work, is "that their daughters, granddaughters, and other women in their families and communities never have to experience what they suffered" (ibid.). Thus, the Q'eqchi' plaintiffs who had developed a strategic emotional community of women with the other Mayan protagonists have now created a geographically local strategic emotional community with the men, women, youth, and children of Sepur Zarco and the surrounding villages.

Decolonizing Emotion: Toward Nos-otras

> Human rights testimonies… risk voyeurism and commodification, and I do not want to minimize those risks. However, the "you" to whom the human rights testimonies are addressed also opens up the possibility of alternative forms of listening, witnessing, and "unforeseen memory"… Human rights testimonies ask us to consider, as Roger Simon puts it in another context, "how and why it would matter if accounts of systematic violence and its legacies were part of [our] memorial landscapes?" We might view this embodiment as an instantiation of the intersubjectivity of memory and witnessing. (Hesford 2011, 122)

As Hesford suggests, processes of listening to and, in her words, witnessing, protagonists' narratives of social suffering and their performances of joy, relief, and connection with one another have generated opportunities for co-constructing knowledge(s) "from the bottom up" as well as multiple opportunities for intersubjective "being-in-the-world." Gloria

Anzaldúa wrote extensively about life at/on/in the multiple borders that she inhabited, from her birth along the US-Mexican border through her death as a distinguished author who embraced multiple subjectivities and positioned herself at their interstices, rejecting the many ways in which she was racialized and linguistically, socially, and heterosexistly marginalized in the multiple homophobic and hegemonic male colonial spaces she occupied as poet, author, Chicana, lesbian. We draw on her idea of *nos-otras* through which she explored the possibilities of reconfiguring the bridge that she initially characterized as the back across which many liberal white feminists walked (Moraga and Anzaldúa 1981) toward reconfiguring the relationships within and across multiple differences and marginalizing borders as possible spaces wherein "home" can be constructed (Anzaldúa and Keating 2002). Widely read for her contributions to decolonizing knowledge generated by Western feminist scholars, she developed an understanding of *mestizaje* that sought to structure the multiple "hybridities" of those who position ourselves or are positioned at the interstices of circulations of power that privilege and marginalize. Her hyphenization of the Spanish-language term *nosotras* wrote into being the possibilities of those separated by chasms of privilege and power coming together toward taking actions for change. As white northern activist scholars, we who have all too frequently positioned "others" invert her construction to recognize that indigenous scholars and knowledge producers have repositioned us as *otras*. And through the activities and actions alongside *ladina*, *mestiza*, and Mayan protagonists described herein, we affirm the possibilities of a strategic emotional community—always in flux and "in formation" and always contested—through which we seek a more just and equitable world.

On Thursday March 10, 2016, in the immediate aftermath of the Sepur Zarco trial, Brinton was reminded of the ways in which the community of women established among the 54 women stretched to include other Mayan protagonists and intermediaries, including ourselves. The Alliance and the Center for Legal Action in Human Rights (CALDH) hosted an event in Guatemala City to celebrate the protagonism of the 15 Q'eqchi' women from Sepur Zarco. As Brinton approached the lawn on which people had gathered, she saw many of the 54 Mayan protagonists whose struggles we had been accompanying and many of the intermediaries from the Alliance. Her eyes were drawn immediately to several Mayan protagonists who knelt on the grass with paintbrushes in hands, developing a mural to celebrate their victory, representing themselves through the familiar floral images and as birds in flight. As she stood observing, one of the Chuj women from Huehuetenango, who had accompanied the Q'eqchi' plaintiffs throughout the trial, came over to her and began to hug her. She was brimming with smiles and just kept patting Brinton on her chest, caressing her heart with a gesture filled with joy, acknowledging that they had walked together. It reminded Brinton of the multiple gatherings we had shared, of how the participants' ways of greeting us as intermediaries had changed over time. The embrace replaced the more traditional Mayan woman's outstretched arm that grazes that of the newcomer to her community. Brinton had previously experienced the rupture of this formalism with the Maya Ixil and K'iche' women with whom she worked in Chajul, a familiarity and familialism that extended beyond those in the organization to the wider circles of women and children who recognized her after so many years of comings and goings in the town. That said, it did not extend to many of the rural villages that she knew less well and had only visited intermittently. Thus she recalled being surprised by the relative speed with which she, Alison, and Fabienne had been "accepted into" the circle of those whose bodies were allowed to touch through an embrace, converting the distance of barely touching arms-length greeting to something much more familiar, an embrace that intimated friendship. But the woman's tapping of Brinton's heart was something Brinton had never before experienced; a gentle embrace, a recognition, a sense of gratitude that traveled between. Brinton was grateful to have shared in a very small part of the long journey that these brave women had initiated together; she experienced this one among the 54 to be enveloping her, bringing her into a celebration of the collectivity of women and men that included, among the many other Maya present, the rural Maya Q'eqchi' of the Sepur Zarco trial and a white Unitedstatesian researcher. They stood together for what felt like 15 minutes until someone who had been trying to pull the disparate subgroups of people apart to initiate the proceedings for the evening succeeded in separating them. This moment of celebration and affirmation filled with emotion and affect does not, of course, negate the multiple contestations and (dis)ruptures in identification described in this chapter. However, it is a glimmer of living into the possibilities of intersubjectively positioning in/as *otras* toward an activist construction of hyphenated community and an embodied performance of *nos-otras*.

NOTES

1. We use the concept of protagonism "to deconstruct dominant psychological discourses of women as 'victims,' 'survivors,' 'selves,' 'individuals,' and/or "subjects." Mayan women are actively engaged in constructivist and discursive performances through which they are narrating new, mobile meanings of 'Mayan woman,' repositioning themselves at the interstices of multiple communities. The term represents person-in-context, invoking the Greek chorus within theater or the 'call-response' within African American church contexts, that is, situating Mayan women dialectically vis-à-vis accompaniers and/or women's community whose empathy is dialogically constitutive of them, that is, of the protagonist" (Lykes and Crosby 2015, 147).
2. This research project was initially approved by York University's Ethics Review Board (May 6, 2009) and the Boston College Institutional Review Board (May 15, 2009), and renewed every year thereafter through 2017. The research was funded by the Social Sciences and Humanities Research Council of Canada (SSHRC), the International Development Research Centre (IDRC), the Faculty of Liberal Arts and Professional Studies at York University, and an Anonymous Grant to the Center for Human Rights and International Justice at Boston College.

REFERENCES

Ahmed, Sara. 2000. *Strange Encounters: Embodied Others in Post-Coloniality*. New York/London: Routledge.

———. 2015. *The Cultural Politics of Emotion*. 2nd ed. New York/London: Routledge.

Anzaldúa, Gloria, and AnaLouise Keating, eds. 2002. *This Bridge We Call Home: Radical Visions for Transformation*. New York: Routledge.

Boal, Augusto. 1985. *Theater of the Oppressed*. Trans. Charles A. McBride and Maria-Odilia Leal-McBride. New York: Theatre Communications Group.

Brownmiller, Susan. 1986. *Against Our Will*. Toronto: Bantam Books.

Buss, Doris. 2009. Rethinking 'Rape as a Weapon of War'. *Feminist Legal Studies* 17 (2): 145–163. https://doi.org/10.1007/s10691-009-9118-5.

CEH (Comisión para el Esclarecimiento Histórico). 1999. *Guatemala: Memory of Silence Tz'inil Na'tab'al*. Guatemala: Guatemala. Retrieved from https://www.aaas.org/sites/default/files/migrate/uploads/mos_en.pdf

Crosby, Alison, and M. Brinton Lykes. 2011. Mayan Women Survivors Speak: The Gendered Relations of Truth-Telling in Postwar Guatemala. *International Journal of Transitional Justice* 5 (3): 456–476. https://doi.org/10.1093/ijtj/ijr017.

———. forthcoming. *Mapping Mayan Women's Protagonism: Accompanying Transitional Justice Processes in Post Genocide Guatemala*. Co-authored Book Manuscript, Under Review.

Crosby, Alison, M. Brinton Lykes, and Brisna Caxaj. 2016. Carrying a Heavy Load: Mayan Women's Understandings of Reparation in the Aftermath of Genocide. *Journal of Genocide Research* 18 (2–3): 265–283. https://doi.org/10.1080/14623528.2016.1186952.

Das, Veena. 2007. *Life and Words: Violence and the Descent into the Ordinary*. Berkeley: University of California Press.

Eng, David L. 2011. Reparations and the Human. *Columbia Journal of Gender and Law* 21 (2): 561–583.

Fine, Michelle. 1994. Working the Hyphens: Reinventing Self and Other in Qualitative Research. In *Handbook of Qualitative Research*, ed. Norman K. Denzin and Yvonna S. Lincoln, 70–82. London: Sage.

Fulchiron, Amandine, Olga Alicia Paz, and Angélica López. 2009. *Tejidos que lleva el alma: Memoria de las mujeres mayas sobrevivientes de violación sexual durante el conflicto armado*. Guatemala: ECAP, UNAMG and F&G Editores.

Granek, Leeat. 2013. Putting Ourselves on the Line: The Epistemology of the Hyphen, Intersubjectivity and Social Responsibility in Qualitative Research. *International Journal of Qualitative Studies in Education* 26 (2): 178–197. https://doi.org/10.1080/09518398.2011.614645.

Grupo de Mujeres Mayas Kaqla. 2014. *Las voces de las mujeres persisten en la memoria colectiva de sus pueblos*. Guatemala: Grupo de Mujeres Mayas Kaqla.

Hartman, Saidiya. 1997. *Scenes of Subjection: Terror, Slavery, and Self-Making in Nineteenth-Century America*. New York: Oxford University Press.

Henry, Nicola. 2009. Witness to Rape: The Limits and Potential of International War Crimes Trials for Victims of Wartime Sexual Violence. *International Journal of Transitional Justice* 3 (1): 114–134. https://doi.org/10.1093/ijtj/ijn036.

Hesford, Wendy S. 2011. *Spectacular Rhetorics: Human Rights Visions, Recognitions, Feminisms*. Durham: Duke University Press.

Impunity Watch and the Alliance to Break the Silence and Impunity (ECAP, MTM and UNAMG). 2017. *Changing the Face of Justice: Keys to the Strategic Litigation of the Sepur Zarco Case*. Guatemala: Impunity Watch and Alianza Rompiendo el Silencio y la Impunidad.

Jaleel, Rana. 2013. Weapons of Sex, Weapons of War. *Cultural Studies* 27 (1): 115–135. https://doi.org/10.1080/09502386.2012.722302.

Jimeno, Myriam. 2010. Emoções e política: A vítima e a construção de comunidades emocionais. *Revista Mana* 16 (1): 99–121.

Kapur, Ratna. 2002. The Tragedy of Victimization Rhetoric: Resurrecting the 'Native' Subject in International/Post-Colonial Feminist Legal Politics. *Harvard Human Rights Journal* 15 (1): 1–38.

Lykes, M. Brinton, and Alison Crosby. 2015. Creative Methodologies as a Resource for Mayan Women's Protagonism. In *Psychosocial Perspectives on Peacebuilding*, ed. Brandon Hamber and Elizabeth Gallagher, 147–186. Cham: Springer. https://doi.org/10.1007/978-3-319-09937-8_5.

Maguire, Patricia. 1987. *Doing Participatory Research: A Feminist Approach*. Amherst: Center for International Education, University of Massachusetts.

Merry, Sally Engle. 2006. Transnational Human Rights and Local Activism: Mapping the Middle. *American Anthropologist* 108 (1): 38–51. https://doi.org/10.1525/aa.2006.108.1.38.

Million, Dian. 2013. *Therapeutic Nations: Healing in an Age of Indigenous Human Rights*. Tucson: University of Arizona Press.

Moraga, Cherríe, and Gloria Anzaldúa, eds. 1981. *This Bridge Called My Back: Writings by Radical Women of Color*. Durham: Duke University Press.

Shaw, Rachel L. 2010. Embedding Reflexivity Within Experiential Qualitative Psychology. *Qualitative Research in Psychology* 7 (3): 233–243. https://doi.org/10.1080/14780880802699092.

Solano, Luis. 2013. Development and/as Dispossession: Elite Networks and Extractive Industry in the Franja Transversal del Norte. In *War by Other Means: Aftermath in Post-Genocide Guatemala*, ed. Carlota McAllister and Dianne M. Nelson, 119–142. Durham: Duke University Press.

Stephen, Lynn. 2017. Bearing Witness: Testimony in Latin American Anthropology and Related Fields. *The Journal of Latin American and Caribbean Anthropology* 22 (1): 85–109.

Taylor, Diana. 2003. *The Archive and the Repertoire: Performing Cultural Memory in the Americas*. Durham: Duke University Press.

Tuck, Eve. 2009. Suspending Damage: A Letter to Communities. *Harvard Educational Review* 79 (3): 409–428. Retrieved from http://hepg.org/her-home/issues/harvard-educational-review-volume-79-issue-3/herarticle/a-letter-to-communities_739.

Velásquez Nimatuj, Irma Alicia. 2016. *Peritaje cultural: Violaciones sexuales a mujeres q'eqchi' en el marco del conflict armado interno (1960–1996) de Guatemala, caso Sepur Zarco, municipio de El Estor, departamento de Izabal*. Unpublished expert witness report presented to the February 2016 Sepur Zarco trial.

Vizenor, Gerald, ed. 2008. *Survivance: Narratives of Native Presence*. Lincoln: University of Nebraska Press.

CHAPTER 9

Women Defending Women: Memories of Women Day Laborers and Emotional Communities

Gisela Espinosa Damián

INTRODUCTION

There are moments of rupture with the past independently of how far or close the past is to the present. The importance lies in the shift in the horizon of meaning that some event signified for the social actors who experienced the past and are living the present. Perhaps something changes every day so that everything will remain the same: In the logic of gatopardism, continuity prevails. Occasionally, however, an event makes a striking break with the routine and is capable of shaking up the horizon that gives meaning to daily existence. That rupture trumps continuity and the resulting fracture enables the historization of the past at a moment when people who witnessed or participated in the event are still living.

This reflection allows me to focus on the memories of five of nine ex-day laborers and members of the *Naxihi Na Xinxe Na Nishi* (Women Defending Women) Civil Association that began organizing in 2004. The Association was founded to defend labor rights and later began defending and disseminating information about reproductive rights and living without violence to women in the San Quintín Valley (henceforth Valley or San Quintín) (Fig. 9.1).

G. Espinosa Damián (✉)
Division of Social Science and Humanities,
Metropolitan Autonomous University-Xochimilco, Mexico City, Mexico

© The Author(s) 2018
M. Macleod, N. De Marinis (eds.), *Resisting Violence*,
https://doi.org/10.1007/978-3-319-66317-3_9

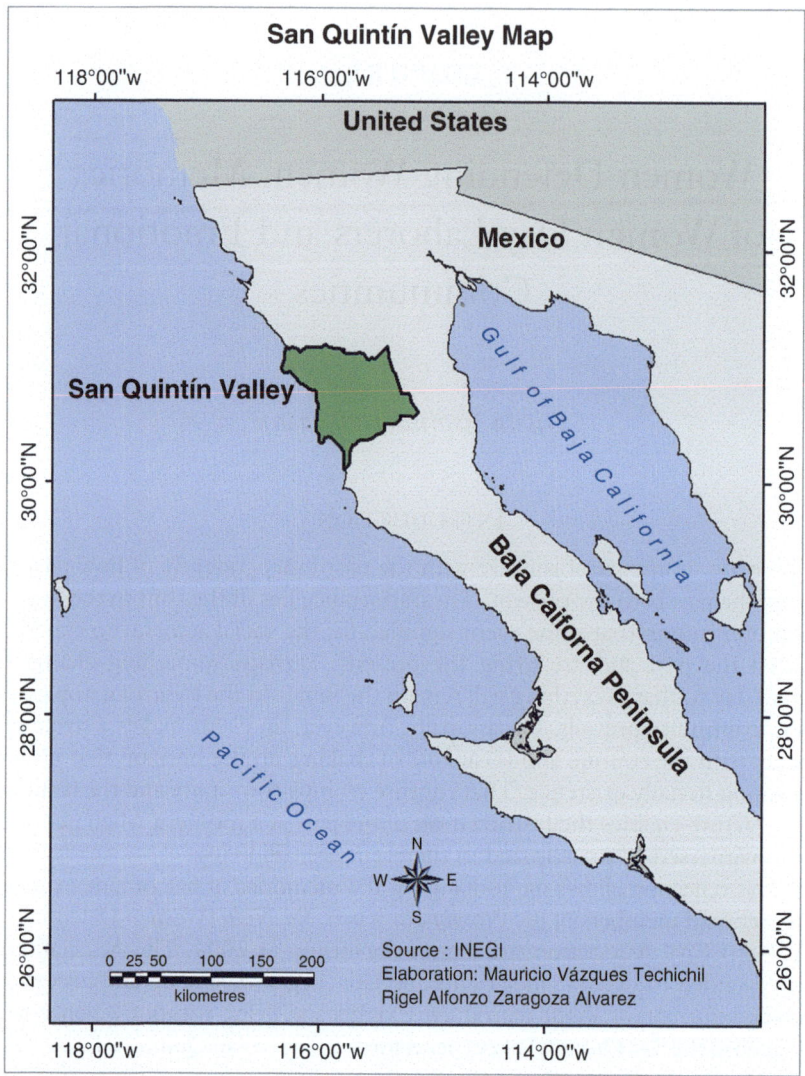

Fig. 9.1 San Quintín Valley map by Mauricio Vázquez Techechil and Rigel Zaragoza Álvarez

In 2012, I began working with the women to systematize their experience in preventing and treating gender violence. It soon became clear that gender-based violence was just one of many forms of violence found in this profitable enclave for agro-exporting corporations. The women shared with me the rupture involved in leaving one's place of origin, how people live in encampments and labor in agricultural fields or in working-class neighborhoods, in a poignant setting where sadness, rage, and human warmth welled up. Perhaps it was not the first time they recalled their experiences, but never before had they done so collectively and for analytical purposes. The women's stories intermingled experiences and emotions, interjections, gazes, and voices tempered by feelings.

My systematization gathers their experiences and insights in preventing and helping to heal gender violence, but a "blind spot" in my academic gaze kept me from explicitly reflecting on emotions during this study. Nonetheless, the tension between the systematic and subjective aspects comes through in this chapter, which is, in turn, an orderly analysis of their working experience and an engaged denouncement of the violence that is involved therein.[1] This text emanates from an analytical-political-emotional convergence—I am included—in which the actors begin to refocus on the meaning of life. When this happens, the "anthropologists' feelings of indignation also intervene" (Jimeno et al. 2011, 276), since we researchers who "work with people who have suffered [...] are immersed and shaped by this emotionally-charged environment" (Jimeno et al. 2015, 27).

Sharing experiences created mutual trust in collaborative work and prepared the terrain for a new undertaking that was affected by a transcendent event in the Valley, that is, the "Day Laborer Work Stoppage" of 2015, whose accounts, images, and vivid recollections inundated social and mass media with examples of unacceptable injustice, past and present. In this turbulent Valley, the Naxihi women awaited my arrival to reflect collectively on the work stoppage and in this context we began to bring two ideas into sharper focus: a project of collaborative research[2] and an exploration in letting the women narrate their own stories of working the fields as day laborers and the accompanying grievances and feelings of injustice, in tandem with demands for social change. Indeed, "subjectivity emerges and manifests itself with particular force in the fissures and, in a moment of confusion, in the ruptures of how everyday memory works, in the restlessness due to something that prompts us to work on an interpretative level in order to find meaning and words that can express it" (Jelin 2002, 35).

From the beginning, our intention was to link the women's memories with projects for change and reach a wider public in order to strengthen actions aimed at labor and social justice. There was a performative intention in the project, in spite of the lack of dramatic representation to connect the women with the wider public. The idea of narrating and writing their memories was not simply to acknowledge or derive some solace in their role as victims, but rather to facilitate production of other realities, establishing contact with readers who could give meaning to their own memories. As Barthes (1994) says, the text becomes real as the reader experiences it. Words produce subjectivity, a concrete way to gain awareness and understand the world.

Indeed, as the women delved into their memories they were led into a labyrinth: They not only recalled memories with a clear political meaning but also moved in an immense field, enveloped by the concerns of another nature, that is, overflowing or repressed emotions and caring for one's image. As we shall see, these narratives are not orchestrated by a single meaning; rather, they are experiences that have been lived with their truth and subjectivities.

The women trusted me as an intermediary that could transform their memories into a text and their suffering into arguments for demanding rights. Personally, I felt privileged by their trust and affection; I was committed emotionally and politically, as I simultaneously tried to keep up the "strong objectivity" (Harding 1996) that acknowledges the hopelessness of being neutral while seeking truth—relative, partial, but truth nonetheless—rigorous and critical knowledge that forces us to stop concealing and recognize that I have my affections, loyalties, and assumptions. In other words, I tried to address the challenges of a situated knowledge.

From this rich panoply of experiences woven from the women's (ongoing) memories and projects, I have chosen five Naxihi women's memories,[3] painful yet hopeful, which have been fashioned into a text, and a pretext, to achieve a better understanding of the relationships between memory and emotional political communities.

Day Laborer Insurrection and Emotional Communities

At dawn on March 17, 2015, the San Quintín Valley awoke in a state of insurrection. There had been protests and movements years before but none with this strength and magnitude: Some 20,000 strikers, according to a conservative estimate, blocked the Trans-Peninsular Highway (the only road connecting the Valley to its most important market, the United States). As a result, the strawberry and vegetable harvests were suspended at a key moment for agribusiness. The movement articulated labor demands that had been unsuccessfully raised time and again for over a quarter of a century. There were also new demands, among them a halt to sexual harassment of women day laborers.

The movement exploded onto the scene with surprising force: Although the leaders of the Alliance for National, State, and Municipal Organizations for Social Justice convened people in several neighborhoods and communities in the Valley, they never thought so many would gather. At dawn on March 17, the movement grew to an unexpected scale. Those who were unaware of the movement quickly discovered its momentum; those who were not going to head out were mobilized, those who had kept quiet shouted and were moved to action by the legitimate reasons for the strike and people's growing enthusiasm.

The prevailing social order that had enshrined extreme exploitation, exhausting workdays, meager pay, social (in)security, and violation of a wide variety of rights had been altered. Those in power had to use the security forces to reimpose (relatively) their control over this "empowered" sector. The movement lasted several months, but over time, internal disagreements over salary negotiations divided leaders and thus the movement itself was fragmented.

The most relevant gains were a wage increase, work foremen were brought under restraint in abusing workers, the workforce was registered (slowly) in the Social Security Institute, and two new trade unions were registered, while calls to organize were tolerated. Yet the split that occurred within this powerful social force was undoubtedly the most painful outcome of the long-lasting mobilization.

The 2015 movement signaled a "before" and an "after." Some of its participants said "nothing was the same afterwards." The social and labor order remained unchanged but labor and social injustices began to be denaturalized on a massive scale. A grassroots force and power, previously unimagined, began to make itself felt. Day laborers began to imagine new possibilities in terms of the meaning of being, of work, and of citizens' rights, while social indignation and solidarity spread beyond the Valley. At that time, a large-scale *emotional community* began to grow: This idea alludes not just to a convergence of emotions, but rather synthesizes the "process of construction that links victims of a violent event with a wider audience.

The ties between community and spectators are based on the building of shared feelings of moral repudiation. Shared indignation bolsters public political involvement" (Jimeno et al. 2015, 251).

The suspicion, or conviction, that another world is possible drew a line between the immediate past and the present; it rent asunder the prevailing "common sense" that for decades had made the Valley into one of the most profitable agro-exporting enclaves in Mexico. The structural violence that defined hierarchies and positions, molded behaviors, created subjectivities and identities consistent with ruthless capitalism, as if profit accumulation were the *meaning* of life for all human beings. There was no great massacre here, no holocaust, just daily quotas of violence that kill people gradually and prevent life from blossoming.

The 2015 movement shook the symbolic and social order: It transformed the fatalism that grievances are inevitable into an actionable feeling of social injustice (Moore 1989, 433). It unleashed other imaginaries regarding the future and made the present into a political and emotional moment from which to gaze to the past and the future with new meaning. One of the deepest changes brought by this event developed and continues to grow in the subjective realm, that is, emotions, feelings of grievance, imaginaries, and social projects; a new subjectivity exists that guides actions. The 2015 movement meant a "rupture" in the time of the day laborer, which had been synonymous with an infinite cycle of work, "until you drop." There are continuities and the effects of the movement have yet to settle out. Something is coming to an end and something else, somewhat blurred, emerges. The present is a time of transition to a moment that is taking shape in the midst of disarray and new surges of energy to organize.

Memories and Flashes of Hope

In this environment in which pessimism and social exploitation are fused together, the testimonies of the Naxihi women inaugurate an opportunity to build a potential collective memory, made up of "shared memories, superimposed, an outcome of multiple interactions, framed by social and power relationships [...] an interweaving of traditions and individual memories, in dialog with one another, in a state of constant flux, with some social organization [...] and with some structure fixed by shared cultural codes" (Jelin 2002, 22).

The collective memory of the Naxihi women is also beginning to challenge and negotiate the meanings of the past vis-à-vis the entrepreneurial narrative of economic success and a governmental narrative of progress and peace. It questions the invisibility and the passivity attributed to women day laborers; for public institutions they are merely a vulnerable population or a statistic; even in the narratives of day laborer movements, women laborers practically do not exist. This demonstrates the complexity of identitary constructions, because the women, as we shall see, have not been passive subjects. But let us not get ahead of ourselves.

The testimonies that appear below were given following the zenith of the day laborer movement, when the Naxihi women were searching for meaningful memories in a mysterious, revolutionary Valley. Benjamin says that when excavating memories—as in archeology—an inventory of discoveries is not as important as the place in the present ground in which memories are stored (Benjamin 2011, 128).

As we acquaint ourselves with the memories of the Naxihi women, we discover what was hidden from one of the most muted voices within subalternized groups. Their testimonies not only heighten our awareness of the particular injustice that women laborers experience and their resistance and rebelliousness, they also reveal the multiplicity of actors and tensions that have permitted such a polarized and inhumane world to exist. In spite of the suffering that left the women with mnemonic scars and notwithstanding that in most memory literature *trauma* and *victims* are key references, as my knowledge grew of the Naxihi women's memories, I realized that their wounds are only part of their story; so are the hope, encouragement, and eros that truly give them the strength to survive their emotional wounds, their trauma, and continue onward restoring their world.

Walter Benjamin (2008), Jenny Pearce (2016), Enzo Traverso (2016), Jimeno et al. (2015), and De Marinis and Macleod (in Chap. 1, this book) confirm my perception and my analytic objective, since, in researching memory, these authors sustain the importance of recovering the goals and bright moments of grassroots power, the ways by which subalternized social actors become political actors and citizens with agency, the creativity and "sparks of hope" (Benjamin 2008, 40) that encourage social struggles, often eclipsed by repression, suffering, and trauma. At times actors are left in the role of victims in spite of their agency and notwithstanding the fact that the promises that lie in the past survive alongside them. In order to excavate their memories of resistance, one is forced to uncover "layers" of what was silenced by conventional historiographies in an effort to give back to the actors their "historical capital" (Pearce 2016), with all its pain and richness.

Collaborative Research

In spite of the restrictions imposed by physical distance, funding, and time,[4] my experience with "Women Defending Women" taught me that producing knowledge and strengthening processes that are clamoring for justice, freedom, non-violence, and acknowledgement involves using collaborative methodologies in which researchers and social actors establish analytic and emotional common ground. Jenny Pearce (2016) had a similar reflection when she spoke of co-participation (researcher and *campesinos*), in order for the social actors to own their "historical capital" through diverse expressions, such as creating a memory museum. Miriam Jimeno et al. (2011, 276) also sustains that ethnography is both an instrument of knowledge and an approach that strives to understand the subaltern's point of view; it is a tool to go beyond the text to joint action, based on "collaborative anthropology" and a "complicity" that at times are hidden in the notion of "participatory observation." I identify with the women based on my experience (Fig. 9.2).

Fig. 9.2 Women Defending Women with the author. Photograph by Alfonso Zaragoza Álvarez

In the case before us, I would like to defend the potential of participatory systematization, which academia esteems to be of minor importance, if it considers it at all. This modest study may unbridle processes of enormous weight, both in the ways knowledge is produced and in the political effects that stem from cooperation between civil organizations and academia.

The Naxihi women transitioned from "participating" to "cooperating"; they changed their position from one of informants to epistemic subjects of the research process and its possible results; the women actively participated in the different phases of the research and are currently undertaking relevant initiatives, such as narrating and setting down their experiences and memories framed by emancipatory social processes.

As an academic who accompanies these processes, I am forced to bring into play my wisdom and experience, while simultaneously recognizing the limits of these factors and facilitating the potential of collectively building knowledge. This type of cooperation enables us to journey down a new path where the shared meaning of the academic, political, and emotional bond is like a guiding light that facilitates experimentation and quests.

The Memories

The five Naxihi women who share their experiences below are Amalia T., a Mixtec, originally from Oaxaca, on the verge of becoming a "senior citizen," who was a traveling day laborer as a young girl. She has a secondary school education and has lived in the Valley for 37 years, where as an adult she worked 14 years as a day laborer. She was the principal promoter of Women Defending Women and is currently a broadcaster on XEQIN, the regional indigenous radio station. Margarita, Patricia, and Amalia S. are 39, 47, and 49 years old, respectively. The three women are originally from the Mixtec region in Oaxaca and were day laborers for over two decades; Margarita studied high school, Patricia finished primary school, and Amalia Sánchez studied secondary school. They have lived in the Valley between 28 and 36 years. Born in San Quintín to Amalia S., Adilene is 26 years old. She is currently studying a postgraduate degree in psychology. As a young girl and adolescent, she was a day laborer. The three elder women, Amalia T., Amalia S., and Patricia have children. The two younger women, Adilene and Margarita, are single and have no children. All five women consider themselves indigenous and three of the five speak Mixtec and Spanish (Fig. 9.3).

Fig. 9.3 Woman day laborer. Photograph by Gisela Espinosa

By gathering the recollections of the Women Defending Women, I socialize the memories of five significant, traumatic, and/or gleaming moments with their similarities and contrasts: Leaving one's place of origin, Arriving at the San Quintín Valley, Working as a day laborer, Studying, and Participating in a social setting. It is not my intention to make "history" in its objectified meaning and validated by all the disciplinary canons (Traverso 2016, 19–20). Rather, my intent is to make inroads to *memory*, to identify fragmentary, disperse, multiple recollections that hardly fit together neatly like jigsaw-puzzle pieces. They overlap and outline a collective memory of what their experience has been:

the difficulties and dreams of women day laborers in the Valley. It is hardly a solitary and objectified account, but rather a diversity of stories and embodied narratives, inevitably marked by subjectivity, previously hidden by *history*.

Leaving One's Place of Origin

Paty is lively, spontaneous, and cheerful. She gave her testimony in the Naxihi meeting room, where my partner and I were present as active "listeners."[5] Our questions, glances, silences, gestures, or laughter were in dialog with her words: a listener participates in a creative work (Jelin 2002, 84–85); Paty's testimony was not a structured and pre-existing archive that can be opened and displayed, but rather was created in interaction with the listeners.

> I was born in San Martín Durazno but grew up in Santiago Juxtlahuaca. I was the youngest of seven brothers and sisters and the only one who was able to grow up, all the rest died; I too was going to die and my dad said, "Look, my daughter, in spite of being a bit of a drunk, I did everything possible to keep you from dying" [...] When I was old enough to remember, I realized that my mom lived with my dad's violence, because he drank a lot, every day, sometimes he would come home and insult my mother, shout at her, beat her, he would say she had a lover [...] it's like he had visions [...] several times we had to sleep in the cornfield to hide, we had to take a mat, and if not, just grab a blanket and run [...] I remember when I was ten my father wanted to marry me off [...] [Once] when I got back from school, my dad was drinking and he said, "my daughter, leave your backpack over there and come sit here because this couple have come and I want to talk to you" [...], and I saw a cardboard box of things like fruit, food [...] but he had had his beers, his liquors, which was his routine. And my dad said, "Look, this husband and wife are going to sell their harvest and they remembered you and they've come to ask for you so you can marry their son" [...] And I said, "But Dad, I don't want to get married." "Well, I say that you're getting married, thank these people who have come to pay their respects and to speak with me, they haven't come to rob and sell you out on the street or anything, or is that what you want?" "I don't want to get married, Dad," I told him. "You have to get married! Because they've brought these things, there's a bottle there which I've already begun to drink." My mother didn't say anything [...] I began to cry and then I quickly decided to go to my godmother's house [...] I was with her something like three days and then my father arrived and asked for

my forgiveness [...] I finished primary school, I really wanted to continue studying but I saw that there wasn't enough money, my mother would say "study." "No," I would say, "I don't want to anymore." I really wanted to be a teacher but I could see that mother was working so hard to sell tortillas; that was her job, to sell tortillas [...] Around 1978 or 1979, we left for Sinaloa and a man said to my father, "Let's go to Baja because there is plenty of work there." We took the train to Mexicali and two years later returned to Oaxaca. [One day] my uncle Mucio arrived and said there was much work and opportunities there, and girls, boys, women work and earn money. Wow, my mom didn't think twice. My dad didn't want to go but finally said, "Okay, if you want we'll go" [...] and so we packed our little bag of clothes [...] I remember, since we lived on a little hill, I looked back and saw my granny, she just sat, my granny, like so, with a little dog (Paty cries), she was looking at us [...] my mother also felt sad when she saw how my granny was being left behind. (Interview with Patricia, September 14, 2015, San Quintín Valley)

The image of Paty's mother is one of resignation and silence until taking a radical decision to leave town; her father has two sides, when sober, he is kind and hard-working, when drunk, he gets *delirium tremens* and turns violent. The godmother is another feminine image, a woman who is able to put a stop to the father's authoritarianism and lend Paty protection and affection like a mother. Paty's granny is a moving character, but in the end helpless and resigned to being abandoned when her family leaves. The place of origin is not an idealized place, rather more a harsh environment, of economic necessity, lack of educational opportunities and options for fulfilling one's dreams. Here, domestic violence coexists with structural violence. So by leaving this environment, the greatest sadness is abandoning her grandmother, but her mother, Paty says, does not think twice, because she believes that in the Valley there may be a way to overcome the difficult life in Juxtlahuaca. It is a heartbreaking moment, but the "sparks of hope" seem to outweigh the loss. Paty cannot imagine the way her life will change as she leaves behind that little hill. Once in the Valley, she works as a day laborer, earns her own income, during the 1980s actively participates in the struggles for a decent wage, chooses a partner, and decides on marriage. She breaks with the future that she might have had in the Mixtec region of Oaxaca and builds new identitary elements that are quite distinct from the mistreated or fatalistic woman. Today, she is a human rights defender.

Arriving at San Quintín Valley

I began coming to Baja California in 1987 when I was 17 [...] I came with my dad to "San Simón el Barrio Pobre," where there were people from my home town; the *Los Pinos* farm gave them a little bit of land next to the highway so people could build their home, with plastic, with pines from the field or branches [...] that's where we lived. I was unaware of the custom of these parts of getting up at three in the morning to make that day's lunch, and I thought that first night, "How will tomorrow be?" [...] My first day at work was pure hell. I hadn't brought more than two sets of clothes. And my aunts said [to my mother], "Now look, we're going to give a scarf to your daughter, we're going to give her a cap because tomorrow she has to dress like this." I remember they taught me how to cover up, I felt I was going to be smothered, I couldn't see [...] It was painfully sad for me, because I brought high-heeled dress shoes and I headed out to the fields wearing those shoes. I already had horribly swollen feet because [...] we arrived in Mexicali on the train, then from Mexicali to Ensenada on a bus, and then from Ensenada to here on a bus. I was totally exhausted because it had been almost eight days, good God! My feet were terribly swollen; It felt like I couldn't even put my shoes on. And in those shoes I went to work, stoop labor [...] In *Los Pinos* there were work crews, each foreman had his group of workers. And then [...] we had to plant. So, as you can imagine, I was doing stoop labor all day with those shoes on. I had a pain in my heart that was hurting me, but I didn't tell my father because I would have stressed him out [...] because my dad would say, "We won't rest, everyday we'll go to work, we'll save money to go back, we won't stay." In the afternoon I hobbled back and my aunts said, "How'd it go, girl?" I was in no mood to talk, I didn't say anything. There were no bathrooms; you had to go out in the field. So I found a spot in the field, relieved myself, and I sat there in the sand, I just sat. Truth be known, I cried bitterly. Why had my dad brought me here? I cried. Why didn't I continue studying? My goals back in my town were different. When I finished secondary school, I was going to study in Yetla de Juárez or in Xochitla where there are technological schools; I wanted to go to those schools. But my dad said no, because we were a large family. My mom had eleven children, one right after the other. And I said to myself, "If I don't help my mom and dad, how are these kids going to live. I have to work," and that's how with all my strength I left to come to San Quintín. At the end of that first day, I ran a fever and I cried, but the next day I returned to plant and suffer in my shoes. (Interview with Amalia S., September 18, 2015, San Quintín Valley)

Amalia's arrival, her shoes, her initial working days profoundly moved me; I felt like the "other" whose cultural frames-of-reference are still unaccustomed to this suffering. Amalia S. tells her story because she knows there is injustice and pain, but I have the feeling that to be able to narrate it, she had to bring her trauma under control, and for me, the impact is still astonishment and shock.

Amalia S. was not consulted on the decision to leave her hometown or go to work but, as the eldest of 11 children, when she was 17 she felt she had to assume responsibility and help cover her family's expenses. She arrived at *Los Pinos*, one of the largest and most profitable farms in the Valley. Amalia suffered terribly due to her unfamiliarity with the route and with her work as a day laborer, a *trauma* that left her speechless the first day. *Trauma*, says Jelin (2002), involves a rupture, a crack, an inability to assimilate what is unlivable, since the social frameworks that have given meaning to experience, to words themselves, are insufficient to understand and explain the traumatic event. Years would have to pass before Amalia S. could verbalize, recount, speak about that pain, or about the questioning that was unspeakable at that moment.

After months working in the fields and saving some money, Amalia S. returned to the Mixtec, but her father's attempt to force her to marry against her will made her rebel: "How can I be married off, how can they turn me over to those persons. I refuse. I know how to earn my daily bread, I know how to stoop over, I learned about suffering and can cover my own expenses." So Amalia S. flees without her father's consent and returns to the Valley where she suffered "hell," not just the first day but over 20 years as a day laborer. In San Quintín, in addition to the traumatic experience that left her with a mnemonic scar, she charted out an independent life, fell in love, had a family and struggled, and struggles, for women's rights. She was not the passive victim, but a woman who fights in what she believes in.

Working as a Day Laborer

Adilene is the daughter of Amalia S. and of a day laborer father who seldom returns from the United States. She is the eldest of three siblings and from a young age was forced to take on the roles of mother and caretaker, since "children around here are very much alone, their parents work all day," she says. But she was also a day laborer as a child, an adolescent, and a young adult, partly to pay for her studies and partly because her father used a pedagogy of horror regarding day labor work.

When I was eight or nine, my parents took me to work [...] on Saturday and Sunday they would take me [...] I remember, they would get me ready, they dressed me and we would get on the bus. On the way there I wouldn't tell them the outrage I felt, because on Saturday and Sunday I wanted to stay home. So I wouldn't speak to them until noon, sometimes I wouldn't have lunch because I didn't want to talk to them [...] I didn't want that life for myself, from the time I set foot in a field, arriving early, the bushes dripping wet and you have to stick your hands in because you can't use gloves... I remember the very first time I went to a farm not far from here, planted with round gourds, Star variety they called them [...] So my dad says, "We're going to work and when you've earned your day you can go home." I said, "Well, okay." Once in the field he said, "They pay 25 pesos a bucket." So I said, "Okay, if I fill about four, I'll have earned my day and I'll leave." So I hurried. The shrubs are very thorny and they wouldn't let us use gloves to avoid damaging the fruit [...] you had to pick the fruit gently so it wouldn't get scratched or anything. Before noon I had filled my four buckets and so I said, "Dad, I've finished, I've done my day, I'm leaving." "No," he said, "you're not leaving until you've done a bed, the furrows. You can't go." And I said, "But you told me..." "If you want to earn more, work, and you'll see what it is to work in the fields," he said. I cried that day because he had deceived me into going [...] I hated Saturdays and Sundays, I hated holidays, I hated suspension days. As vacation time approached it was hell to think I was going to the fields. It was very painful for me; I can say that it was a traumatic experience. To avoid using a skirt over my pants, the way women day laborers did, so nobody could see their butts, I would wear very long sweatshirts but I didn't like to. I felt I was choking, "Mom, I'm choking, I can't stand this." And she would say, "You have to get used to it, huh, you'll get used to it." (Interview with Adilene, September 20, 2016, San Quintín Valley)

Adilene is finishing up her master's degree. She overcame the trauma stemming from that experience as a young girl, adolescent, and young woman. She was able to escape from the field work she hated so much due to her very strong convictions. Although her parents encouraged her to study, they also wanted her in the fields: "You have to get used to it." If learning how to do stoop labor and suffering allowed Amalia S. to get out of an imposed marriage and begin to take her future into her own hands, her daughter Adilene rejects that learning and rebels. "If I had stayed in the fields I would now be married and with kids, life in the fields is very different," she says. It is startling to feel the power of this young woman, her resistance to authoritarianism, her ability to reflect and create new meanings of life that her words and experiences express. Not only has she studied with great sacrifice, she has taken unusual decisions within the Valley environment, such as not becoming a mother, in spite of pressure from society and her family: "I'm not going to take a risk just because society says you have to be a mother [...] just to satisfy them." She is light years away from the conventional family, patriarchal power, and even her mother's cultural spectrum when Adilene suggests, "Mom, get to know other people, give yourself the opportunity, I don't want you waiting around for my dad when he may not ever show up." It is interesting to see that a mother and daughter share a working space; both promote and defend women's rights. Both were rebels, even though there are generation gaps and tensions. Today Adilene, now a psychologist, helps women suffering from violence and undoubtedly one of her duties has been to reflect deeply about the violence she suffered.

Adilene shared her testimony in a small doctor's office; the setting was warm and intimate. Several times tears welled up as I felt her pain and admired her rebelliousness and critical abilities.

STUDYING

Margarita's family arrived in the San Quintín Valley in 1979. "I just remember that first night my mom covering me with newspapers as I watched the sky with so many stars. We slept on the street." Her meaningful memories during infancy? Work as a day laborer: "I began working when I was eight"; sexual harassment of boy and girl day laborers: "Every time I see that Bimbo bread ad I remember an older person in charge of the crew of children and in exchange for a piece of bread with peanut butter he would feel up the girls and boys"; the camps: "we spent a lot of time at the camps, you see lots of things there that you don't even want to think about"; her father: "My father in the United States, when he'd show up, he'd just drink, spend money, and beat up my mom." When she was 17, she worked at *El Milagro* farm. They asked if she wanted to become a crew foreman. At first she refused because she thought workers would not pay attention to her, but [management] convinced her and she was a foreman for two years. They offered her a better position in the experimental field counting pea seeds, but "I told them no, I couldn't even count to 20."

At that time it was summer vacation and many students worked at *El Milagro* [...] I had just turned 18. A guy who studied at the UABC[6] began talking to me and it dawned on him that I didn't know how to read so he told me about the INEA.[7] That day I went home with determination [...] There were guests and my dad, he's a different person when someone's visiting... I told him I wanted to go to the INEA. "Do whatever you want" [...] and I picked up a notebook, a pencil, and off I went [...] afterwards I wasn't able to move for two days after the beating he gave me, but, what do you think I did? [she asks me]. The next day I went to school! In a year I finished primary and secondary school, at the age of 19. Then I heard there was a new school and off I went again to talk to my family, I wanted to learn [...] I told my *compañeras* that I hadn't suffered discrimination because I was indigenous but because I didn't know how to read. At work there was a secretary and, goodness! Did she ever bully me! [...] You're so dumb! And I said, I'm going to push on! I'm going to study!, but my dad [said], no, that wasn't for me, not so much because I was a woman but because he thought that school wasn't a place for poor people. My dad told me, "Every week as long as you turn over the full check, do whatever you want with your life." The first day at school was very difficult, because the following day my dad took away my backpack and notebook and said, "Get to work. Why are you losing time at a place that isn't meant for you?" [...] I was wearing a rather old pair of pants and I went off to school [...] they told us that we were going to have lots of teachers and then they asked "who knows English?" And I said, "No, this isn't for me." Really, I stood up and left [...] I was crossing the highway when I bumped into a guy from El Rosario, real handsome [...] "Hey!", he said to me, "Where you going? We've just arrived." "I'm leaving," I told him. Obviously I was shattered. "But why?" And he began to talk and talk and talk, com'on, let's go, and this and that. And I went back! That guy never finished. For me, having gone to school was one of the most beautiful things in my life [...] Graduation day arrived and I said to my dad, "I'd like you to be there with Mom, to accompany me." He said no, but I insisted. "Well," he said, "if you're not ashamed to be seen with us, with your dad all dirty." And that's how he went, after work, in his day laborer clothes [she laughs]. When he arrived at the school, an elderly gentleman said to my dad, "It's great that our sons and daughters are graduating! I hope they will continue, so many people would like to see their children graduating from high school, our children have now grown up, but it's great they made the decision." And many things began to come out. Goodness! My dad was so moved, the tears began to roll. Afterwards he bought me a stuffed bear and said, "I'm taking you out to eat," and so we went and had some tacos. (Interview with Margarita, September 15, 2015, San Quintín Valley)

What obstacles does a young woman day laborer have to overcome to study? It is not simply a matter of facing the exclusionary effects of structural violence and ethnic discrimination. Margarita does not perceive the intersection of these two factors: She maintains that people do not discriminate against her because she is indigenous but because she is illiterate, without noticing that perhaps not knowing how to read has to do with being born an indigenous woman. We exchanged thoughts about this. Beyond recognizing that one's ethnic and class origins have implications in terms of lack of access to schooling and, later, overcoming the lag becomes a monumental task, we should note how the internalization and defense of one's status as an excluded person work in the social structure.

The father's discourse, attitudes, behavior, and violence point to a performative affirmation of a social status that specifies that Margarita is "out of place" at school, since studying "isn't for poor people." Classism is assimilated as a weapon pointed against oneself is a structuring structure, a *habitus*, which is recreated and becomes an obstacle for a woman day laborer who wishes to study and become someone. Thus, in Margarita's case, finishing high school is a feat that involved both combining studying with an exhausting day-labor job and facing her father's violence and irrationality in opposing her education.

Margarita's memories regarding her material and symbolic battles, her objective and subjective obstacles, do not lead her to victimize herself, even though she has undoubtedly been a victim. Today she is able to verbalize traumatic moments in addition to convictions and decisions. Her feelings of indignation and rage have been transformed into a positive force for making her dreams come true, in spite of her father's convictions. As Amaranta Cornejo (2016) says, rationality, emotionality, and corporality are interwoven social constructions from where we know and act.

Suffice it to say that Margarita's memory is similar to that of thousands of young people who currently study or have studied in the Valley. Unlike her father, most mothers and fathers probably want their children to study in order to free them from having to do exhausting agricultural work. San Quintín residents know from experience that day-labor work is not a future to aspire to and so education becomes "the hope" in the social imaginary.

Margarita laughs easily, her gaze is inquisitive and strong. Like other Naxihi women, she recounts painful moments, social and family injustices. Seemingly, to survive her ordeal, she has become strong and rebellious and as such is able to narrate, while smiling, so much pain; meanwhile, emotions well up in me.

Participating in a Public Sphere

I've been a day laborer since I was nine. My parents took me from one place to the next, Veracruz, Sinaloa, Baja California, United States. Later, even though we wanted to, we were unable to return to Oaxaca. So here we stayed. One day, a woman from our region said to me, "I'd like to invite you to sign up for a course to become a midwife," and so I went with her, I did my social service in the Social Security [Institute], in the camps [...] Then a doctor told me, "Hey, Amalia, you speak Mixtec well. Do you know they're going to start a radio here in San Quintín? Why don't you go and ask for work?" [...] And I replied, "I haven't studied," I just had the INEA secondary-school degree and was married with four children [...] I started working at the radio and had the opportunity to attend a course in Mexico City. At the hotel I stayed at, some indigenous women were also there for a meeting.[8] I wanted to stay; I talked to the radio manager and he gave me permission. I was delighted! And there I heard that we women have a right to land, to health, to education… a right to the forest, that we have to care for the environment, and much more. Back then I didn't know anything [...] especially that we women have rights. I returned to San Quintín with so much enthusiasm [...] I felt I was flying through the air, almost as if I couldn't (she laughs) touch the floor [...] I saw many things and had so many thoughts in my head. Then I said, "We can organize ourselves," because the women had said that we as women can organize and together achieve so much [...] So we organized as a group of women handicraft makers [...] to regain our culture in terms of our dress; we were 18 women. And then, wow! I ran into a problem: husbands. "So where are you going? Amalia is crazy, she's stirring up the women," and similar things. And look, first I was able to get my husband to understand that I too could participate and do things. He'd get jealous. Once [...] he locked the door because I was worked up and going out late at night. So I began giving him some simple pamphlets on rights and human rights, and all those things, you know? (She laughs) So we realized that women were afraid of their husbands and I thought, we're indigenous and indigenous men have authority. Why? Because women give it to them. I was scared but I went door to door to invite other women. We also did community work during our military service [...] Then other women began to seek us out. On the radio I talked about women's rights, we recorded spots about violence, discrimination. And men would say, "Oh no, Amalia is talking about women's rights, what wrong with her? She's got to stop!" Other women began to seek me out: "Imagine, the general foreman, who's in charge of the crew, the one who counts the number of tomato buckets, did so-and-so to me…" We've had and continue to have sexual harassment in the fields, but no one ever denounces it. There is so much to do in San Quintín! People don't know their labor rights, nowadays just a bit, but back then nothing [...] in 2004 I sought out help and found Semillas[9] in order to establish ourselves [as a civil association]. Factor-X, a group that works in the maquiladoras in Tijuana, came to train us, but our situation as day laborers is very different from that in the maquiladoras [...] we began to do spots, pamphlets, set up information tables, bumper stickers, workshops, day-long activities on women's labor rights.... (Interview with Amalia T., September 2015, San Quintín Valley)

Our dialog with Amalia T. took place at the radio station. I felt a generational bond and a kind of mutual complicity and understanding throughout the interview.

Amalia T. was a key person in destabilizing the conventional order and sowing curiosity and organization in the San Quintín Valley. A series of fortunate circumstances placed her at the right place at the right time, but nothing would have happened if Amalia did not possess communication skills, speak two languages, establish social relationships easily, spot flashes of hope in the midst of a tumultuous world, or have enthusiasm and imagination to think the unthinkable and create new realities to change things in a positive direction. Although Amalia was also a girl day laborer, suffered in the agricultural fields, had little formal schooling, and married a jealous and narrow-minded man, that is, although she had painful or traumatic experiences, Amalia emphasizes those moments in which she sees a small opening, a possibility: She learned about midwifery, became a radio broadcaster, acquainted herself with women's rights, found Semillas, trained in labor rights, even the military service opened new possibilities. The story of Women Defending Women would lack meaning without Amalia T.

Clearly, Amalia T.'s chance encounter with the Continental Meeting of Indigenous Women and rights-based discourse leaves a deep impression in her vision of the world and her subjectivity. And it is interesting that the radiant and hopeful past and the creativity of the indigenous women of the hemisphere remained etched in the memory of a key person and had an impact on the isolated day laborer Valley of San Quintín. Organizing women in a social space where a woman's only "justification" for leaving the house is to do day labor is equivalent to violating the symbolic and social order that upholds patriarchal power at home and in the fields.

Currently, Amalia T.'s broadcasting duties prevent her from permanently accompanying the Naxihi women, but at the radio station she is able to open space and support the work of the group. Hers is an important and inspiring figure as she guides and counsels, and for these reasons she is not only a founder but a vital part of the team.

Conclusions

The memories and emotions analyzed herein do not come from unbridled violence, a holocaust, a massacre; rather, they are the result of persistent, naturalized suffering, past and present. It is this anguish that explodes emotionally and politically in 2015, upending and delegitimizing the inhumane conditions fostered by entrepreneurs in the San Quintín Valley. The work stoppage motivates the need to remember, to ground in multiple memories, the grievances, the feelings of injustice, grassroots rage, and demands for justice, a life with dignity, and labor and human rights.

The day laborer insurrection of 2015 shapes a political-emotional community that brings together a wide range of actors from different settings, that is, local, regional, national, and international. In an even smaller setting, micro emotional and political communities thrive, with their own distinctive elements, such as the Naxihi women, affected by their experiences, suffering, and gender aspirations. The feeling of helplessness and frustration when trying to implement their aspirations or decisions regarding living partners, maternity, migration, working as a day laborer, studying or participating in a public space..., sheds light on both structural violence—classist and racist—that affects male day laborers too, and the gender violence and patriarchal order that seek to control women's lives.

Rebelliousness and the wish to shed the role of victims reinforce the shift in feelings from resignation, helplessness, or the inevitability of grievances, to feelings of injustice and plans that involve social actions. It is no coincidence that all of the Naxihi women were day laborers and currently struggle for women's human and labor rights. An emotional convergence and a series of critical reflections have steered them in this direction. Although their shared emotions guide their collective actions, we should avoid "emotionalizing" their history, that is, attributing everything to emotions. Contacts with other actors and discourses have been relevant: the rights-based discourse, new perspectives, and the infectious enthusiasm that one of the main Naxihi organizers took away from the Continental

Meeting of Indigenous Women; discourses regarding injustices, social and labor rights, and the indignation that grew stronger with the work stoppage; reflections on gender violence and women's rights with other civil associations; reflections, analysis, collaborative studies, and proposals for action that arose with this chapter author; all of the above affected by intersubjectivity, not just emotional or subjective, strengthens their actions with a rights-based and emancipatory perspective. The performative nature of the process is connected by emotions, but also by language, readers, concepts, and social imaginaries nurtured by very different perspectives.

For a researcher such as myself, who has dealt with research-action methodologies, and who for years has recognized that emotions, reasons, and actions form a complicated melting pot, I had not undertaken an analysis of this link within social processes. It has been a challenge to delve into the notion of *emotional communities* in order to shed light on my understanding of the experience of this small community of Women Defending Women and myself. As I finished this text, I felt that without this accrual of desires and emotions, this subjective, epistemic, and political wager that led us to work collaboratively and excavate the women's memories would have been impossible.

It remains to be seen if the testimonies that came out of this teamwork do in fact have an influence in shaping and strengthening people who are willing to commit to goals of justice, lives with dignity, and fulfillment of day laborer rights, especially among women day laborers. In other words, will this potentially conceivable "we women," perhaps provisional and brief, be a link or a bridge to build political-emotional communities on another scale?

Notes

1. The systematization of their experience is available in Espinosa Damián, Gisela. 2013. *Naxihi na xinxe na xihi. Por una vida libre de violencia para las mujeres en el Valle de San Quintín, Baja California*. México: UAM, CDI, *Naxihi na xinxe na xihi*-Mujeres en Defensa de la Mujer.
2. The forthcoming book, *Vivir para el surco. Trabajo y derechos en el Valle de San Quintín*, coordinated by two members of Naxihi na xinxe na xihi, Esther Ramírez and Amalia Tello, together with Gisela Espinosa (UAM-X), is the end result of this collaborative research.
3. Nine testimonies were given with this idea in mind.

4. My university teaching and related activities require prolonged stays in Mexico City. I need a full day to travel to the San Quintín Valley and another day to return. The distance, time, and cost involved do not allow me to make frequent trips to the region.
5. My partner, Juan Manuel Aurrecoechea, began participating in 2015 as an *acompañante* and assistant in document research and in technical aspects of the project. Juan Manuel was present during four of the five interviews discussed herein and participated by asking questions, commenting, and becoming involved in the process.
6. UABC, Autonomous University of Baja California.
7. INEA, National Institute for Adult Education.
8. Amalia T. is referring to the Second Continental Meeting of Indigenous Women, held in Mexico City in 1997.
9. Sociedad Mexicana Pro Derechos de la Mujer (Mexican Society for Women's Rights), a feminist organization that supports women's projects in the areas of health, decent work conditions, autonomy, justice.

References

Barthes, Roland. 1994. *El susurro del lenguaje*. Barcelona: Paidós Comunicación.
Benjamin, Walter. 2008. *Tesis sobre la historia y otros fragmentos (Introducción y traducción de Bolívar Echeverría)*. México: Itaca-UACM.
———. 2011. *Denkbilder. Epifanías en viajes*. Buenos Aires: El cuenco de Plata.
Cornejo Hernández, Amaranta. 2016. Una relectura feminista de algunas propuestas teóricas del estudio social de las emociones. *Interdisciplina* 4 (8): 89–104. January–April.
Harding, Sandra. 1996. *Ciencia y feminismo*. Madrid: Morata.
Jelin, Elizabeth. 2002. *Los trabajos de la memoria*. Buenos Aires: Siglo XXI.
Jimeno, Myriam, Ángela Castillo, and Daniel Varela. 2011. Experiencias y recomposición social en Colombia. *Sociedades e Cultura* 2 (14): 275–285.
Jimeno, Myriam, Daniel Varela, and Ángela Castillo. 2015. *Después de la masacre: emociones y política en el Cauca indio*. Bogotá: Universidad Nacional de Colombia, Instituto Colombiano de Antropología e Historia.
Moore, Barrington. 1989. *La injusticia: bases sociales de la obediencia y la rebelión*. México: IIS-UNAM.
Pearce, Jenny. 2016. The Past Is Not History: Co-constructing an Historiography of Resistances in El Salvador. In *Conflicto Armado, Justicia y Memoria. Tomo 'Teoría Crítica de la Violencia y Practicas de Memoria y Resistencia'*, ed. Enan Arrieta Burgos, 125–156. Medellín: Editorial Universidad.
Traverso, Enzo. 2016. Memoria e historia del siglo XX. In *Archivos y memorias de la represión en América Latina*, ed. María Acuña, Patricia Flier, Miriam González Vera, et al., 17–29. Santiago de Chile: LOM Ediciones-FASIC.

INTERVIEWS

Adilene, September 20, 2016.
Amalia S., September 18, 2015.
Amalia T., September 16, 2015.
Margarita, September 15, 2015.
Patricia, September 14, 2015.

Index[1]

NUMBERS & SYMBOLS
19th September committee (Mexico), 59
30th anniversary of the earthquake, 58, 59, 65, 72
  See also Mexico City earthquake

A
Abarca, Cuauhtémoc, 59, 65, 66
Abject, 9, 156, 157
  and abjection, 157, 159n8, 173
Abu-Lughod, Lila, 5
Acevedo, Sebastián, 8, 45, 99–119
ACIN, *see* Association of Indigenous Councils of Northern Cauca
Acompañantes (volunteers), 8, 13, 125, 129, 137, 209n5
Acosta, Gerson, 28, 33
Actor for Change Consortium (Guatemala), 169
Acts of remembering, 73
  See also Remember

ADEPAC, *see* Association for the Development of Central America
Affect(s)
  affectivity, 11, 16, 157, 158
  circularity of affects, 149–151
  and politicization of affect, 9, 78, 83
  See also Political affective community(ies)
Affective Turn, The, 11, 157
Afro-Colombians, 23, 28, 30–32, 36
Ahmed, Sara, 1, 10–12, 144, 176, 178
Alameda (Chile), 100, 108
ALDHU, *see* Latin American Human Rights Association
Aldunate, José, S. J., 100, 103–106, 110, 111, 118n10
Alexander, Jeffrey, 26, 33
Allende, Salvador, 99, 108
Alliance to Break the Silence and Impunity (Guatemala), 173
Alliance for the National, State and Municipal Organization for Social Justice (Mexico), 191

[1]Note: Page numbers followed by 'n' refer to notes.

Alta Verapaz (Guatemala), 125, 139n9, 169
Andalzúa, Gloria, 166
APPO, *see* Popular Assembly of the Peoples of Oaxaca
Archbishop Romero, 83
Arendt, Hannah, 24, 26, 46, 50n3
Ariza, Marina, 10
Armed struggle (Nicaragua), 3, 79, 83, 86, 88
Army (Guatemala), 124–126
Arroyo, Sergio Raúl, 64
Association for the Development of Central America (ADEPAC), 134
Association of Displaced Peasants and Indigenous People of the Naya Region (Asocaidena) (Colombia), 30
Association of Indigenous Councils of Northern Cauca (ACIN) (Colombia), 30, 38, 41
AUC, *see* Autodenfensas Unidas de Colombia
Audience, 1, 5–8, 11, 17, 26, 32, 33, 35, 37, 47, 48, 55, 57, 70, 112, 113, 115, 128, 166, 167, 173, 175–179, 191
Autodenfensas Unidas de Colombia (AUC) (Colombia), 37, 41
Autonomous University of Baja California (UABC), Mexico, 203
Autonomy, 145, 146, 150, 158, 158n2, 158n3, 159n4, 166, 209n9
and autonomous organizing, 61
See also Indigenous people
Aylwin, Patricio, 102
Ayotzinapa (Mexico), 45, 58, 66, 70, 72
Azaola, Elena, 2, 143

B
Backhurst, David, 73
Ballesteros, Juan Antonio, 110, 119n14
Barthes, Roland, 190
Bastian Duarte, Ixkic, 8, 140n13
Benjamin, Walter, 4, 14, 78–84, 92, 94, 95n2, 95n3, 101, 104, 106, 117, 193
Beverley, John, 14, 15
Body
and embodied pain, 170
racialized bodies, 176
Bogotá (Colombia), 34
Bolton, Roberto Father, 104, 105, 107, 109, 110
Borgoño 1470, torture center (Chile), 99
Bourgois, Philippe, 2, 144, 149
Boy Scouts, 60
Brinton, Lykes, 18, 168, 181, 182
Burke, Peter, 105
Butler, Judith, 12

C
Cacica Gaitana, 36, 39
CALDH, *see* Center for Legal Actions in Human Rights
Calima Block of the AUC (Colombia), 37
Calveiro, Pilar, 3, 16, 105, 126
Campesinos, 9, 18, 85, 123, 129, 135, 138, 153, 194
See also Peasants
Canadian University Service Overseas (CUSO), 134, 135
Cárdenas, Cuauhtémoc, 61
Carlson, Marvin, 12
Carmelita Rosario, Maya Achi' catechist, 15

Carpio, Salvador Cayetano (Marcial), 82
Castillejo Cuéllar, Alejandro, 17, 148
Castillo, Ángela, 112
Catholic University (Chile), 108, 115
Cauca Province (Colombia), 24, 31, 41, 42, 50n9
Cauca's Regional Indigenous Council (CRIC) (Colombia), 32, 34, 36, 38–40, 50n9
CCPP, *see* Commission of Guatemalan Refugees
CEAR, *see* Special Commission for Attention to Refugees
CEH, *see* Historical Clarification Commission
Central Nacional de Investigaciones (CNI) (Chile), 118n9
Center of the History of the Salvadoran civil war (El Salvador), 84
Center for Legal Actions in Human Rights (CALDH) (Guatemala), 181
Chajul, El Quiché, 168
Chalatenango (El Salvador), 9, 18
Chicago boys (Chile), 3
Chile
  and Chile Committee for Human Rights, 102, 119n11
  MCTSA, 101, 109, 112–115, 117
  military dictatorship, 4, 8, 101, 102
  National Commission for Truth and Reconciliation, 102
  President Aylwin's transitional government, 102
  recent history of resistance, 101
  torture, 99–117
  Valech and Rettig reports, 102
  videos, 104
Chimaltenango (Guatemala), 170
Ching, Erick, 93
Christian communities, 99, 104, 108

Christian Federation of Salvadoran Peasants (FECCAS) (El Salvador), 88
Chuj, 170, 172
  See also Indigenous People
Circularity of affects, 149–151
  See also Affect(s)
Circularity of emotions, 12
  See also Emotion(s)
Citizen action, 24, 27, 46, 112
Civil Self-Defense Patrols (PAC) (Guatemala), 139n4, 139n9
Clough, Patricia, 11, 144, 157
CNDH, *see* National Commission of Human Rights
CNI, *see* Central Nacional de Investigaciones
CNMH, *see* National Center of Historical Memory
CNRR, *see* National Commission of Reparation and Reconciliation
Coc Teul, Francisco, 130
Coello, Teresa, 124, 126, 127, 129–131, 134, 137
Cold war, 2, 126, 127
Collaborative research, 2, 5, 8, 9, 13, 194, 195, 208n2
Collazos, Lisinia, 31–33, 37, 38, 42
Collective memory, 13, 17, 105, 117, 192, 193
  See also Memory
Colombia
  and commemorations, 23–49
  forced displacement, 4, 26
  Indigenous Councils, 38
  Kitek Kiwe, 46
  Nasa People, 7
  Naya massacre, 46, 50n1
  paramilitary groups, 26, 37
  victim, 23–49
Colorado Nates, Oscar, 64

COMADEP, see Meso-American Office for Development and Peace
COMAR, see Mexican Commission for Attention to Refugees
Commemoration, 4, 5, 15, 24–28, 31, 33, 34, 36–44, 46–49, 59, 113
Commission of Guatemalan Refugees (CCPP) (Guatemala), 124, 131, 133
Committee of Surviving Memory (El Salvador), 78
Communitas, 149, 157
Communities of Populations in Resistance (CPR) (Guatemala), 127, 139n5
Community Studies and Psychosocial Action Team (ECAP) (Guatemala), 169, 173, 177
Connerton, Paul, 25
Continental Meeting of Indigenous Women, 206, 207
Conversatorios (conversations) (methodology), 93
Coordinator of the Residents of Tlatelolco (Mexico), 59, 62, 65
Cornejo Hernández, Amaranta, 7, 12, 204
Counterinsurgency policy (Guatemala), 125
CPR, see Communities of Populations in Resistance
CRIC, see Cauca's Regional Indigenous Council
Crónica, 8, 53–74
Crosby, Alison, 9, 13, 16–18, 57, 135, 149, 168, 171, 173, 175, 183n1
Cuban Revolution, 2
Cubitt, Geoffrey, 92
CUD, see Victims Coordinating Council
CUSO, see Canadian University Service Overseas

D
Das, Veena, 1, 12, 144, 154, 172
Day laborer movement, San Quintín (Mexico), 193
and Day laborer work stoppage (Mexico), 189
De Cortina, Jon, 85
De la Madrid, Miguel, 60
De la Rosa Osorno, Juana, 63–65
Deleuze, Gilles, 11
De Marinis, Natalia, 9, 12, 15, 47, 78, 145, 150, 159n8, 193
Democracy, 63, 134
Denzin, Norman, 113
Department of Protection of Citizens' Rights (Colombia), 34
Development Hubs, 127, 139n4
DINA, see *Dirección de Inteligencia Nacional*
Dioceses of San Cristóbal de las Casas (Mexico), 131
Dirección de Inteligencia Nacional (DINA) (Chile), 118n9
Doiron, Fabienne, 9, 13, 16, 18, 135, 168
Democratic Revolutionary Party (PRD) (Mexico), 65
Drug trafficking (El Salvador), 85
Duarte, Rolando, 126, 130
Durán, Diego, 53
and Durán Códex, 53

E
ECAP, see Community Studies and Psychosocial Action Team
Elías Trochez Educational Center (Colombia), 28
El Mercurio, newspaper, 100
El Milagro, farm in San Quintín Valley, 202
ELN, see National Liberation Army

El Porvenir, newspaper, 124
El Salvador
  and guerrilla, 82
  historiography of resistance, 77–96
  Museum of Historical Memory,
    Arcatao, 80, 90
  Peace accords, 83
  post Cold War, 85
  Salvadoran revolution, 78, 83–85,
    88, 93
  Salvadoran war, 93
Emotional community (Barbara
  Rosenwein's concept), 6
Emotional community(ies)
  and the concept of emotional
    community(ies), 1, 2, 7, 26,
    45, 55, 57
  political emotional community(ies),
    207, 208
  the process of creating emotional
    community(ies), 24, 47, 49, 55
  strategic emotional community(ies),
    54, 57, 58, 63, 72–74, 101,
    116, 117, 164–166, 168–173,
    175, 177, 179–181
  strategic emotional political
    community(ies), 8, 45,
    53–74, 114
  See also Political affective
    community(ies)
Emotional histories, 77–96
Emotion(s)
  and cultural force of emotions, 11
  emotional commitment, 27
  emotional connectors, 70
  emotional involvement, 27
  emotional links, 45, 112
  fear, 83, 101, 114, 117, 158
  feminization of emotion, 176
  feminized emotions, 107, 176
  indignation, 114
  love, 107, 111, 114, 117

moral indignation, 36, 49
sadness, 17, 144, 158
suffering, 17, 54, 112–115, 207
terror, 101
See also Pain
Empathy, 4, 9, 17, 27, 37, 47, 63,
  107, 114, 144, 151, 167, 183n1
Eng, David, 166, 172
Episcopate Committee Against
  Torture (Chile), 107
Espinosa, Gisela, 8, 139n7, 208n2
Espinosa, Mónica, 39
Ethnography, 5, 194
EZLN, *see* Zapatista Army of National
  Liberation

F
Fals Borda, Orlando, 18
False positives (Colombia), 36
FAR, *see* Rebel Armed Forces
Farabundo Martí Liberation
  Movement (FMLN) (El
  Salvador), 79, 84, 85
Fassin, Didier, 17, 46
FECCAS, *see* Christian Federation of
  Salvadoran Peasants
Federation of the Relatives of the
  Disappeared (FEDEFAM)
  (Venezuela), 15
Felman, Shoshona, 74n2, 109
Feminist Participatory Action Research
  (PRA), 12, 165
Field Worker's Union (UTC)
  (El Salvador), 88
Fine, Michelle, 166, 167
Flashes of history, 14, 81, 89
  See also History
Flashes of memory, 101, 104, 117
  See also Memory
FMLN, *see* Farabundo Martí
  Liberation Movement

Forced displacement, 4, 8, 9, 26, 123, 144, 147–149
and mass displacement, 125
Foucault, Michel, 19n5
FPL, *see* Popular Forces of Liberation
Freire, Paulo, 18
Fulchiron, Amandine, 170
FUSADES, *see* Salvadoran Foundation for Economic and Social Development

G
Galtung, Johan, 2
GAM, *see* Mutual Support Group
Garment Workers' Union (Mexico), 62
Gender, 2, 9, 10, 16–18, 54, 55, 168, 172, 176, 178, 207
and gender violence, 189, 207, 208
See also Gender justice
Gender justice, 172, 178
See also Justice
General Giap, 82
Genocide (Guatemala), 125
post-genocidal Guatemala, 167
Goldwater, Mike, 87
Granek, Leeat, 167
Green, Linda, 146
Group of Relatives of the Disappeared (Chile), 108, 139n6
Guanacos (water cannons) (Chile), 100
Guatemala
and armed conflict, 126
counterinsurgency, 125
genocide, 125
mass displacement, 125
massacre in Ixcán, 15
Maya Q'eqchi' Women, 164
post-genocidal Guatemala, 167
refugees, 14, 137
Ríos Montt Régime, 169

Sepur Zarco Trial, 165
sexual violence, 56, 165
Tribunal of Conscience, 56
Guattari, Felix, 11
Guerrilla (El Salvador), 82, 84
See also War in El Salvador
Guevara, Che, 82

H
Halbwachs, Maurice, 17, 105
Halley, Jean, 11, 144, 157
Hamacher, Werner, 81, 82
Haraway, Donna, 18, 144
Harding, Sandra, 190
Hartog, Francois, 46
Harvey, David, 3
Henry, Nicola, 173
Hernández, Aída, 18, 144, 175
Hesford, Wendy, 165, 166, 172, 175, 180
High Risk Court (Guatemala), 164
Historical Clarification Commission (CEH) (Guatemala), 125, 127, 169
Historiography, 78, 80–82, 94
historiography of resistance, 78, 94
See also History
History
historiography, 78, 80–82, 94
historiography of resistance, 78, 94
recent history, 2, 5, 13, 14, 101, 105, 106, 115, 117, 128, 138
See also Flashes of history
Hivos, aid agency, 134
Hobsbawn, Eric, 105
Huehuetenango (Guatemala), 125
Human condition, 26, 155
Human Rights
and documenting Human Rights violations, 164

Human Rights violation,
143, 144, 172
International Human Rights Law, 34
International Rights regime, 172
Human Rights Unit (Colombia), 34
Hyphen, 166, 167, 173
and epistemology of the *hyphen*, 167
Hyphen of relationality, 173

I

IAHRC, *see* Inter-American Human Rights Commission
Impunity Watch, 163, 165, 173–175, 179, 180
Indigenous Council (Colombia), 30, 32, 38, 44, 50n2
Indigenous guard (Colombia), 34, 38
Indigenous people
  Chuj, 129, 170, 172, 182
  indigenous Council (Colombia), 30, 32, 38, 44, 50n2
  Indigenous Guard (Colombia), 34, 38
  Kahnawake Mohawks, 74
  Kaqchikel, 170, 171
  K'iche', 136
  Mam, 129, 170
  Maya, 15, 74, 177, 182
  Maya Q'eqchi' women, 164
  Mixtec, 67, 74, 158n1, 195, 198, 200, 205
  Naxihi Women, 195
  Nahua, 74
  Nasa, 4, 7, 15, 23, 24, 28, 32, 36, 39, 50n4, 74
  Ndembu, 149
  Popti', 129
  Q'anjob'al, 129
  Triqui, 143
  See also Autonomy

Indignation
  emotions, 4, 107, 114, 150
  and moral indignation, 26, 36, 47, 49, 114
  shared indignation, 36, 48, 192
  See also Moral repudiation
Indios, 30
INEA, *see* National Institute for Adult Education
Injustice, 15, 39, 43, 46, 114, 125, 149, 189, 191–193, 200, 204, 207, 208
Inter-American Human Rights Commission (IAHRC), 159n6
Inside/outside metaphors, 116
Institutional Revolutionary Party (PRI) (Mexico), 61, 145, 146
Intermediary(ies), 164–173, 175, 177, 178, 181, 182, 190
International Humanitarian Law, 33
Inter Pares (Canada), 168
Intersectionality
  and intersection of gender, "race", social class, nationality, 168
  intersectional identities, 169
Inter-subjective relationship, 167
Ixcán (Guatemala), 129–131
Ixmucané, organization (Guatemala), 136

J

Jalok U (Guatemala), 179
Jasper, James, 1, 10
Jelin, Elizabeth, 1, 16, 155, 189, 192, 197, 200
Jimeno, Myriam, 1, 4–10, 13, 15, 18, 19n3, 25, 27, 46, 51n14, 54, 55, 65, 112–114, 125, 134, 138, 144, 155, 159n7, 164, 189, 192–194

Juárez, Karen, 178, 199
Justice, 3–5, 7, 13–18, 25–27, 32–34,
  37, 38, 40, 41, 44, 47, 49,
  51n16, 83, 91, 103, 109, 112,
  116, 117, 127, 130, 135, 144,
  148, 153–156, 158, 158n2, 168,
  171, 173, 178–180, 190, 191,
  194, 207, 208, 209n9
  transitional justice, 14, 16
  See also Gender justice
Jutiapa (Guatemala), 129
Juxtlahuaca, Oaxaca (Mexico),
  146, 197, 198

K
Kahnawake Mohawks, 74
  See also Indigenous people
Kapur, Ratna, 173
Kaqchikel, 171
  See also Indigenous people
Kershaw, Baz, 113
K'iche, 136
  See also Indigenous people
Kitek Kiwe (Colombia), 4, 5, 24–29,
  31–39, 42–47, 113

L
La Jornada, newspaper, 58, 64, 65,
  70, 71
La Laguna (Colombia), 30, 33, 34, 38
Las Flores, municipality (El Salvador),
  85–87, 89, 90
Latin American Human Rights
  Association (ALDHU)
  (Ecuador), 109
Las Vueltas, municipality
  (El Salvador), 87
Law 1448 of 2011 (Colombia), 37
Law of Justice and Peace, decree 1290
  of 2008 (Colombia), 32

Le Breton, David, 10, 26
Levi, Primo, 155
Liminality, 149
Lira, Elizabeth, 15
Listeners
  empathetic listeners, 17, 45, 57, 58,
    64, 66, 101, 164, 165, 172,
    173
  process of listening, 180
  See also Witness
Local Popular Power (PPL)
  (El Salvador), 79, 80, 86, 89–92,
    95n6
López, Angélica, 136
Los Pinos, farm in San Quintín Valley,
  199, 200
Lutz, Catherine, 5, 10–12
Lykes, Brinton, 9, 13, 15–18, 57, 135,
  149, 165, 167, 168, 171, 172,
  175, 183n1

M
Macleod, Morna, 4–6, 8, 13, 14,
  45, 47, 55, 65, 102, 104,
  113, 114, 134, 139n11,
  140n12, 193
Maguire, Patricia, 171
Malkki, Liisa, 149
Mam, 129, 170
  See also Indigenous people
Maritimes-Guatemala Breaking the
  Silence Network, 168
Mass displacements (Guatemala), 125
Massacre, 3–5, 7, 8, 15, 23–28,
  31–37, 39, 41, 42, 45, 50n4, 72,
  89, 102, 125, 132, 145, 147,
  169, 192, 207
Maya, 182
  See also Indigenous people
Maya Q'eqchi' women, 182
  See also Indigenous people

MCTSA, see Sebastián Acevedo Movement Against Torture
Memorial, 68, 72, 180
  See also Memory
Memory
  flashes of memory, 101, 104, 117
  historical memory, 54, 78, 85, 87
  memorial, 34, 68, 72, 180
  and 'memory boom, 78
  memory communities, 93
  Native people's memory, 74
  reserves of memories, 79
  social memory, 17, 53–74, 128
  turn to memory, 92
  See also Collective memory
Memory and Human Rights Museum (Chile), 104, 106
Merriam-Webster Dictionary, 73
Meso-American Office for Development and Peace (COMADEP) (Mexico), 124, 130, 131, 134, 136
Mestizaje, 181
Mexican Commission for Attention to Refugees (COMAR) (Mexico), 124
Mexican Society for Women's Rights, 209n9
Mexican solidarity committee, 131
Mexico
  and agro-exporting corporations, 189
  crónica, 8, 53, 54, 58, 72, 74
  day laborers in San Quintín, 8
  forced displacement in Oaxaca, 144, 147–149
  gender violence, 189, 207, 208
  indigenous people, 61, 143–158
  Mexico city earthquake testimonies, 54, 58
  Oaxaca, 143–158
  paramilitaries, 146, 150
  Poniatowska, Elena, 58, 59, 62, 74

Mexico City earthquake, 54, 58–60
  See also 30th Anniversary of Mexico City earthquake
Mexico City's Social Security Baseball Park (Mexico), 68
Mingas (Colombia), 33, 35, 36, 50n11
  and *minga* (protest) (Colombia), 34
Mining projects (El Salvador), 86
MINUGUA, see United Nations Mission to Guatemala
Mixtec region, Oaxaca (Mexico), 158n1, 195, 198
Moneda, Palacio de la (Chile), 108
Monsivaís, Carlos, 61–63
Moore, Barrington, 192
Moral communities, 49
Moral repudiation, 192
  See also Indignation
Movement of unification and Struggle of Triqui People (MULT) (Mexico), 145, 158n4
MTM, see Women Transforming the World
MULT, see Movement of unification and Struggle of Triqui People
Museo de la Ciudad (Mexico), 59, 64, 65, 72
Museum of Historical Memory, Arcatao (El Salvador), 80, 90
Mutual Support Group (GAM) (Guatemala), 127

N
Nada, Nadie: Las voces del temblor (Nothing, Nobody: The Voices of the Mexico City Earthquake), 58
  See also Poniatowska, Elena
NAFTA, see North American Free Trade Agreement
Nahua, 74
  See also Indigenous people

Nasa, 15, 23, 24, 28, 32, 36, 39, 74
  See also Indigenous people
National Army (Colombia), 34, 37, 51n13
National Autonomous University of Mexico, 68
National Center of Historical Memory (CNMH) (Colombia), 50n1
National Commission of Human Rights (CNDH) (México), 159n6
National Commission of Reparation and Reconciliation (CNRR) (Colombia), 31, 32, 34
National Commission for Truth and Reconciliation (Chile), 102
National Commission on Political Imprisonment and Torture (Chile), 102
National Democratic Front (Mexico), 61
National Institute for Adult Education (INEA) (Mexico), 203, 205
Nationalist Democratic Organization (ORDEN) (El Salvador), 88
National Liberation Army (ELN) (Colombia), 41, 50n4
National Public Prosecutor Office (Colombia), 34
National Union of Guatemalan Women (UNAMG), 68, 165, 169, 173, 179
National University of Chile, 103
National Victims' Day (Colombia), 37
Navaro-Yashin, Yael, 11, 144, 157, 159n8
Naxihi women (Mexico), 189, 190, 192, 193, 195, 204, 207
Naxihi Xinxe Na Nishi (Association Women Defending Women) (Mexico), 187
Naya massacre, 35, 39, 46, 47, 50n1
  See also Massacre

Naya region (Colombia), 28, 29, 31, 33, 35, 37, 40
Ndembu, 149
  See also Indigenous people
Neoliberalism, 3, 13
Niezen, Ronald, 113, 114
Non-governmental organizations (NGOs), 85, 124, 130, 134, 135, 137
Non-repetition, 33, 41
Nora, Pierre, 79, 92
North American Free Trade Agreement (NAFTA), 3
North Vietnamese military, 82
Nos-otras, 13, 57, 166, 180–182
  See also We-others

O
Oaxaca (México), 143–158
Ocular epistemology, 166, 175
ORDEN, see Nationalist Democratic Organization
Orellana, Patricio, 102–104
Oxfam, 134

P
PAC, see Civil Self-Defense Patrols
Pain, 5, 6, 9, 11, 12, 15, 36, 48, 57, 62, 68, 70, 84, 127, 128, 134, 138, 144, 148, 150, 151, 154, 156–158, 172, 175, 178, 179
  and embodied pain, 170
  See also Emotions
Paramilitaries
  and *paracos* (Colombia), 28
  paramilitaries groups (Colombia), 27, 37
  paramilitary forces (Guatemala), 125
Parissi, Rosa, 99, 104, 105, 111, 119n11

Peace accords (El Salvador), 83
Peace accords (Guatemala), 8
Pearce, Jenny, 2, 4, 9, 14, 18, 82, 193, 194
Peasants, 23, 31, 34, 35, 40, 79, 80, 82–94, 95n6, 96n7
   See also Campesinos
Performance
   and performative actions, 26, 101, 108, 117
   performative acts, 15, 36, 43, 158
   performative events, 26, 49
   theatrical performance, 101
Petén (Guatemala), 123, 124, 132, 135, 136
Pinochet, Augusto, 3, 45, 99–117
Pinzón, Mónica, 177
Polígono 14, Ixcán (Guatemala), 131
Political affective community, 9, 78, 154–157, 159n7
   See also Affect
Political emotional community, 207
   See also Emotional communities
Pollak, Michael, 17
Poniatowska, Elena, 45, 53–74
   See also Nada, Nadie: Las voces del temblor (Nothing, Nobody: The Voices of the Mexico City Earthquake)
Popayán (Colombia), 24
Popti, 129
   See also Indigenous people
Popular Assembly of the Peoples of Oaxaca (APPO) (Mexico), 155
Popular education, 18, 124, 134
Popular Forces of Liberation (FPL) (El Salvador), 79, 82, 95n5, 95n6
Popular Unity Party (UP) (Chile), 103
Positioned subject, 11
   See also Researcher's positionality
PPL, *see* Local Popular Power
PRD, *see* Democratic Revolutionary Party
PRI, *see* Institutional Revolutionary Party
Probúsqueda(El Salvador), 85
Proceso, magazine, 62
Promise Land, 87, 88, 93
Protagonism, 164, 167, 181, 183n1
Public denouncements, 143, 144
   and Public denunciations, 16, 47

Q
Q'anjob'al, 129
   See also Indigenous people
Quetzal, La (Guatemala), 132, 133, 136
Quiché, El (Guatemala), 168
Quilcué, Aída, 34
Quintín Lame, 43

R
Rappaport, Joanne, 13, 42, 74, 101, 114, 116, 144
Raspachín (Colombia), 28–30
Razack, Sharene, 57
Rebel Armed Forces (FAR) (Guatemala), 136
Recent history, 2, 13, 14, 105, 106, 115, 117, 128
   See also History
Reflexivity, 166–169
Refugees
   refugee camps, 28, 83, 93, 135
   refugee return, 8, 125
Remember, 16, 26, 28, 72, 73, 78, 81, 100, 111, 131, 133, 135, 197–199, 201, 202
   and remembering person, 81
   See also Acts of Remembering
Reparation, 7, 18, 32, 33, 38, 44, 46, 47, 51n16, 164, 165, 170–173, 179

Researcher's positionality, 167
  See also Positioned subject
Resistance
  and narratives of resistance, 78
  peasant resistance in El Salvador, 83
  resistance subjectivity, 82, 83
  See also Historiography of resistance
Retting Report (Chile), 102
Revolutionary National Guatemalan Unity (URNG) (Guatemala), 124, 126, 136
Reyes Girón, Esteelmer Francisco, 164
Reyes Mate, Alfonso, 46
Ricoeur, Paul, 16
Ríos Montt regime (Guatemala), 169
Rosaldo, Renato, 11, 144
Rosenwein, Barbara, 6, 7, 119n15
Ruiz, Samuel Bishop, 131

S

Sabido Ramos, Olga, 10
Salas, Pablo, 112, 114
Salvadoran Foundation for Economic and Social Development (FUSADES) (El Salvador), 85
Samuel, Raphael, 73, 91, 93
San Quintín Valley (Mexico), 8, 187, 190, 196, 198–203, 206, 207, 209n4
Santander de Quilichao (Colombia), 30, 31
Scheper Hughes, Nancy, 2, 144, 149
Sebastián Acevedo Movement Against Torture (MCTSA) (Chile), 8, 99, 100, 102–117, 118n10
Sepur Zarco (Guatemala)
  Sepur Zarco Military Outpost, 164
  and Sepur Zarco trial, 16, 57, 163–182

Sexual violence
  and sexual harassment, 191, 205
  sexual slavery, 164
Shaw, Rachel, 167
Shaw, Rosalind, 58
Shoah, 24
Sieder, Rachel, 18
Silber, Irina, 85
Simpson, Audra, 74
Sindicato de Costureras "19th September" (Mexico), 61
Situated knowledge, 18, 144, 190
  researchers' positionality, 167
  See also Positioned subject
Socialism (Chile), 3
Social movements, 1, 10, 14, 55, 56, 117, 168
Social Security Institute (Mexico), 191
Sociodrama (methodology), 28
Solidarity, 4, 7, 8, 15, 27, 44, 47, 57, 61–63, 78, 83, 90, 91, 108, 111, 112, 114, 117, 124, 130–132, 135–137, 145, 147, 148, 150, 151, 153, 157, 158n4, 168, 191
Sparks of hope, 4, 80, 91, 94, 193, 198
Special Commission for Attention to Refugees (CEAR) (Guatemala), 124
Speed, Shannon, 18, 144
Stephen, Lynn, 8, 13, 14, 16, 45, 54, 56, 73, 101, 104, 114, 117, 138, 155, 164, 178
Stolen, Kristi Anne, 130
Strategic emotional community(ies), 57, 58, 63, 101, 116, 117, 164–166, 168, 169, 171, 173, 175, 177, 179–181
  and strategic emotional political community(ies), 8, 45, 53–74, 114
  See also Emotional communities

Suffering, 5, 6, 17, 43, 45–47, 54, 55, 57, 59, 64, 78, 91, 106, 112, 113, 115, 134, 149, 155, 170, 172, 178, 180, 190, 193, 200–202, 207
See also Emotion(s)
Systematization (methodology), 195

T
Tattay Bolaños, Pedro, 19n2
Taussig, Michael, 146
Taylor, Diana, 1, 12, 113, 138, 154, 170
Terror, 12, 15, 17, 101, 143–148, 154, 156, 157
  emotions, 101
  See also Violence
Testimony
  documentation of testimonies, 56, 73
  knowledge transmission, 56
  and "live" testimonies, 176
  oral narratives, 54, 56
  oral testimony, 45, 53, 54, 73, 93
  public testimony, 24, 26, 53, 55, 73
  testify, 109, 175
  testimonial moment, 155
  testimonial narratives, 14, 57, 58
  testimonial traces, 16, 17, 143–158
  testimonio, 14, 67
  witness, 7, 14, 16, 148, 157, 174
  See also Video
Theidon, Kimberly, 17, 18, 149, 156
Theology of liberation, 83
The'wala (Colombia), 28–30, 39
Tierradentro (Colombia), 36, 42
Tikal (Guatemala), 123
Timba (Colombia), 30, 31
Timbío, municipality (Colombia), 34

Time
  and future, 74
  and past, 8, 74
  and present, 8, 74, 192
Tlatelolco massacre, 45
Tlatelolco (Mexico), 45
Todd, Molly, 85
Toéz (Colombia), 30
Torture, 8, 15, 38, 45, 88, 99–117, 173
  See also Violence
Transitional justice, 16, 172
  See also Justice
Trans-Peninsular Highway, 191
Trauma
  trauma experts, 17, 148
  and trauma narration, 33
  See also Violence
Traverso, Enzo, 13, 78, 105, 106, 127, 196
Tribunal of Conscience (Guatemala), 56, 173, 175, 177
Triqui, 15, 143–145, 147, 149, 151, 155–157
  and Triqui region, 145, 154, 156, 158n1
  See also Indigenous people
Truth commissions, 18, 103, 109, 113, 127
  and truth commission in Chile, 102
Truth-telling, 18
  See also Testimony
Turner, Victor, 12, 149

U
UABC, *see* Autonomous University of Baja California
UBISORT, *see* Unity for Social Welfare of the Triqui Region
UN, *see* United Nations

UNAMG, *see* National Union of Guatemalan Women
UNHCR, *see* United Nations High Commission for Refugees
Union Coordinator of Earthquake Victims (Mexico), 62, 65
Unit of Justice and Peace (Colombia), 37
United Nations (UN), 127
United Nations High Commission for Refugees (UNHCR), 124, 126
United Nations Mission to Guatemala (MINUGUA) (Guatemala), 127
Universidad del Cauca (Colombia), 34
University of Chapultepec (Mexico), 72
Unity for Social Welfare of the Triqui Region (UBISORT) (Mexico), 145
Uribe, Álvaro, 35
URNG, *see* Revolutionary National Guatemalan Unity
US Agency for International Development (USAID), 85
UTC, *see* Field Workers' Union

V

Valdez Asig, Heriberto, 164, 176
Valech Report (Chile), 102
Valech, Sergio Monsignor, 102, 103
Varela, Daniel, 13, 15, 18, 112
Vela, Manolo, 125, 139n1, 139n3
Velásquez Nimatuj, Irma Alicia, 177
Vicaría de la Solidaridad (Chile), 108
Victim
 and millenary victims, 39
 victim-focused mobilization (Colombia), 25
 victimhood, 93, 175, 176
 victim-witness, 155
Victims Coordinating Council (CUD) (Mexico), 64, 65

Víctores, Mejía (Gen.), military regime, 139n6
Vienna in Solidarity with Guatemala (Guatemala Solidarität Wien), 133
Video
 time, 176
 videos circulate, 104
 See also Testimony
Villa Grimaldi, torture and detention center (Chile), 115
Villegas, René García, 103, 104
Violence
 gender violence, 189, 207, 208
 sexual violence, 16, 56, 103, 145, 147, 148, 150, 164, 165, 169–171, 173, 180
 state violence, 3, 13, 130
 and structural violence, 13, 151, 192, 198, 204, 207
 terror, 12, 148
 torture, 103
 trauma, 49
 violent representations, 164
 See also Emotion(s)
Voice that breaks the Silence, The, (radio station) (Mexico), 146, 158n3
von Ranke, Leopold, 81

W

Wake up the Neighborhood (Mexico), 62
War in El Salvador
 guindas, 87, 89
 See also Guerrilla (El Salvador)
We-others, 57
 See also Nos-otras
Witness
 and crisis of witnessing, 164, 165, 172

expert witness, 7, 13, 16,
  155, 166, 174,
  176–178
public witness, 53
testify, 17, 109, 166,
  174–176
victim-witness, 155
witnesses, 128, 134, 151, 154–157,
  174–177
See also Listener
Women Defending Women (Mexico),
  187–208
Women Transforming the World
  (MTM), 173, 179

X
Xamán massacre, 139n9
  See also Massacre
XEQIN, radio station (México), 195

Y
Yat, Demecia, 163, 174, 175, 180

Z
Zapatista Army of National Liberation
  (EZLN), 158n2
Zacapa (Guatemala), 129

The manufacturer's authorised representative in the EU is Springer Nature Customer Service Centre GmbH, Europaplatz 3, 69115 Heidelberg, Germany. If you have any concerns regarding our products, please contact ProductSafety@springernature.com

Printed and bound by CPI Group (UK) Ltd, Croydon, CR0 4YY
23/03/2026
02076738-0002